RECENT

BRITISH PHILOSOPHY:

A REVIEW, WITH CRITICISMS;

INCLUDING

SOME COMMENTS ON MR. MILL'S ANSWER TO SIR WILLIAM HAMILTON.

BY

DAVID MASSON.

NEW YORK:
D. APPLETON AND COMPANY,
443 & 445 BROADWAY.
1866.

The substance of the greater portion of the following pages was delivered, in the form of lectures, at the Royal Institution of Great Britain, in Albemarle Street, on the afternoons of March 21, 23, and 28, in the present year.

London, *June*, 1865.

CONTENTS.

CHAPTER I.

PAGE

A SURVEY OF THIRTY YEARS, ... 9

CHAPTER II.

THE TRADITIONAL DIFFERENCES: HOW REPEATED IN CARLYLE, HAMILTON, AND MILL, ... 30

I.—The Psychological Difference, ... 33

II.—Cosmological Differences, ... 53

III.—The Ontological Difference, ... 70

CHAPTER III.

EFFECTS OF RECENT SCIENTIFIC CONCEPTIONS ON PHILOSOPHY, ... 142

CHAPTER IV.

LATEST DRIFTS AND GROUPINGS, ... 195

I.—Native Seniors, ... 195

II.—British Comtism, ... 200

III.—Mr. Bain and Mr. Herbert Spencer, ... 207

IV.—Hamiltonianism and its Modifications, ... 216

V.—Mr. Ferrier and a British Hegelian, ... 221

VI.—Swedenborgianism and "Spiritualism," 233

VII.—Mr. Mill on Sir William Hamilton, ... 245

RECENT BRITISH PHILOSOPHY.

CHAPTER I.

A SURVEY OF THIRTY YEARS.

By *recent* British Philosophy I mean the Philosophy of this country during the last thirty years. But what do I mean by British *Philosophy* during that period? You have all a general notion of what I mean. I mean the aggregate speculations during that period of some of our ablest British minds in what are vaguely called "the moral sciences"—their aggregate speculations on those questions of most deep and enduring interest to man which have occupied thoughtful minds in all ages of the world, which are handed on from age to age, and which each generation, however much of previous thought concerning them it may inherit and preserve, has to revolve over again for itself. It has been proclaimed among us, indeed, that Philosophy in this sense has at length happily ceased to exist—that great Pan is dead. I do not believe it; and, if I did, I should be sad. Whatever nation has given up Philosophy—I will be bolder, and, using a word very much out of favour at present, I will say whatever nation has given up *Metaphysics*—is in a state of intellectual insolvency. Though its granaries should be bursting, though its territories should be netted with railroads, though its mills and foundries should be the busiest in the world, the mark of the beast is upon it, and it is going the way of all brutality.

Britain, notwithstanding temporary misrepresentations of her, is not yet in this state. We have not, it is true, and we have not had for a long while, the reputation among our continental neighbours of being a nation caring much for Philosophy. The Germans, in particular, have long pitied us on this account. It is more than forty years since one of their greatest thinkers publicly denounced us by pointing out that England was the only country in Europe where the word Philosophy had become synonymous with natural science, where the barometer and thermometer were spoken of as "philosophical instruments," and where a so-called *Philosophical Journal* treated of agriculture, housekeeping, cookery, and the construction of fire-places.* Historically it might be shown

* Hegel as quoted by Mansel, *Metaphysics*, p. 4, note.

that this very degradation of the word Philosophy among us arose from what was originally a philosophical conception and may have been a good one. Not the less was the taunt well deserved. And, though we may have been recovering since then, our recovery, it must be admitted, has been very gradual.

Exactly thirty years ago Mr. John Stuart Mill could write as follows: "England once stood at the head of European Philosophy. Where stands she now? Consult the general opinion of Europe. The celebrity of England, in the present day, rests upon her docks, her canals, her railroads. In intellect she is distinguished only for a kind of sober good sense, free from extravagance, but also void of lofty aspirations. . . . Instead of the ardour of research, the eagerness for large and comprehensive inquiry, of the educated part of the French and German youth, what find we? Out of the narrow bounds of mathematical and physical science, not a vestige of a reading and thinking public engaged in the investigation of truth *as* truth, in the prosecution of thought for the sake of thought. Among few except sectarian religionists—and what they are we all know—is there any interest in the great problem of man's nature and life; among still fewer is there any curiosity respecting the nature and principles of human society, the history or the philosophy of civilization, or any belief that from such inquiries a single important practical consequence can follow?" *

Even at the time when Mr. Mill wrote these words I cannot but think they described matters as somewhat worse than they really were. When I remember that Coleridge and Bentham and Mackintosh were then but recently dead, that Mr. Mill's own eminent father was yet alive, and that the poet Wordsworth, no less the philosophic sage than the poet, survived as an honoured recluse, I cannot think that the tradition of our national faculty in philosophy had become then so utterly extinct. Possibly, however, the educated mind of Britain *had*, about thirty years ago, sunk to its lowest in respect of interest in philosophy, or any general notion of what philosophy might be. For Mr. Mill was not the sole British thinker who then looked round with something of this conviction. Other voices had been crying in the wilderness. Mr. Mill's senior, Sir William Hamilton, had strongly uttered the same complaint. "The present contrast," he had written in 1830, "which the philosophical enthusiasm of France exhibits to the speculative apathy of Britain is anything but flattering to ourselves. The new spirit of metaphysical inquiry which the French imbibed from Germany and

* Review of Professor Sedgwick's Discourse on the Studies of Cambridge, 1835; reprinted in Mill's *Dissertations*.

Scotland arose with them precisely at the same time when the popularity of psychological researches began to decline with us; and now, when all interest in these speculations seems here to be extinct, they are there seen flourishing in public favour with universality and vigour corresponding to their encouragement." *

Should another authority be wanted to the same effect, it may be found in writings of Mr. Carlyle at about the same date. "It is admitted on all sides," he had written in one of his Essays as early as 1829, "that the Metaphysical and Moral sciences are falling into decay, while the Physical are engrossing, every day, more respect and attention. In most of the European nations there is now no such thing as a science of Mind; only more or less advancement in the general science, or the special sciences, of Matter. The French were the first to desert Metaphysics; and, though they had lately affected to revive their school, it has yet no signs of vitality. Among ourselves the Philosophy of Mind, after a rickety infancy, which never reached the vigour of manhood, fell suddenly into decay, languished, and finally died out with its last amiable cultivator, Professor Stewart. In no nation but Germany has any decisive

* Art. on the Philosophy of Perception, *Edin. Review*, Oct. 1830; reprinted in Hamilton's *Discussions*.

effort been made in psychological science, not to speak of any decisive result." * In this passage, notwithstanding a difference in the tone from those written almost immediately afterwards by Hamilton and Mill, there is substantially the same complaint.

Now, certainly, the concurring testimonies of three such minds may be taken as evidence, if not that Philosophy was then at a lower ebb than usual in Britain, at least that such British Philosophy as was current did not come up to the standard of the best critics, whether judging by their own requirements and aspirations, or by comparison with other nations.

Let us admit, then, that thirty years ago the philosophical credit of Britain was justly low in Europe. Has the state of affairs been changed since then? Surely, to some extent, it has. Those three critics themselves, as we all know, were not content with crying in the wilderness. Even while they were so crying, they had begun their own best efforts that the wilderness should rejoice and blossom. Hamilton, the eldest of them, had begun, in his maturity, to put forth, from his seclusion in Edinburgh, those occasional essays, the fruits of long previous thought, the very titles of which took away people's breath, which

* Article "Signs of the Times," *Edin. Review*, 1829; reprinted in Carlyle's *Miscellanies.*

probably not twenty persons in Britain could intelligently read, but which, where they were read, astonished by their profundity and erudition, and seemed to herald a new era in formal speculation, if only by reinstating difficulty where men had been taking their ease. Carlyle, the second in age, had already put forth, in the same periodical or in others, those earlier essays of his in which, though they were in form literary or biographical, there was evidently the working of a great new philosophical force, and the deep assumption of a new set of fundamental principles. He had also published his *Sartor Resartus*, in which, under such a poetico-grotesque guise as confounded all precedent, and took both phantasy and reason by storm, he compelled readers to behold his principles and their developments in something like system.

Finally, Mill, the youngest of the three—he was but twenty-nine years of age when he wrote the passage which I have quoted—had for several years been writing, in the *Westminster* and other Reviews, articles from which it was to be inferred that, when his courageous and truth-loving father, and that father's friend Bentham, should be gone from the earth, they would leave behind them, in this heir of their hopes, one fit to be an expositor of their ideas through another generation, but who was likely rather to look right and left in that generation for himself, and to honour his descent, not by mere adhesion to what he had inherited, but by an open-mindedness that should even solicit contrary impressions, and push on passionately, at every break of light, in the quest of richer truth. If the history of London during the last reign and the present should ever come to be written, the historian might be reminded of one building in it, now no longer extant, of which rather particular mention might be desirable. It was the dingy old India House in Leadenhall Street, of whose many interesting legends it is now certainly not the least interesting that, thirty years ago, young John Mill, not so well known to the general public as he has been since, had there his official room, to which, along intricate passages, friends and admirers of his, seeking his conversation, would find their way on late afternoons.

If I have individualized Mill, Carlyle, and Hamilton as the persons in whom, if in any, there was the likelihood, thirty years ago, of a new movement in British Philosophy, I have not done so without good reason. Whatever other men, seniors or coevals of these three, may be named as having co-operated with them, either as urging views of their own, or as continuing the older philosophic influences (and I, for one, think that the beneficial influence of Coleridge was not exhausted at his death), certain it is that it is to Carlyle, Hamilton, and Mill that all would point as having been the most prominent leaders of free or uncovenanted British speculation during the last thirty years. Probably first in the order of effect came Carlyle, in all whose writings, historical or other, down to the last, there have been veins and blasts of that philosophy which the earliest of them announced, and the resistless diffusion of which, and even of the phrases and idioms in which it was couched, over the entire surface and through the entire speech of these islands, is a phenomenon not soon to be forgotten. Hamilton's influence was long more local and obscure. But, for twenty years, he was teaching Logic and Metaphysics to large classes in the University of Edinburgh; and thus, as well as latterly by publications bearing his name, there was shed through educated British society some recognition of his system of thought, and a certain Hamiltonian leaven which is still working. Mill, too, has more than fulfilled his promise. To his *Logic*, published in 1843, there have succeeded his other well-known works, and with such accumulated effect that, at the present moment, it may be said that it is Mill, as a Philosopher, that is in the ascendant in Britain. It is Mill that our young thinkers at the Universities, our young legislators in Parliament, our young critics in journals, and our young shepherds on the mountains, consult, and quote, and swear by.

But, of course, in every year since these three men first stepped out as leaders, there have been additions to the procession which they headed—in some cases, perhaps, of mere recruits to one or other of them, but, in others, of independent mind reasserting previous forms of thought, or even of such marked originality that they already divide attention with the leaders, and, when the head of the column has wound round the hill, they in their turn will seem the chiefs.

What the French or the Germans might think of these late efforts of ours, if presented to them collectively, is, indeed, still a question. Not only do we labour under the disadvantage of being an insular people, removed from the centre—a thing which tells in philosophy more than it once did; but it can hardly be said that the majority of those among us who have betaken themselves systematically to philosophy have taken the necessary pains to acquaint themselves with what have been gone through and settled before, within accessible ground, on the subjects of their research. As presenting in a vivid light the possible effects on our recent philosophical literature of these two causes in combination—our geographical insularity and our deficiency of learning—I will quote a sentence or two from one of the last metaphysical works published in Britain. "What we shall take leave to name the *historic pabulum*," says this resolute writer, "this alone is the appointed food of every successive generation, this alone is the condition of the growth of spirit; and, this food neglected, we have a generation that but vacillates—vacillates, it may be, even into temporary retrogression. This last is the unfortunate position now. The *historic pabulum*, passing from the vessel of Hume, was received into that of Kant, and thence finally into that of Hegel; but from the vessels of the two latter the generations have not yet eaten. This is the whole—Europe (Germany as Germany is itself no exception) has continued to nourish itself from the vessels of Hume long after the *historic pabulum* had abandoned it for another and others. Hence all that we see. Hume is our Politics, Hume is our Trade, Hume is our Philosophy, Hume is our Religion—it wants little but that Hume were even our Taste. . . . In short, the only true means of progress have not been brought into service. The *historic pabulum*, however greedily it has been devoured out of Hume, has been left untouched in the vessel of Hegel, who alone of all mankind has succeeded in eating it all up out of the vessel of Kant." *

You see what the writer means. There have been three, and but three, all-comprehensive European

* The Secret of Hegel: being the Hegelian System and Origin, Principle, Form, and Matter. By James Hutchison Stirling. 2 vols. London, 1865. Introd. pp. lxxiii. lxxiv.

thinkers during the last century—Hume in Britain, and Kant and Hegel in Germany. You may fancy them as three buckets or reservoirs, one behind the other in a line, with intervals between them—Hume stationed in his completeness at about the year 1770, Kant at about the year 1800, and Hegel at about 1830. There have been other philosophers in all countries during the century, of some one of whom the historian of Philosophy may be bound to take account; but, as respects philosophic result, they have, one and all of them, been but as saucers and pannikins ranged by the sides of the great buckets or in the intervals between them. There is nothing worth having in the pannikins that is not in the buckets; and there is a vast deal in the buckets—or, at least, in the last two—that has never got into the pannikins. Then why go to the pannikins for philosophy? It is not only Britain, it will have been noted, that the writer accuses of this folly of not drawing its philosophy from the main. But it is clearly our recent British philosophizing that he has chiefly in view. He thinks *it*, above all, inadequately informed with the true hereditary pabulum, and therefore either unconsciously retrogressive, or, at best, beside the point, and needlessly repetitive. He thinks it made up, as he otherwise expresses it, of "contingent crumbs" from unknown tables.

To all this what shall we reply? We may reply that we are, or, at least may be, fully informed from Hume, and that this, on the critic's own principle, is something, seeing that it limits the distance to which we need go back. We may reply that surely some sufficient knowledge of Kant has been possessed by some of our thinkers and scholars since Kant lived, and has been digested in recent British speculation. We may reply that, if Hegel remains unknown, save in a specimen-phrase or two, by reason of his terrible abstruseness, one or two of the intermediates and purveyors between Kant and Hegel—such as Fichte and Schelling—have not been without interpreters. We may reply that, as Hegel's date is 1830, it is about time, in the nature of things, that there should be a fourth European bucket somewhere, superseding Hegel; that, as Britain produced the first, it is not out of possibility that she may repeat her feat and produce the fourth; and that towards such an achievement a knowledge of Hegel may be essential, but not a head-splitting knowledge of Hegel, or a knowledge of all Hegel, or even a worshipping or believing knowledge of Hegel. No disrespect is implied to Hegel. But, whatever Hegel may have been, he was not everybody collectively. As Mr. Artemus Ward said to his American countrymen about the Negro, we ought perhaps to think of him as an important kinsman, but not surely as our grandfather, uncle, aunt in the country, wife, sisters and brothers, and several of our first wife's relations, all in one. A good deal of the world of mind was and is to be seen out of Hegel—a good deal even of what went to make Hegel. May not British thought, starting as it can do from Hume, and with the power of taking Kant in the way, make a leap to all intents and purposes beyond Hegel without actually putting both its hands on Hegel's bended back? Did not Hume evolve *his* abstract philosophy from but an ounce or so of transmitted material in the way of previous system—chiefly, indeed, by persistent native meditation on one final doctrine of one previous thinker?

Granted that larger knowledge is necessary now for anything really relevant to present intellectual needs, and the very largest knowledge for anything thorough and complete. Still may it not be possible that in these insular British mists, in these sometimes clear British airs, amid the suggestive bustle of this rich British life, and under British stars that speak of Infinity no less than do the German, diligent and serious British minds may have of late years been ruminating, without any express aid from Hegel, ideas and conclusions of worth to us, and which even Hegel's countrymen might be glad to get?

All this, and more to the same effect, might be

said by way of making it probable beforehand that our recent philosophy, if not consummate, need not have been mainly retrogressive, or all merely repetitive and beside the point. But, after all, the best method is to examine it. If saucers and pannikins are all that we have, let us at least take an inventory of our saucers and pannikins.

CONSPECTUS OF RECENT WRITINGS AND WRITERS.

[*Not brought beyond March*, 1865.]

SIR WILLIAM HAMILTON (*nat.* 1788—*ob.* 1856):—Article, *Philosophy of the Unconditioned*, in the Edinburgh Review, Oct. 1829; article, *Philosophy of Perception*, in the same Review, Oct. 1830; article, *Logic*, in the same Review, April, 1833; and other articles, from 1829 onwards;—all republished collectively in 1852 as Sir William Hamilton's *Discussions.*—Edition of Reid's Works with *Notes and Dissertations* (incomplete), 1846.—*Lectures on Metaphysics*, in 2 vols., 1859, edited from Hamilton's manuscripts by Mansel and Veitch.—*Lectures on Logic*, 2 vols., 1860, similarly edited.

MR. CARLYLE (*nat.* 1794):—Articles, *State of German Literature* and *Signs of the Times*, in the Edinburgh Review, 1827 and 1829; and other Essays, from that date downwards, reprinted as *Miscellanies.*—*Sartor Resartus*, 1833–'4. All his other writings to the present time; but, perhaps most particularly, for the expression of theory, or for criticism of theories, his *Heroes and Hero-worship*, 1840, his *Past and Present*, 1843, his *Latter-day Pamphlets*, 1850, and his *Life of Sterling*, 1851.

MR. JOHN STUART MILL (*nat.* 1806):—Articles in the Westminster Review and other periodicals from 1832 onwards (including a celebrated Essay on Bentham, 1838, and a sequel on Coleridge, 1840), reprinted as Mill's *Dissertations and Discussions*, 2 vols., 1859.—*A System of Logic, Ratiocinative and In-*

ductive, 2 vols., 1843.—*Principles of Political Economy*, 2 vols., 1848.—Essay *On Liberty*, 1859.—Essay *On Utilitarianism*, 1863.

De Quincey (*nat.* 1786—*ob.* 1859). Through many of De Quincey's Essays there runs a subtle vein of speculative thought, derived from Wordsworth and Coleridge, or on the whole continuing and prolonging their philosophic influence.

Archbishop Whately (*nat.* 1787—*ob.* 1863). Among various writings, subsequent to his *Logic*, published in 1826, may be noted his *Annotations to Bacon's Essays*, 1856, and his *Annotations to Paley*, 1859.

George Combe (*nat.* 1788—*ob.* 1858):—*The Constitution of Man*, 1828; *System of Phrenology*, 1836; and other Phrenological Writings.

Mr. Isaac Taylor (*nat.* 1789):—*Natural History of Enthusiasm*, 1829; and, in a numerous series of subsequent works, perhaps more particularly his *Physical Theory of Another Life*, 1839, his *Elements of Thought*, 1843, his *Restoration of Belief*, 1853, and his *Ultimate Civilization*, 1860.

Rev. Dr. Whewell (*nat.* 1794):—*Philosophy of the Inductive Sciences*, 1840; *Elements of Morality*, 1845; *Lectures on the History of Moral Philosophy in England*, 1852; *The Platonic Diologues for English Readers*, 1859—1861; etc.

Dr. Arnold (*nat.* 1795—*ob.* 1842). The influence of Arnold on English speculative thought may be still traced in eminent disciples or admirers of his in the English Church.

Mr. Samuel Bailey (Author of "Essays on the Formation and Publication of Opinions," 1821, and of "Essays on the Pursuit of Truth," 1831):—*A Review of Berkeley's Theory of Vision*, 1842; *A Theory of Reasoning*, 1851; *Letters on the Philosophy of the Human Mind*, 1855—1863.

Dr. John Henry Newman (*nat.* 1801). Of the speculative system that underlies Dr. Newman's Theology and Ecclesiasticism, and reveals itself more or less in the whole series of his writings, some interesting and rather precise glimpses are given by himself in his last publication, *Apologia pro vitâ suâ*, 1864.

Miss Harriet Martineau (*nat.* 1802). Two of Miss Martineau's works to be particularly noted in connexion with recent British Philosophy are her Correspondence with Mr. Atkinson *On the Laws of Man's Nature and Development*, 1851, and her condensed Translation of *Comte's Positive Philosophy*, 2 vols., 1853.

Rev. F. D. Maurice (*nat.* 1805). In the long series of Mr. Maurice's works, all pervaded by his characteristic mode of thought, may be specially noted his *History of Moral and Metaphysical Philosophy* in the Encyclopædia Metropolitana, reissued now in several separate volumes; his *Theological Essays*, 1853; and his two volumes of controversy with Mr. Mansel, entitled, *What is Revelation?* (1859), and *Sequel to the Inquiry, What is Revelation?* (1860).

Mr. F. W. Newman (*nat.* 1805):—*The Soul: Her Sorrows and Aspirations*, 1849; *Phases of Faith*, 1850; and other writings.

Mr. Benjamin H. Smart:—*Thought and Language: an Essay, having in view the Revival, Correction, and Exclusive Establishment of Locke's Philosophy*, 1855.

Professor De Morgan (*nat.* 1806):—*Formal Logic*, 1849; and occasional parts of his other acknowledged writings.

Sir George Cornewall Lewis (*nat.* 1806—*ob.* 1863):—*Essay on the Influence of Authority in Matters of Opinion*, 1849; *On the Methods of Observation and Reasoning in Politics*, 1852.

Professor James F. Ferrier (*nat.* 1808—*ob.* 1864). Various Metaphysical Papers in Blackwood's Magazine; and *Institutes of Metaphysic, or Theory of Knowing and Being*, 1854.

Professor Patrick C. Macdougall:—*Contributions to Philosophy*, 1852.

Mr. Henry Rogers:—Essays in the Edinburgh Review and other periodicals, republished collectively 1850–'55; *The Eclipse of Faith* (in reply to Mr. F. W. Newman), 1852; and *Defence* of same (in rejoinder to Newman), 1854.

Alfred Tennyson (*nat.* 1810). To those who are too strongly possessed with our common habit of classifying writers into kinds, as Historians, Poets, Scientific and Speculative Writers, and so on, it may seem strange to include Mr. Tennyson in this list. But, as I have advisedly referred to Wordsworth as one of the representatives and powers of British Philosophy in the age immediately past, so I advisedly named Tennyson as succeeding him in the same character. Though it is not power of speculative reason alone that constitutes a poet, is it not felt that the worth of a poet essentially is measured by the amount and depth of his speculative reason? Even popularly do we not speak of every great poet as the exponent of the spirit of his age? What else can this mean than that the philosophy of his age, its spirit and heart in relation to all the great elemental problems, finds expression in his verse? Hence I ought to include other poets in this list, and more particularly MR. BROWNING and MRS. BROWNING, and the late MR. CLOUGH. But let the mention of Mr. Tennyson suggest such other names, and stand as a sufficient protest against our absurd habit of omitting such in a connexion like the present. As if, forsooth, when a writer passed into verse, he were to be abandoned as utterly out of calculable relationship to all on this side of that boundary, and no account were to be taken of his thoughts and doings except in a kind of curious appendix at the end of the general register! What if Philosophy, at a certain extreme range, and of a certain kind, tends of necessity to pass into poesy, and can hardly help being passionate and metrical? If so, might not the omission of poets, purely as being such, from a conspectus of the speculative writers of any time, lead to erroneous conclusions, by giving an undue prominence in the estimate of all such philosophizing as could most easily, by its nature, refrain from passionate or poetic expression? Thus, would Philosophy, or one kind of Philosophy in comparison with another, have seemed to have been in such a diminished condition in Britain about the year 1830, if critics had been in the habit of counting Wordsworth in the philosophic list as well as Coleridge, Mackintosh, Bentham, and James Mill? Was there not more of what might be called Spinozism in Wordsworth than even in Coleridge, who spoke more of Spinoza? But there hardly needs all this justification, as far as Mr. Tennyson is concerned, of our reckoning *him* in the present list. He that would exclude *In Memoriam* (1850), and *Maud* (1855), from a conspectus of the philosophical literature of our time, has yet to learn what philosophy is. Whatever else *In Memoriam* may be, it is a manual, for many, of the latest hints and questions in British Metaphysics.

MR. ARTHUR HELPS:—*Essays written in the Intervals of Business*, 1841; *Friends in Council*, first series, 1847; second series 1859; etc.

MR. WILLIAM SMITH (of Edinburgh):—Translations of various works of Fichte, separately published, and collected in two volumes (with a Memoir) as *The Popular Works of Fichte*, 1844.

MR. J. D. MORELL:—*History of Speculative Philosophy in the Nineteenth Century*, 1846; *Lectures on the Philosophical Tendencies of the Age*, 1848; *Philosophy of Religion*, 1849; *Elements of Psychology*, 1853; *Introduction to Mental Philosophy*, 1862.

MR. G. H. LEWES:—*Biographical History of Philosophy*, 1845 (second edition, 1857); *Comte's Philosophy of the Positive Sciences* (an abridged exposition of Comte), 1847.

DR. J. GARTH WILKINSON:—*A Popular Sketch of Swedenborg's Philosophical Works*, 1847; *Emanuel Swedenborg: A Biography*, 1849; *The Human Body and its Connexion with Man*, 1851.

ARCHBISHOP THOMSON:—*An Outline of the Necessary Laws of Thought: A Treatise on Pure and Applied Logic.*

REV. CHARLES KINGSLEY:—*Phaethon, or Loose Thoughts for Loose Thinkers*, 1852; *Alexandria and Her Schools*, 1854; with speculative views in his *Miscellanies* and his writings generally.

PROFESSOR MANSEL:—*Prolegomena Logica*, 1851; *Lecture on the Philosophy of Kant*, 1856; *Limits of Religious Thought* (Bampton Lecture), 1858, and Controversy with Mr. Maurice thereon; *Metaphysics* (reprinted from the Encyclopædia Britannica), 1860.

HENRY THOMAS BUCKLE:—*History of Civilization in England*, 2 vols., 1857, 1861.

PROFESSOR JAMES MCCOSH (Belfast):—*Intuitions of the Mind Inductively Investigated*, 1860 (new edition, 1865).

MR. HENRY CALDERWOOD:—*The Philosophy of the Infinite;*

with special reference to the Theories of Sir William Hamilton and M. Cousin: 2d edition, enlarged, 1861.

PROFESSOR ALEXANDER BAIN (of Aberdeen):—*The Senses and the Intellect*, 1856 (2d edition, 1864); *The Emotions and the Will*, 1859; *On the Study of Character*, 1861.

PROFESSOR A. C. FRASER (Sir William Hamilton's successor in the chair of Logic and Metaphysics in Edinburgh):—*Essays in Philosophy*, 1856; *Rational Philosophy in History and in System*, 1858; and various philosophical articles in the North British Review.

REV. DR. JOHN CAIRNS:—Article *Kant* in the 8th edition of the Encyclopædia Britannica; *Examination of Professor Ferrier's Theory of Knowing and Being*, 1856; *The Scottish Philosophy Vindicated*, 1856; and various occasional Essays.

PROFESSOR THOMAS SPENCER BAYNES (St. Andrews):—*An Essay on the New Analytic of Logical Forms*, 1850; Translation of the *Port Royal Logic*, with Introduction, 1851; *Sir William Hamilton* ("Edinburgh Essays"), 1856.

PROFESSOR JOHN VEITCH (Glasgow); Joint-Editor with Dr. Mansel of Sir William Hamilton's Lectures; author of *Memoir of Dugald Stewart* in collected edition of Stewart's Works; also of other occasional writings.

MR. RICHARD LOWNDES:—*An Introduction to the Philosophy of Necessary Beliefs*, 1865.

MR. HERBERT SPENCER:—*Social Statics*, 1851; *Principles of Psychology*, 1855; *Essays*, reprinted from periodicals (1st series 1858; 2d series 1863); *Education*, 1861; *First Principles* (the 1st volume of a System of Philosophy now in progress), 1862.

MR. JAMES HUTCHINSON STIRLING:—*The Secret of Hegel: Being the Hegelian System in Origin, Principle, Form, and Matter.* 2 vols., 1865.

APPENDIX. Under this head may be included a number of items of which it is difficult to take account in a more special manner. (1) There is the extensive recent literature of so-called "Spiritualism" or "Spirit-Manifestations"—a literature partly of native production, but to a great extent imported from America. In a conspectus like the present, which is statistical and not critical, at least a reference to this literature is demanded, in order to bring before us the actual state of affairs. (2) There have been importations from America of works of quite a different speculative kind, of which Draper's *History of the Intellectual Development of Europe* (1863) may stand as an example. (3) Among ourselves there is a large quantity of speculative thought, of all varieties of tendency, diffused through current Essay-writing in periodicals, or through much of our higher prose-literature not professedly philosophical. Mr. Froude, for example, who might have been named specially in the list with reference to some of his earlier writings and to more recent individual Essays, comes into the list not less distinctly through his "History." Criticisms and discussions recognisable by a characteristic mode of philosophical thought, and sometimes of expressly philosophical nature, might be brought together, with but little trouble, from some of our leading periodicals, and associated, if I am not mistaken, with the name of Mr. Fitzjames Stephen. Finally, not to multiply names, a distinct vein of philosophical opinion, and of criticism of prevailing opinion, has made its appearance in the Essays of Mr. Matthew Arnold.

It is of recent British Philosophy as represented to the eye in this conspectus of recent writers and writings that I mainly propose a review in the chapters which follow. The nature of the references made will indicate on what writers my knowledge enables me to lay the stress, and what others I have in view but slightly.

CHAPTER II.

THE TRADITIONAL DIFFERENCES: HOW REPEATED IN CARLYLE, HAMILTON, AND MILL.

Our conspectus presents us, certainly, with a sufficient medley. For an adequate review of the course of recent British speculative thought as it is there represented, we should have to disentangle those separate tissues or movements of speculative inquiry which have received separate names according to the objects with which they are mainly conversant. We should have to take account separately of recent British Psychology, of recent British Logic, of recent British Ethics, of recent British Jurisprudence, of portions of recent British Theology, and of what has been done under such heads as the Philosophy of Art, the Philosophy of History and Politics, and the Science of Education. In each of these divisions of Philosophy certain names would occur as peculiarly prominent; nor, in pursuing the views of all thinkers in each, is there any limit to the subdivisions that might be necessary.

A survey of this kind is obviously not what we can attempt here. We must employ some much more summary method. Instead of trying to grasp the extensive body of recent British Speculation, we must, if possible, seize it at the very nape, where the trunk and limbs are united with the head. That such a method need not be impossible is indicated by the fact that the different departments of speculative inquiry are obviously interconnected. It is rare to find a thinker that does not pass from one department to another; and he only is spoken of as a systematic philosopher whose scheme of thought has taken some account of them all. What does this imply but that there are for every philosopher certain root-principles, the thinking-out of which in all directions and in all kinds of conjunctions constitutes his very business as a philosopher? Let there be a difference between two thinkers as to their root-principles, and this difference will shoot its correspondences into all the subjects about which they speculate. Further, if any set of differences as to root-principles can be pointed out as repeating itself among philosophers generally, we have here a means of classifying philosophers into schools. Our concern, then, is to see whether we can lay our hands on any set of ultimate differences which seem to have been constant or recurring in philosophy. If we can do so, we shall have an instrument for our purpose.

The ultimate differences among philosophers hitherto are to be sought in Metaphysics proper. It is in the views they take of certain metaphysical questions that philosophers, first of all, or most essentially of all, part company. But Metaphysics is a terrible bugbear of a word in these days. You know the popular definition: When A talks to B, and B does not know what A is saying, and A himself does not very well know either, but both B and A keep up the pretence and nod to each other wisely through the fog—that is Metaphysics. We are all dearly in love with the Physics; but we cannot abide the *Meta* prefixed to them. Perhaps it is a pity. There are some who would not object to see the beautiful Greek word dancing out again in its clear pristine meaning, and naming thoughts and objects of thought which must be eternal everywhere whether there is a name for them or not, but which it is an obstruction and beggarliness of spirit not to be able to name. We need not go farther than Shakespeare for our warrant:

> "The golden round
> Which fate and *metaphysical* aid doth seem
> To have thee crowned withal."

Surely a word that Shakespeare used, and used so exactly and lightly, need not ever be un-English. But there is no use in rowing against the stream; and, till there is a restitution of the word Metaphysics to its English estates, perhaps it is best to get on as much as possible without it. I will try to do so at present. And yet I do not know that you will thank me, or think I have hit on any great improvement as respects perspicuity, when you hear what I propose to substitute. I believe, then, that the differences among philosophers hitherto may be resolved ultimately into (1) a difference of *Psychological Theory*, accompanied by (2) certain differences of *Cosmological Conception*, all subject to or ending in (3) a difference in respect of *Ontological Faith.* Here are three phrases, each more uncouth, it must seem at present, than the single term "Metaphysics," whose meaning I distribute among them. But I will do my best to explain each, and, in doing so, to make the reason for such a triplicity of terms apparent.

I.

THE PSYCHOLOGICAL DIFFERENCE.

All that we know comes to us in what we call Mind or Consciousness. We may differ as to what Mind is—as to the origin of this strange thing, or power, or organism, or mode of existence, which we call Consciousness, and as to the gradations in which it may be found actually appearing up to Man, or may be imagined as ascending beyond Man. Nay, we may differ even as to the ultimate scientific necessity of that distinction between Mind and Matter, Soul and Body, which has come down sanctioned by immemorial usage, and pervades all our language. But we all talk of Mind; nor, with whatever reserve of liberty to speculate what it is, or how it came to be, can we do otherwise. Nothing is known to us except in and through mind. It is in this Consciousness, which each of us carries about with him, and which, be it or be it not the dissoluble result of bodily organization, is thought of by all of us not under any image suggested by that organization, but rather as a great chamber of aërial transparency, without roof, without walls, without bounds, and yet somehow enclosed within us, and belonging to us—it is within this chamber that all presents itself that we can know or think about. Except by coming within this chamber, or revealing itself there, nothing can be known. Whatever may exist, only as much as can break through into this sphere, or send a glimmering of itself into it, exists for our intelligence. From the farthest ends of space, from the remotest moment of time, whatever fact, object, or event would be known by me as happening or existing, or as having ever happened or existed, can be so only by having itself announced, somehow or other, within this present room or chamber which I call my mind. That comets are at this moment pursuing their curves at mighty distances unseen from our Earth; that there was a period when the Earth was a cooling mass of hot matter not yet habitable by organisms known to us; that there came a later period when it was possessed by strange saurians and other animal forms now extinct; that there once lived a Julius Cæsar; that the Earth is a spheroid; that there is an Australian Continent—for any of these conceptions or beliefs my sole warrant lies in corresponding facts of my own consciousness. The Universe, past, present, and to come, rolls into my ken only through my mind. On this ground of Consciousness then, as the repository, storehouse, or conventicle of all knowledge, all philosophers take their stand—even those who end by explaining Consciousness itself as a temporary result or peculiarly exquisite juncture of the conditions which it employs itself in recalling and unravelling. So far there is no difference among philosophers, no division into schools. Should any one attempt to set up as a philosopher on any other ground, it could only be because he did not understand the use of terms.

But let us advance a step. What is the origin of all those multitudinous ideas, notions, or informations which flutter through our Consciousness—which rise there, at our bidding or without our bidding, in all sorts of combinations, and out of which we construct our knowledge or beliefs as to what has been, or is, or is to be? Whence come the ideas into our minds that we find there, and that constitute our intellectual stock? Is any portion of our knowledge of a different origin from the rest, and of a different degree of validity in consequence of that different origin? On this question there has been a polar antagonism among philosophers since there were philosophers in the world. In nothing have philosophers, in nothing have men at large, differed so essentially as in the answers they have given, knowingly or implicitly, to this question. Here is that difference of *psychological theory* wherein, as I have said, we must look for the first split among philosophers, and the explanation of further discrepancies. The history of Philosophy hitherto has been mainly a struggle, varying in form from age to age, but not in substance, between two radically opposed psychological theories.

According to one school or series of philosophers hitherto, all our knowledge, all our notions, all our beliefs, are derived solely from Experience. There is a streaming into our minds, through the senses, of multiform impressions from the external world, which are combined within the mind by laws of association, and are discriminated, classified, analysed, recollected, grouped, and what not, till they form the entire miscellany of our facts, cognitions, and habits, and even our highest principles, propositions, axioms, and generalizations. All that is in Man—all that he calls Truth (let it be even mathematical truth, or his highest notions of right and wrong, or any ideas he may have of beauty, or nobleness, or even Deity)—is but a deposit or induction from the circumstances in which Man is placed. Had these conditions been different, the deposit would have been different. All truth, therefore, is contingent or historically arrived at. There is no such thing as innate or *à priori* truth, or direction to truth; and any higher certainty that some truths may possess over others is but the consequence of a wider, more perfect, and more frequently repeated induction. Such, more or less clearly recognized, avowed, and argued from, has been the theory of one school or series of thinkers since Philosophy began. It is usually called the *Empirical* theory, or the theory of *Sensationalism.* The former name (though it unfortunately has reproachful associations) is only intended to imply what the philosophers in question avow when they say that they own no other origin of our knowledge than Experience; and the latter name only expresses what has also been admitted by the most thorough of these philosophers—to wit, that the assertion that all our knowledge originates in experience is tantamount to the assertion that it all comes into the mind through the channels of the senses. "*Nihil est in intellectu quod non prius fuerit in sensu*" ("Nothing is in the intellect which has not before been in the senses") is the formula of this class of philosophers, propounded by some of themselves, and adopted by others in describing them. Another of their phrases is that the mind is to be conceived as originally a *tabula rasa*, or white paper, containing no characters whatever, but receiving whatever is inscribed upon it wholly from without.*

To this view, however, there has been, on the part of other philosophers, a continued opposition. There have always been philosophers who maintained that there is another source of our knowledge than Experience or Sense—that there are notions, principles, or elements in our minds which could never have been fabricated out of any amount of experience, but must

* The objection to the word *Sensationalism*, as defining the theory of the resolvability of all Truth, or Knowledge, or Faculty, into Experience, is that some who hold the theory would repudiate such a name for it. The objection to the name *Empiricism* is that it imports mere popular prejudice into a philosophical question, by calling up associations with the word "Empiric" as used in an opprobrious sense. As Mr. Mill has used the adjective "Experiential" as unexceptionably conveying the meaning for which a word is sought (Article on Comte in *Westminster Review*, April, 1865), perhaps the substantive *Experientialism*, though crude to the ear, might be brought into use.

have been bedded in the very structure of the mind itself. These are necessary beliefs, *à priori* notions, innate ideas, constitutional forms of thought, truths which we cannot but think.

> "Yet hath the soul a dowry natural,
> And sparks of light some common things to see,
> Not being a blank where nought is writ at all,
> But what the writer will may written be.
>
> "For Nature in Man's Heart her laws doth pen,
> Prescribing Truth to Wit, and Good to Will;
> Which do accuse, or else excuse, all men
> For every thought or practice good or ill.
>
> "And yet these sparks grow almost infinite,
> Making the world and all therein their food,
> As fire so spreads as no place holdeth it,
> Being nourished still with new supplies of wood." *

There have been various forms of this doctrine, some of them confused and mystical enough. But amid all the diversities there is recognisable a common psychological theory, contradictory of that of Sensationalism. It is known as the theory of *à priori* ideas, necessary beliefs, or latterly as the theory of *Intuitionalism* or *Transcendentalism.* By this last name is implied the supposition that there are elements of knowledge, the

* Sir John Davies's Poem "On the Soul," written in 1592.

origin or reason of which transcends or lies beyond the horizon of historical conditions.

Discerned in the ancient world in the form of Aristotelianism *versus* Platonism, traceable through the middle ages in the controversy between the Nominalists and the Realists, this opposition of philosophies has been bequeathed into our modern times, and has represented itself in Britain as well as in other countries.

It is difficult to determine certainly, as regards Bacon (1561—1626), on which side he would have ranged himself. He rather abstained from grappling with the question at all, as too recondite for his purposes, and preferred going out with his whole strength on the exposition of a method in which either set of thinkers might find satisfaction. Yet the general tenor of Bacon's writings leaves an impression as if he had given a splendid impulse to Empiricism, and tried to commit the British nation to a contented futurity in that faith. Among Bacon's British contemporaries, however, there were not wanting respectable defenders of the other psychological theory. And if, on coming on to the next generation, we find, in the powerful figure of Hobbes (1588—1679), an undoubted and avowed champion of Empiricism in its most pronounced form, it is only to see around him resolute maintainers of the contrary philosophy in such men as SIR THOMAS BROWNE (1605—1682), HENRY MORE (1614—1687), CUDWORTH (1617—1688), and the Cambridge Platonists.

But then there arose LOCKE (1632—1704), the "Father of English Philosophy," as he has so generally been called. *He* certainly did pledge his nation, if any man could do such a thing, to a futurity that should reject from its philosophic faith every rag or vestige of the doctrine of innate ideas. He is indeed hazy in his language whenever he seeks to define what he means by his cardinal principle that all our ideas originate in experience—hazier, considerably, even than Hobbes had been. For he seems to avoid or deny the conclusion that this would leave but one ultimate original of our knowledge—to wit, sensations of external objects; and he expressly constitutes another source of knowledge under the name of "Reflection," the "Internal Sense," or the cognizance which the mind has of its own proceedings. But critics of his language on this point have shown, I think, that it can have no meaning unless it implies a surrender of Locke's own principle. By self-consciousness, or the mind's reflection on its own proceedings, the mind certainly knows of these proceedings; but the very question is, whence these proceedings proceed. The mere knowledge of the proceedings, if this is all that Locke means by "Reflection," cannot be a source, in the first instance, of any part of the proceedings. If material is once brought into the mind, the mind may keep a register of what it does with such material; but this mere keeping of the register cannot be spoken of as an independent source of any of the material. In short, though it may be against Locke's will, his Empiricism cannot stop short of Sensationalism, and this has been seen and avowed by his most consistent disciples. "The mind is a blank organism, receiving sensations from without, and knowing and registering what it does with them" —in some such form as this must the radical proposition of Locke's philosophy be expressed; and, if the phrase "blank organism" be unintelligible, it can only be, I apprehend, because the radical proposition of the Empirical philosophy, as hitherto propounded, is really unthinkable. If knowledge is worked-up sensation, then quite as important a constituent of knowledge as the aggregate of sensation that has been worked up is the *mode* in which it has been worked up; and this refers us to the structure of the working-up machine, or mind itself, as having contributed its pressure to the result.

Little wonder, then, that, notwithstanding the power with which Locke's philosophy has transmitted itself in England—a power so great that Lockism and its developments have been recognized abroad as peculiarly the English philosophy—it has never been without assailants in England itself. "The question in dispute could not," as Mr. Mill well says, "so long have remained a question, if the more obvious arguments on either side had been unanswerable."* CLARKE (1675—1729) and BUTLER (1692—1753) were English representatives of the *à priori* philosophy, contemporary with Locke, or near his time. Abroad, in DESCARTES (1596—1650), in SPINOZA (1632—1677), and in MALEBRANCHE (1638—1715), there had been more systematic and illustrious maintainers of the principle of such a philosophy; and their influence had not been unknown in Britain. But what was considered the staggering blow to the Lockian philosophy for the time came from the German LEIBNITZ (1646—1714). "*Nihil est in intellectu quod non prius fuerit in sensu*," was his famous retort upon the maxim of the Sensationalists, "*nisi intellectus ipse:*" "Nothing is in the intellect which has not before been in the senses—unless it be the intellect itself." This epigram of Leibnitz has been ridiculed as meaningless; but it seems to me to have been, in its time, one of the most perfect aphorisms ever uttered. At all events, it defined with surprising exactness the work that remained to be accomplished by another

* Essay on Coleridge, 1840, reprinted in Mill's *Dissertations.*

German, and a greater than Leibnitz, if the world were not to be given over to Lockism and to what Lockism might lead to.

In Britain there had arisen a beautiful-minded Berkeley (1684—1743), who, accepting the notion that the sole furnishing of the mind consists of sensations, but alarmed at certain consequences which he saw, or foresaw, from the prevalent use of that notion, sought to set matters right by denying that the mind had any right to pursue its sensations beyond its own walls, or to attribute them to any real external world of matter. What I am conscious of, all that I really know of, is sensation *in* my mind, and not any external material world beyond my mind; and if you, for your part, adopt the gross and purely gratuitous supposition of such a world, I feel myself both far more faithful to experience, and in possession of a creed far more glorious and solacing when I reject all your external material world—all your hills, and seas, and trees, and stones, and stars—as anything more than existences or motions in some mind or minds! Not that these images, so dear to all of us, are meaningless! What if they are possessed so familiarly by all of us in common, and occur over and over again with such constant regularity, only because they are hieroglyphic and sacramental of the one unseen Spirit and Father of all, ceaselessly communicating His nature and will to His creatures in such well-chosen and sufficient symbols?

But hardly had Berkeley thus made his assertion of Mind or Thought as the only legitimately conceivable reality in the Universe, when there came a HUME (1711—1776), with his simple ruthlessness, to show that, on the principles of philosophic reason, even this reality must vanish from the universe, and not a rack be left to float in the void. This succession of ideas, which is called Mind and which is all that is really known, has *it*, when you investigate sufficiently, any substratum of real continuous being? Is not Mind, too, if you come to that, a hypothesis beyond the facts? Is there any certainty, any substantiality at all, anything but an illusive series of phantasms flitting in a vague nothingness of Time and Space?

Doubt had in Hume reached its extreme limits. Far as the eye could reach, there was nothing but desolation, or at the utmost a phantasmagory of merely empirical co-existences and successions floating over a pit of Nonentity. Aghast at this result of philosophy, radical thinkers everywhere set themselves, as by a common impulse, to a re-examination of that psychological theory of Empiricism itself to which, it was generally seen, the result was to be credited. On Locke's theory of Experience as the one ultimate origin or reason of knowledge, no answer to Hume seemed possibly forthcoming; all the possibilities in that direction seemed to have been exhausted and evaporated by Hume's criticism. If there was to be a rebuilding at all of any edifice of human certainty on the desolated space which Hume had swept, it could only be on a foundation laid afresh in some form of the psychological theory opposed to Locke's—the theory of necessary beliefs, or of *à priori* constituents of knowledge. This is what makes Hume's name so great, and his epoch so important, in the history of European philosophy—that, having exhibited the one of the two competing psychological theories in its uttermost developments, and these such as the soul could not abide in, he occasioned everywhere a disposition to revert to the other theory and take it on trial.

In Hume's own country, while his philosophy was yet flowing fresh and cold from the fountain-head, Reid, who was his senior by a year (1710—1796), but whose philosophical activity was first called forth by him, offered that sober, and, if not subtle, yet rich and grave "Philosophy of Common Sense," the essential character of which was that it fell back on a supposed equipment of necessary beliefs or elements of knowledge, given in the very structure of the mind itself, and not historically or empirically collected.

Reid left his foundation of necessary beliefs in a somewhat chaotic and questionable state; but he at least established in North Britain, while Hume was alive or well remembered, a philosophy of some sort, that might witness to the possibility of a theory of necessary beliefs against the persevering Lockism of South Britain. For, in England, the Empirical Philosophy of Locke, either ignoring its seeming self-explosions in the developments given it by Berkeley and Hume, or else voting these seeming self-explosions to be no self-explosions at all, but only blazes of irrelevant metaphysics kindled on the road by a fantastical Irishman and a dialectical Scotchman, but not interrupting the road anything to speak of for practical purposes—in England, I say, Locke's philosophy had been persevering triumphantly as if nothing were the matter. HARTLEY (1705—1757), ABRAHAM TUCKER (1705—1774), PRIESTLEY (1733—1804), and PALEY (1743—1805), were all Lockians—differing among themselves, to be sure, and not thinking Locke's views by any means final, but accepting his main principle as intact by anything that had happened, and acting on it in their different ways.

Nay, there was a waft into England of a more thorough-going Sensationalism than it might have of itself been able to excogitate out of Locke. This was that philosophy of the French CONDILLAC (1715—

1780) whcih some regard as only Lockism compelled to know itself, and which, boldly reducing the mind to the single function of animal sensibility, declared all knowledge, all habit, all faculty, all belief, to be but "transformed sensation." With but Reid's sober bequest of a so-called Scottish Philosophy of Common Sense to antagonize all this mass of English and imported Sensationalism, what was Great Britain to do? The help which British Transcendentalism, left at such odds, was calling for, was to come to it from without—was to come to it from that quarter from which the entire Europe of the eighteenth century was to derive its intellectual refreshing. Now it was that there arose that fellow-countryman of Leibnitz who was to remember his famous aphorism against Locke, "*nisi intellectus ipse*," and was to give it a significance and explication still wider in the world.

The Critical Philosophy of KANT (1724—1804) has been spoken of as that one event of modern times which is comparable for the dimensions of its spiritual effects to the French Revolution in the political order of things. Of what Kant did all have now some general idea. Feeling, as Reid had done, that the inanity into which Hume had dissolved everything was a dreariness which the human soul could not sustain, he addressed himself to the same task as Reid, but by a different method, in an atmosphere freer from prejudice, and with a profounder reach of spirit. The result was that he reported the mind to be no mere blank organism, receiving sensations and registering its own proceedings with them (even were such a representation thinkable in its very terms), and no mere concretion of transformed sensations round a still-active centre of mere sensibility, but an organism of very definite powers and structure, flung from a fathomless unknown into the world of sensible and historical conditions, and seizing and interpreting these conditions according to "forms" native to itself and of *à priori* origin. Sensibility itself had its forms—Space and Time not being external existences, but structural habits of the perceiving mind; the Understanding proper had its forms—certain modes in which, and in which alone, it could think of things; nay, a-top of the Understanding, or forming its supreme part, was a certain highest faculty, which might be called Reason, having a structural relation to three boundless, unknowable, and yet necessarily-asserted objects—the World, the Soul, and God.

But, if Kant thus substantially reasserted the theory of Transcendentalism against that of Empiricism, he did so in a way that set aside much of the previous philosophizing of the Transcendentalists, and prescribed to Transcendentalism in future a more modest behaviour. By his very use of the phrase "necessary *forms* of thought," as at least an alternative for the phrase "innate *ideas*" till then generally in use, he removed a stumbling-block. He thus brought into clearer view the essential assertion of Transcendentalism—to wit, that the structure or *à priori* capability of the organism, called Mind, which works up the material given in sensation, has at least as much to do with the worked-up result, called Knowledge, as the material itself. But, by the same means, he disowned and cleared away the numerous theosophic and metaphysical systems which previous Transcendentalists had offered to a disgusted world in the name of Transcendentalism—systems which had, in many cases, consisted in first asserting the principle of "innate ideas," and then offering as an authentic collection of these "innate ideas" some set of very definite and locally-elaborated propositions of some small particular person. This two-edged character of Kant's Philosophy has been sympathizingly remarked upon by a British expositor. "The result of Kant's Critical Philosophy," he says, "was that, against the Sceptics, a whole system of knowledge, underived from experience, was proved to exist in the mind, and that, against the Dogmatists, this knowledge was declared to give no hold, at least so far as speculation is concerned, over the nature of things, or metaphysical truth. The Kantian Philosophy thus substitutes for positive Metaphysics a criticism of pure Reason, explaining why there can be none, and at the same time vindicates those elements of knowledge that beget metaphysical inquiry from sceptical rejection and contempt." *

But no man can be final in this world; and the German followers of Kant proceeded less on the restricting lesson of his teaching than he would perhaps have wished. FICHTE (1762—1814) and SCHELLING (1775—1854), not to speak of HEGEL (1770—1831), went on certainly into varieties of a tolerably positive Metaphysics in the name of Transcendentalism, though of kinds that would never have existed but for Kant, and that referred themselves to Kant; and it is the aggregate of their speculations and those of others, along with Kant's, that we think of now as the German Philosophy.

This Philosophy had been long in progress before any influence from it was felt within our islands. Such easier native philosophizing as lay in the continuation and further development of the hereditary Lockism of England, partially antagonized by the Scottish Philosophy of Reid, had sufficed for British purposes. Surviving Priestley and Paley as a universally recognized representative of British Empiricism,

* Dr. Cairns: Art. *Kant*, Encyc. Britannica: 8th edit.

though a representative of novel and unique figure, was BENTHAM (1749—1834); beside whom, with more of the keen faculty of the pure psychologist, appeared JAMES MILL (1773—1836). Admired and respected through the island, on the other hand, as the classic expositor of Reid's homely Scottish Philosophy in its own territory, was DUGALD STEWART (1753—1828); the brilliant aberration from whom of his pupil THOMAS BROWN (1778—1820) was compensated by the greater, though eclectic, consistency of MACKINTOSH (1765—1832). On the whole, though the meeting of the two opposed tides was visible, it was rather in a kind of would be commingling than in any very violent conflict; and, but for the appearance of one spokesman for Transcendentalism, of a richer genius constitutionally than the thinkers of the Scottish School, and in secret correspondence with that new German Philosophy of which they knew little or nothing, Benthamism in Britain would have had no adequate counteractive. This was COLERIDGE (1772—1834), whose philosophical function may be defined by saying that through him there was transmitted an opportune suffusion of Kant and Schelling into England, as of light softened through a stained-glass medium, and that into this suffusion he also resumed whatever of Anglo-Platonism had been floating, long neglected, in the works of old English

Divines. At the back of Coleridge, however, in all this, if one looked rightly, was to be seen, abetting him in the main, if criticising him in particulars, the massive personality of WORDSWORTH.

II.

COSMOLOGICAL DIFFERENCES.

Thus have I traced down, to the exact point of its connexion with the British present, that struggle of the two opposed Psychological Theories in which, in Britain as in every other country, so much of the essence of the history of Philosophy is involved. Let us now attend to that second difference, or set of differences, among philosophers which I described as a difference or differences of *Cosmological Conception.* Not the less because the view which I want here to bring out is susceptible of popular exposition, and may be invested with popular associations, am I disposed to set some store by it.

By "cosmological conception" I do, in effect, mean very much that general image of the totality of things which each one carries about with him, and which is sometimes spoken of more grandly as his "theory of the universe." The beauty of the thing for our purposes is that every one has it. A "psychological theory" is a learned luxury, which the immense majority of people may go from their cradles to their graves without consciously possessing; but every one has a "cosmological conception," though he may not be aware of it under that pedantic-looking name. Yon cottager who spins at her own door has *her* "cosmological conception," *her* working-image of the world she lives in. There is a past of mystery, all opaque beyond her own immediate memory or the traditions of her kith and kin, save where the Bible lights up a gleaming islet or two in the distant gloom; there is a present of toil and care, not without help from on high; and a little way on the hour is thought of when body and soul shall be severed—the one to its rest under the church-yard-grass, the other to that heaven above the stars where loved ones that have gone before will mayhap be seen again:

> "We'll meet and aye be fain
> In the land o' the leal."

And, from the cottager upwards, we have endless variations of the cosmological conception, according to character and knowledge, and yet with wondrously little difference in the main. Not that the variations are without significance. That image of the totality of things which any one carries about with him, and under the power of which he is continually living and acting, is, all-in-all, the most comprehensive expression of his whole being and its acquisitions. It embodies more of himself than his utmost reason, however trained it may be, can reduce into thesis or proposition. For every thing in him goes to make it—the very feelings, and longings, and last impressions or inspirations which his reason has not yet organized; it is tremulous to every touch of new fact, or reading, or meditation. The "cosmological conception" of any man, his sensuous image of the world, would be, if we could get at it, the truest abstract or representation of his whole mind or philosophy.

It is to be expected, in the case of philosophers, that the cosmological conception shall be visibly in accord with the psychological theory. This, however, has not always happened. The history of philosophy presents curious instances in which the cosmological conception of a philosopher has seemed to be grander than his set of avowed principles; or, on the other hand, the propagandist of propositions of glorious capability has been seen dwelling personally in a cosmological conception little better than a hut. Hence, in the case of any philosopher, the necessity of taking account, if possible, of his cosmological conception as well as of his psychological theory; and hence, again, the necessity of having at least some general classification of the cosmological conceptions that have prevailed among philosophers, wherewith to supplement or correct our mere distribution of them, on the grounds of psychological theory, into the two schools of Transcendentalists and Empiricists.

A classification of systems of philosophy according to the cosmological conceptions governing them has actually been made. It is founded on a consideration of the differences among philosophers as to what that totality of existence is which is to be accepted as really vouched for by Mind. All agree, as we have said, that mind is the sole voucher for anything; but philosophers are divisible into schools according to the various views they have taken of the constitution of that phænomenal Universe, that Cosmos, that total round of things, of which we have a recurring assurance in every act of perception, and which is orbed forth more or less fully for each man in his wider contemplations.

The popular or habitual conception of mankind in general is that there are two distinct worlds mixed up in the phænomenal Cosmos—a world of Mind, consisting of multitudes of individual minds, and a world of Matter, consisting of all the extended immensity and variety of material objects. Neither of these worlds is thought of as begotten of the other, but each of them as existing independently in its own proper nature and within its own definite bounds, though they traffic with each other at present. Sweep away all existing minds, and the deserted Earth would continue to spin round all the same, still whirling its rocks, trees, clouds, and all the rest of its material pomp and garniture, alternately in the sunshine and in the depths of the starry stillness. Though no eye should behold and no ear should hear, there would be evenings of silver moonlight on the ocean-marge, and the waves would roar as they broke and retired. On the other hand, suppose the entire fabric of the material Universe abolished and dissolved, and the dishoused population of spirits would still somehow survive in the imaginable vacancy. If this second notion is not so easy or common as the first, it still virtually belongs to the popular conception of the contents or constitution of the Cosmos. The conception is that of a Natural Dualism, or of the contact in every act of perception of two distinct spheres, one an internal perceiving mind, and the other an external world composed of the actual and identical objects which this mind perceives.

On the first exercise of philosophic thought, however, this conception is blurred. An immense quantity of what we all instinctively think of as really existing out of ourselves turns out, on investigation, not to exist at all as we fancy it existing, but to consist only of affections of the perceiving mind. The redness of the rose is not a real external thing, immutably the same in itself; it is only a certain peculiar action on my physiology which the presence of an external cause or object seems to determine. Were my physiology different, the action would be different, though the cause or object remained the same. Indeed, there *are* persons in whom the presence of a rose occasions no sensation of redness such as is known to me, but a much vaguer sensation, not distinguishable from what I should at once distinguish as greenness. And, as colour is thus at once detected as no external independently-existing reality, but only a recurring physiological affection of myself and other sentient beings like myself, so with a thousand other things which, by habit or instinct, I suppose as externally and independently existing. When I imagine the depopulated Earth still wheeling its inanimate rotundity through the daily sunshine and the nocturnal shadow, or one of its bays still resonant in moonlit evenings with the roar of the breaking waves, it is because, in spite of myself, I intrude into the fancy the supposition of a listening ear and a beholding eye analogous to my own. It is only by a strong effort that I can realize that a great deal at least of what I thus think of as the goings-on of things by themselves is not and cannot be their goings-on by themselves, but consists at the utmost of effects interbred between them and a particular sentiency in the midst of them. But the effort may be made; and, when it is made repeatedly, in a great many directions, and with reference to a great many of the so-called properties of matter, the inevitable result for the philosophic mind is that the popularly-imagined substance of a real external world finds itself eaten away or corroded, at least to a certain depth. So far philosophers are agreed. It is when they proceed to consider to *what* depth the popularly-imagined substance of the real external world is thus eaten away, or accounted for, that they begin to differ.

Some philosophers, departing as little as may be from the popular judgment, suppose that, however much of the apparent external world may be resolved into affections of the subjective sentiency, there still remains an objective residue of such primary qualities as extension, figure, divisibility, mobility, etc., belonging to external matter itself, and by the direct and immediate cognizance of which the mind is brought face to face with external substance and knows something of its real goings-on. Philosophers of this school are known generally as REALISTS. More numerous, however, are those who, not allowing an objective and independent reality even to the so-called primary qualities of matter, but believing them as well as colour, odour, or savour, to be only affections of the sentiency, deny that the mind is in any sense brought face to face with real external things such as they seem in the act of perception. To thinkers of this school there has been given the general name of IDEALISTS.

This broad distinction of Philosophers cosmologically into REALISTS and IDEALISTS is so far convenient enough. Cosmologically, or in respect of this present Universe of ours, with its dualism of Mind and Matter, every man must declare himself either a Realist or an Idealist, if he understands the meanings attached to these terms. The distinction has reference solely to his notion of the so-called external or material world in its relations to the perceiving mind. If he abides, though only in part, by the popular conception, and regards the material world as a substantial reality independent of the perceiving mind, and which the mind, according to its powers, presses against and directly apprehends in every act of perception, then he is a REALIST. If, on the other hand, he cannot see that there need be asserted any external material world with such characters as we attribute to it, but supposes that our unanimous agreement in the imagination of such an external world is merely a habit of our own sentiency, projecting its own ideas or affections outwards and giving them a body, then he is an IDEALIST.

The mere distribution of Philosophers, however,

into the two great orders of Realists and Idealists does not answer all the historical requirements. Each order has been subdivided, still on cosmological grounds, into two sections. Among Realists, the *Materialists* or *Materialistic Realists* have been distinguished strongly from the *Dualistic Realists*, called also *Natural Realists.* Similarly, among Idealists, there has been a large group of what may be called *Constructive Idealists*, distinguishable from the *Pure Idealists.* But this is not all. Not only by this subdivision of each of the orders, still on cosmological grounds, into two sects, are we provided with the four sects of *Materialists*, *Natural Realists*, *Constructive Idealists*, and *Pure Idealists;* but (by bringing considerations into the classification which, I think, are not exclusively cosmological) these four sects have been flanked by two extreme sects, called respectively *Nihilists* and *Pantheists.* The doctrine of these last is called also, in recent philosophical language, the doctrine of *Absolute Identity.*

Thus six systems in all, professedly cosmological, have figured in the past history of Philosophy. Let us re-enumerate them in the arrangement which will be most convenient for us in the sequel, adding such further explanations as may seem necessary.

(1.) There is the system of *Nihilism*, or, as it may be better called, *Non-Substantialism.* According to this system, the Phænomenal Cosmos, whether regarded as consisting of two parallel successions of phænomena (Mind and Matter), or of only one (Mind or Matter), resolves itself, on analysis, into an absolute Nothingness,—mere appearances with no credible substratum of Reality; a play of phantasms in a void. If there have been no positive or dogmatic Nihilists, yet both Hume for one purpose, and Fichte for another, have propounded Nihilism as the ultimate issue of all reasoning that does not start with some *à priori* postulate.

(2.) There is the system of *Materialism*, or *Materialistic Realism*. According to this system, a certain sum-total of real existence is assumed as underlying the conscious succession of ideas, but the seeming dualism or co-ordinate independence of two worlds, one of Mind and the other of Matter, is got rid of by supposing Matter to be the primordial unity, and Mind to be, or have been, educed from it. There have been avowed Materialists among philosophers, of whom Hobbes is an early English example. But many have been called Materialists who have really not been such; nor, if we consider the contradictory varieties of thought which may exist within one apparent drift of speculation, ought the name, while odium attaches to it, ever to be applied to any one without his own permission.

(3.) There is the system of *Natural Realism* or *Natural Dualism*. According to this system, while Mind or Spirit is regarded as an undoubtedly real essence, or substance, or energy of one origin and nature, the extended Material World in the midst of which this Mind or Spirit seems to find itself, and with which it seems to have commerce, is also assumed as a distinct reality, and not as a distinct reality of some highly-removed sort, acting upon us illusively through mediate signs and impulses, but as actually very much that solid and substantial world which we get at through our senses. There have been varieties, however, cruder and finer, of this Natural Realism. What do mankind in general believe? They believe that the material world is exactly and in every respect the world which our senses report to us as external to ourselves. They believe that the rocks, the hills, the trees, the stars, that we all see, are not mere hieroglyphics of a something different from themselves and from us, but are really what is there. That outer vastness of space in which orbs are shining and wheeling is no mere representation or visionary allegory of something; it is the thing itself. This is, and always has been, the popular belief of mankind in general. All mankind may therefore be described, generally, as Natural Realists. But, strange to say, Natural Realism has been the system of but one or two modern philosophers—among whom Reid is named as a type. Nay, more, among these philosophers it is not the popular form of the belief that is entertained. Mankind in general suppose sweetness, shrillness, colour, etc., to be qualities inherently belonging to the objects to which they are attributed, while the philosophers who are Natural Realists admit that at least these so-called "secondary qualities" of objects have no proper outness, but are only physiological affections—affections of the organs of taste, hearing, sight, &c., produced by particular objects. Thus the Natural Realism of philosophers is itself a considerable remove from the Natural Realism of the crude popular belief. It does not, with the crude popular belief, call the whole apparent external world of sights, sounds, tastes, tacts, and odours, the real world that would be there whether man were there or not; but it descries in that apparent world a block or core, if I may so say, which would have to be thought of as really existing, even if there were swept away all that consists in our rich physiological interactions with it.

(4.) There is the system of *Constructive Idealism.* It may be so called to distinguish it from the more developed and extreme Idealism presently to be spoken of. According to this system, we do not perceive the real external world immediately, but only mediately —that is, the objects which we take as the things actually perceived are not the real objects at all, but only vicarious assurances, representatives, or nuntii of real unknown objects. The hills, the rocks, the trees, the stars, all the choir of heaven and earth, are not, in any of their qualities, primary, secondary, or whatever we choose to call them, the actual existences out of us, but only the addresses of a "something" to our physiology, or eductions by our physiology out of a "something." They are all Thoughts or Ideas, with only this peculiarity involved in them, that they will not rest in themselves, but compel a reference to objects out of self, with which, by some arrangement or other, they stand in relation.

Difficult as this system may be to understand, and violently as it wrenches the popular common sense, it is yet the system into which the great majority of philosophers in all ages and countries hitherto are seen, more or less distinctly, to have been carried by their speculations. While the Natural Realists among philosophers have been very few, and even these have been Realists in a sense unintelligible to the popular mind, quite a host of philosophers have been Constructive Idealists. These might be farther subdivided according to particular variations in the form of their Idealism. Thus, there have been many Constructive Idealists who have regarded the objects rising to the mind in external perception, and taken to be representative of real unknown objects, as something more than modifications of the mind itself—as having their origin without. Among these have been reckoned Malebranche, Berkeley, Clarke, Sir Isaac Newton, Tucker, and possibly Locke. But there have been other Constructive Idealists, who have supposed the objects rising in the mind in external perception to *be* only modifications of the mind itself, but yet, by some arrangement, vicarious of real unknown objects, and intimating their existence. Among such have been reckoned Descartes, Leibnitz, Condillac, Kant, and most Platonists. The general name "Idealists," it will be seen, properly enough includes both the classes as distinct from the Natural Realists, inasmuch as both classes hold that what the mind is directly cognizant of in external perception is only ideas. But, inasmuch as these ideas are held by both classes, though under divers hypotheses, to refer to real existences beyond themselves, and distinct from the perceiving mind, the thinkers in question may also properly enough be called Realists or Dualists, though not "Natural" Realists or Dualists. They occupy a midway place between the Natural Realists and the philosophers next to be mentioned.

(5.) There is the system of *Pure Idealism*, which abolishes Matter as a distinct or independent existence in any sense, and resolves it completely into

Mind. Though this system is named in the scheme, for the sake of symmetry, and as the exact antithesis to Materialism, it is difficult to cite representatives that could be certainly discriminated from the merely Constructive Idealists just mentioned on the one hand and from the school of philosophers next following on the other. Fichte is, perhaps, the purest example.

(6.) There is the system of *Absolute Identity.* According to this system, Mind and Matter are phænomenal modifications of one common Substance. The whole Cosmos, both of Matter and of Mind, is referred to a one Absolute Entity, of which it is to be conceived as but the function, activity, manifestation, or forthrushing. This system, it will be noted, is at the opposite extreme from Nihilism. It is the system of Spinoza, and also, though with a difference, of Schelling.

In this classification of Philosophical Systems from one point of view I have followed, with some little liberty of rearrangement and change of expression, the best recent authority on the subject.* Objections

* Sir William Hamilton's *Discussions* (Articles "Philosophy of Perception" and "Idealism"); also his *Lectures on Metaphysics* (i. 293—297); but particularly his *Dissertations on Reid* (748, 749, and 816—819). In these portions of Sir William's writings, his classification of Philosophical Systems from the point of view of the Doctrine of External Perception is turned over and over again in all sorts of ways, and with all sorts of side-lights. I have taken his authority for the

may be taken to the classification even in respect of what it was intended for; nor, whatever may be its worth as respects the past, do I think that it provides, as it stands, a sufficient means of recognizing and naming the various working cosmological conceptions now extant among philosophers, and of which it might be desirable to take account.* But it goes so far. It brings out, at all events, what I wished to bring out—to wit, that we can have by no means an adequate collective view of the philosophers of our time, so long as we trust to a mere preliminary division of them, however accurate, into Empiricists and Transcendentalists. Behold what crossings and matchings, both of Empiricism and Transcendentalism, in-

facts, but have modified and rearranged the classification to suit it to my purpose in the text.

* For example, a very prevalent form of cosmological conception among thinkers of the present day is one which, if I am not mistaken, it would be difficult to assign to any one of the six systems enumerated. It is a compound of *Materialism* with *Constructive Idealism.* A very large number of thinkers, if I am not mistaken, always think of Mind as bred out of Matter, and yet, when they study this Mind as perceiving and taking cognizance of that World of Matter out of which it has been bred, do not allow that it grasps the reality at all, but only that it substitutes for the reality a hypothetical construction of its own affections. Sentiency, they think, is the child of Matter, but has never beheld, nor can behold, the real face of its mother. Are there not also millions of forms and degrees of sentiency, from the lowest of living creatures up to man, each apprehending the world according to a different measure of capacity? Is the dog's world—*i. e.* the construction of his own affections to which the dog attributes an external reality—the same, even so far as it goes, as his master's?

calculable beforehand, in even the cosmological classification so suggested to us! Empiricists among the Idealists, side by side with Transcendentalists! On the other hand, Transcendentalists in almost all the six classes, and even in those where we should expect only Empiricists! What if there should be such a thing even as a Transcendental Materialist, or a Materialistic Transcendentalist? I am not concerned here with what ought to be possible or impossible in cosmological conception consistently with either of the two psychological theories. My statement is that a philosopher may have a working cosmological conception which could not be reconciled with his avowed psychological theory if he would think that theory consistently out, or respecting which, at all events, his opponents give him this assurance. In short, as there have been strange crossings and matchings of the psychological theories with the prevailing cosmological conceptions in the past, so there may be in the future. And what if we were still farther to complicate the intertexture by introducing, even at this point, the theological element? There have been Atheistic as well as Theistic Idealists; there have been Theistic as well as Atheistic Empiricists; there are in the world some whom rough popular speech does not hesitate to describe as Transcendental Atheists; and, as there have been examples of what might be called Theistic

Materialism in the past, what if something still describable by that name should exist somewhere at present, throwing stones both at Atheism and Pantheism?

III.

THE ONTOLOGICAL DIFFERENCE.

Mind or Consciousness, whatever it may be, is that organism in the midst of all things through which all our knowledge of all things must come. Philosophers, therefore, may make a study of *that;* and they have done so under the name of Psychology. Round this organism, howsoever related to it, is the vast and varied Cosmos, or phænomenal and historical Universe, which the organism reports to us as hung in Space and voyaging through Time. Philosophers may make a study of *that;* and such a study would be Cosmology. But, beyond this whole phænomenal Universe or Cosmos which has the Mind of Man in its midst, it has been the passion of Philosophy to assert or speculate a transcendent Universe, or Empyrean of Things in Themselves, of Essential Causes, of Absolute or Noumenal, as distinct from Phænomenal, Existence. What enspheres the Cosmos, what supports it, of what absolute reality underneath and beyond itself is it significant, of what Absolute Meaning is it the expression, the allegory, the poem?

May not the entire Phænomenal Cosmos, hung in Space and voyaging through Time, be but an illusion—and this whether we consider it to be, within itself, a play of Matter alone, or of Spirit alone, or of both Matter and Spirit? If we feel that it is not, on what warrant do we so feel? In what tissues of facts and events, material or moral, in this phænomenal Space-and-Time World shall we trace the likeliest filaments of that golden cord by which we then suppose it attached to a World not of Space and Time; and how shall we, denizens of Space and Time, succeed in throwing the end of the cord beyond our Space-and-Time World's limits? Is the Cosmos a bubble? Then, what breath has blown it, and into what Empyrean will it remelt when the separating film bursts? Asking these questions in all varieties of forms, Philosophy has debated the possibility of an *Ontology*, or science of things in themselves, in addition to a Psychology and a Cosmology. These two are sciences of the Phænomenal, but *that* would be a science of the Absolute. It would be the highest Metaphysic of all, and, indeed, in one sense, the only science properly answering to that name. It would be the science of the Supernatural. Can there be such a science? A question this which seems to break itself into two—Is there a Supernatural? and can the Supernatural be known? It is the differences that have shown themselves among philosophers in their answers, express or implied, to these questions that I have in view under the name of their differences in respect of *Ontological Faith.*

The Ontological difference is intertangled with the Psychological and Cosmological differences, and a discussion of *them* always brings *it* into sight. Most probably, if matters were fully reasoned out, all the three sets of differences might be knit together, and it might be shown that adhesion to one of the two psychological theories involved, in strict consistency, an obligation to a particular mode of cosmological conception, and that this again involved obligation to a particular form of ontological faith. But the minds even of philosophers, coming at separate times on questions which are really inter-related, do not always march up to them in the same state of feeling, but sometimes bring forces to the front in one case which remain in the background in others. Hence, just as it seemed impossible to infer with any precision from our knowledge of a philosopher's theory of the Origin of our Ideas in which of the six systems of conception as to the constitution of the Phænomenal Universe he might be found ranking himself, so neither from a philosopher's psychological theory nor from his cosmological system would it be safe, as things go, to infer his ontological faith.

Take the first ontological question. *Is* there an Absolute, a Supernatural, or is the Phænomenal Universe all that exists? It might seem that only the Transcendentalist would be entitled to a strong affirmative to this question. His very theory of the Mind of Man, as an organism bringing with it into the Phænomenal World ideas or structural forms of *à priori* origin, refers one, if it has any meaning, to a Supernatural World or Empyrean, out of which the Mind of Man is to be conceived as having proceeded, and from which it still carries recollections or shreds of affinity. From the Empiricist on the other hand it might seem that the only answer to be expected to the question is, "I do not know, nor can any man know." As all knowledge, according to the Empiricist, is the product of experience, and as there cannot have been and never can be experience of anything beyond the bounds of Experience, the assertion of an Absolute or Supernatural, save in the sense of "the yet unknown" or "all that nobody yet knows anything about," would seem to be incompetent to the Empiricist. And yet there have been most positive Theists and Theologians among the Empiricists—firm and even dogmatic believers in an Absolute; and there is nothing that such Theistic and Theological Empiricists have resented more than the assertion of Transcendentalists that their Theism was irreconcileable with their Empiricism, and that they had no right to leap to the conclusion of an Infinite Intelligence beyond the world or in it from the observation of ever so much of worldly watch-making.

If thus, practically, the ontological creed of a philosopher, even in its first article, cannot be always inferred from his psychological theory, neither can it be safely inferred from the form of his cosmological conception. If any one could assert "There *is* no Absolute," surely it might be the Nihilist, who has analysed away both Matter and Thought, and attenuated the Cosmos into vapour and non-significance. Yet, from the abyss of a speculatively reasoned Nihilism more void than Hume's, Fichte returned by a convulsive act of soul—which he termed *faith*—an intense, a burning, a blazing Ontologist. *A fortiori*, the Materialist has not seen that he need deny an Absolute. Regarding the Cosmos, considered within itself, as wholly a development of Matter, he has not always thought himself debarred, any more than other people, from assuming an Absolute from which this Cosmos of developed matter may have its metaphysical tenure. For Natural Realists, again, and for either Constructive Idealists or Pure Idealists, the belief in a supernatural is obviously easy and congenial. Analysing the double series of phænomena which he finds in the Cosmos, and coming in each case upon a substratum of ultimate reality—in the one upon a Thinking Substance constituted in such and such a manner, and in the other on an extended and resisting Substance of Matter diversely constituted—the Natural Realist feels as if at both points he were actually grating on the rock of the Absolute. He feels himself at both points in contact with some immeasurable Real Existence, beyond all phænomenal Nature, and yet determining it and projected into it.

With the Constructive Idealist it is the same, save that, as his notion of Matter is more impalpable and hypothetical than that of the Realist, his sense of contact with the Supernatural is concentrated rather in his notion of the necessity of a real noumenal origin for the grand phænomenon of Consciousness. In this, the Pure Idealist, for whom the Universe resolves itself wholly into this single phænomenon, may well outdo his more hesitating brother. All that is, was, or will be in this Space-and-Time World is, according to the Pure Idealist, but the organized, consolidated, and transmitted aggregate of the thoughts of the Minds within it. All the more, therefore, must that power of thinking which has involved itself in such a vast cocoon of wonders be itself conceived as originating in the fiat of some Absolute Cause. And yet, as in the end, it is only a felt necessity or compulsion of thought that either Realists or Idealists can plead when they assert a Supernatural beyond the Phænomenal, and as this feeling of necessity or compulsion is itself liable to alternations of strength and weakness, both Realists and Idealists will be found to have wavered greatly in respect even of that first article of any ontological faith which would simply aver a Supernatural and stop there.

Thus Shelley, the very principle of whose life and poetry was philosophical Idealism, seemed willing, throughout a great part of his life, not only to be thought of, but to think of himself, as an Atheist. And so it is quite conceivable that a Natural Realist, even when grappling the rock of an Absolute through his ultimate investigations of the two orders of cosmical phænomena whose distinctness he recognizes, should have moments of doubt whether it is a rock he is grappling, or only an illusion. In short, only those whose interpretation of the Cosmos merges in a metaphysical doctrine of Absolute Identity would seem to have got hold of a cosmological principle which, in itself, and without aid from any act of the soul not allowed for by its own terms, would positively and continuously presuppose and assert a Supernatural. With them, Nature *is* the Supernatural in one of its moments. The Cosmos does not swim in an Empyrean from which it is divided by any film, but is that very state or embodiment of the entire Empyrean which has been attained up to this instant. The Phænomenal is the life of the Absolute.

It is when we pass, however, to the second question propounded towards an Ontology that the interest grows most vivid. It being supposed that an Absolute exists, is any knowledge thereof possible to Man? Here, of course, leaving out of sight all who would actually deny that there is an Absolute, and also all whose position in respect to that prior question is that they think an *Ay* or a *No* to it equally absurd, we need attend only to those who, in whatever manner, stand by an affirmative to that prior question. What has been the history among *them* of the farther question as to the cognisability of this affirmed Absolute of things? The history of the question, we may say confidently, has consisted in a continuous, emphatic, and nearly unanimous iteration of a negative answer to the question, accompanied all the while by modes of thought, speech, and conduct, in which a positive answer to it, and very definite forms of a positive answer, have been practically assumed.

The almost unanimous assertion of philosophers, since philosophy began, has certainly been to the effect that in no form is an Ontology, or knowledge of things in themselves, possible to Man. It has been the assertion not only of philosophers, but of the most devout and most dogmatic of theologians. That the finite cannot apprehend or conceive the Infinite; that neither matter nor mind can be known in its essence; that all man's knowledge can only be relative and according to the measure and mode of his intelligence; that any attempt of human thought to transcend the phænomenal world is only as if a bird should hope to soar above that element the beating of its wings in which is the very cause of its soaring at all; that it is blasphemy to think that God is as we can think Him to be—in these and a thousand other ways the thing has been stated. The Socratic definition of the highest human wisdom—that it is the most assured knowledge of our own inevitable ignorance—has been repeated, in this connexion, till it is the best-known of philosophical maxims.

The only loudly-heard voice from antiquity proclaiming the possibility of an Ontology seems to be that of Socrates's disciple, Plato. The far-famed *Idealism* of Plato is, in fact, a theory of the cognisability of the Absolute.* Our Phænomenal World, Plato

* Here we may note the confusion of practice in the use of the word *Idealism*. It is used in three different senses, and in combinations of these. First, Transcendentalism in Psychology, inasmuch as it avows a belief in innate ideas, or necessary forms of thought, is sometimes called Idealism. Secondly, there is the more accurate and now the philosophically accepted use of the term, which identifies Idealism with a particular form of Cosmological Conception—that, to wit, which resolves all material phænomena into subjective affections, or affections or ideas of Consciousness. This is the

loves to fancy, is not so utterly and hopelessly disconnected from the Absolute World of Noumena, Ideas, or Things in Themselves, but that for the pure and persevering reason a passage from the one to the other may be possible. He taxes his gorgeous imagination for ways of representing his notion of this transcendent possibility. Human Life or the Cosmos of Man, he says in one place, may be likened to a dungeon or cave, the inmates of which are chained, with their faces towards the interior wall, and incapable of turning round. Lo! on the wall on which they gaze there flit strange shapes and phantasmagories—the phænomena of this world. Voices also are heard which they, the beholders of the phantasmagories, attribute to the phantasmagories, and connect with them as well as they can. For the phantasmagories on the wall, and the accompanying voices, are

sense in which the term has been employed, unless where there is indication to the contrary, throughout the text. But, thirdly, there is Plato's Idealism, which includes much more than mere Psychological Idealism, and is quite different from Cosmological Idealism. It is an Ontological Idealism, or a theory how the phænomena of this world may be but reproductions or disguises of the ideas or essential realities of a Supernatural World, or Empyrean of things in themselves. There has been no end of misstatements arising, even in histories of Philosophy, from inattention to these different meanings of the word Idealist. Philosophers have been spoken of as Idealists who were Idealists only in one of the senses and by no means in the others. Nay, when a thinker declares of himself that he is an Idealist, it is still necessary to ask in which of the three senses, or in what combination of them, he uses the term.

the sole realities to these tenants of the cave. But what if they could turn their faces round towards the entrance to the cave, where it communicates with a larger and freer world? Then would they begin to surmise differently. For along the mouth of the cave, though separated from it by an embankment, there lies a bit of roadway, on which persons belonging to that freer world are ever passing and repassing, carrying images or what not, and talking to each other the while; and beyond the roadway there is a blazing light; and the phantasmagories on the inner wall of the cave are but shadows of the tops of the images which the pedestrians on the bit of roadway in front of the cave are carrying past it; and the voices heard and attributed to the shadows are the voices of the invisible bearers of these images.

Thus in our World of Sense, all those phænomena whi h seem realities to us, are but the shadows and echoes of real objects and ongoings in an unseen World of Archetypes, Ideas, or Self-subsisting Intelligences. If we could but turn round! Nay, what are philosophers but those who do contrive somehow to turn round, and even though dazzled at first, to work their way to such a full glimpse of the Archetypal World as that they can bring back a report of it to the other dwellers in the cave, and press upon them that explanation of the phænomena of the cave which the report furnishes? Or, again, as an alternative to this theory of Archetype and Shadow, expounded in some parts of Plato's writings, we have, in others, his theory of Reminiscence. Man, though now the denizen of this World of Sense, has had a former and grander life in the Empyrean of Ideas, and when here he investigates truth and arrives by contemplation at the pure ideas or forms of phænomena, these are but recollections or recoveries more or less faint, of the knowledge familiar to him in his former existence. Those *à priori* elements of knowledge, which Plato, as the supreme Transcendentalist of antiquity, contended for so strongly under the name of Ideas, were, therefore, in his language, *à priori* in a very special sense. They were fragments of a former Absolute Existence, actually shivered through our life amid the phænomena of sense; and it was the very business of Philosophy to seek for the fragments and to piece them together. Wordsworth here is but a renderer of the Transcendentalism of Plato:

"Our birth is but a sleep and a forgetting:
The Soul that rises with us, our life's Star,
Hath had elsewhere its setting,
And cometh from afar;
Not in entire forgetfulness,
And not in utter nakedness,
But trailing clouds of glory do we come
From God, who is our home."

Allowance being made for the exuberance of Plato, and for the perplexity as to some parts of his final meaning arising from his very exuberance, it seems inevitable to conclude that *he* did not limit the possibilities of Philosophy to a Psychology and a Cosmology, but regarded it as the very work of Philosophy to push on through these to an Ontology, or Science of Absolute Truth. Now, in this matter, men in all time, or at least Transcendentalists in all time, have felt with Plato, even while reasoning with Aristotle. If an Ontology is an impossibility for the human spirit, a Transcendentalism that should not root itself in an assumed Ontology seems equally an impossibility. What has been the history of the Soul of the World but a rage of Ontology? Why have there been wars, why have there been martyrdoms, but because one Supernaturalism sought to put down another? What has genius been, what has religious propagandism been, but a metaphysical drunkenness? Conceive a spiritual teacher coming forward, and, in reply to questions as to the certainty of his doctrine, owning that he knew it only to be cosmologically true, but whether true absolutely he could not tell. Would not his virtue seem to be gone from him in the very act of the confession?

Above all, if he were a Transcendentalist, contending for necessary and universal elements or ideas in the human reason, and if, when put to it, he were to admit that he knew even this mental organism, this Soul with its necessary ideas of God and Right, only and exclusively as a phænomenon, and dared not affirm whether its necessary ideas had a basis in the eternal nature of things or not, would not this diffidence be his ruin? But it never so happens. Men do proceed on the notion that what they know to be true *has* a foundation in the nature of things. Transcendentalists cannot use their phrase "*à priori* elements of the human soul" without implying strenuously not only that these elements come out of some priority, but that they are *bonâ fide* intentions of that priority, and not deceptions. But what is this but to profess to know something about the Absolute? It is not only to assert that there is an Absolute and stop there (which would itself be something); it is also to assert something very specific of the Absolute—to assert a something equivalent to what, in human speech, is called veracity.

And yet, rationally, the Absolute is incognisable, unthinkable! How is this? What is the reconciliation? There has been one almost invariable answer. "The sphere of Faith transcends the sphere of Reason." There is, it is said, an organic necessity of man's nature, or of his nature in certain moods, which compels him to believe much that he cannot know.

It is by Faith, it is said, and not by Reason, that we can refer the laws of our own consciousness, or the constitution of the material world around us, to a valid origin or purpose in Absolute Being; it is by Faith, and not by Reason, that we can even assert an Absolute at all, except as a mere blank, or negative, or paralysis of knowledge. Faith, and not Reason, is that condition of spirit in which Man, by his nature, must ever ponder the ultimate problems. And so it is at this point that Christian Theology comes in, and, showing her credentials, offers instruction. But even she presents herself not as capable of theorizing the Absolute for human reason, but only as the bearer of a special message. Whatever authority she may assume as she proceeds with her teachings, her opening address to man, when he first questions her metaphysically, is but as that of Raphael to Adam, when he began, at Adam's request, the narrative of the events of that supra-mundane Universe which had preceded Man's:—

"High matter thou enjoinst me, O prime of Men,
Sad task and hard! For how shall I relate
To human sense the invisible exploits
Of warring Spirits; how, without remorse,
The ruin of so many, glorious once
And perfect while they stood; how, last, unfold
The secrets of another World, perhaps

Not lawful to be revealed? Yet, for thy good,
This is dispensed; and what surmounts the reach
Of human sense I shall delineate so,
By likening spiritual to corporal forms,
As may express them best—though what if Earth
Be but the shadow of Heaven, and things therein
Each to other like more than on Earth is thought?"

In no modern philosopher is the attitude of Psychological Transcendentalism to the question of the possibility of an Ontology presented more interestingly than in Kant. He was, as we have seen, the refounder of Transcendentalism in modern Europe. In an age when Empiricism seemed to have taken universal possession, and killed out its opposite, he reproclaimed that opposite. As the result of an investigation of the human mind more exact and profound than had ever been undertaken before, he reasserted the mind to be an organism of certain structural or *à priori* capabilities, or forms of operation, which necessitated its mode of commerce with all matter of experience, and the notions, thinkings, and beliefs that might accrue from that commerce. Nay, as the supreme *à priori* elements of human reason, he recognised the ideas of three supra-sensuous or trans-conscious objects—God, the Soul, and the World. In the Soul of Man, at its very highest, what was perceived, as structural and connate, was a straining after these three objects of trans-conscious enormity. And yet, in answer to the question whether, after all, this might not be a mere straining into vacuum, a delusive grappling towards objects in an ocean of no objects, Kant declared speculative reason to be impotent. Here was the sceptical side to his Transcendental Philosophy. As to the fact of an organic and necessary grappling of the mind in search of an Absolute he had no doubt; but as to the positive existence of an Absolute to answer the grappling, and much more as to the nature of the being of such an absolute, if it existed, he had nothing to say, in the name of Reason, but that Reason could say nothing. A rational Ontology or Metaphysic was impossible. Only in the phænomenal world did Man's reason live, move, and have its being; not an inch beyond that world could it chase any phænomenon whatever—not even the momentous phænomenon of its own constitution. Objectively, therefore, the Absolute was nothing more than a name for Unknowableness—Inconceivability. Subjectively, however, or as a regulative principle or fact of the mental organism itself, the notion of an Absolute, or the instinctive straining towards the Unknowable, was to be considered as something more for Man than mere nescience. In this position Kant left the question, appending to his philosophy of the Pure Reason a philosophy of the Practical Reason, wherein Man, returning from his hopeless attempt to outfly the phænomenal, might take consoling refuge.

Here it is that the post-Kantian philosophers of Germany refused to abide with Kant. The post-Kantian movement, as represented in Fichte, Schelling, and Hegel, was a strenuous exertion for the recovery of Ontology as that without which all the Psychology and all the Cosmology in the world would be little better than blindman's buff. Thus, in the speculative philosophy of Fichte, there were two stages. The first landed him in pure Subjective Idealism, or that system which, annihilating the Cosmos, save as the externalizing of one's own thoughts, may be said to have merged Cosmology utterly in Psychology. Ontology itself, if there could be such a science, was also merged in Psychology—for either the only all-in-all or Absolute was that Self of which the Cosmos was a poem, or, if there was a transcendent Absolute which had spun the Self which spun the Cosmos, Self could not mount back to it. Dissatisfied, however, with this state of things, or with the resolution which he began to think inevitable of his Subjective Idealism into Nihilism, Fichte was latterly ravished with the notion of a doctrine which should start with an Ontology from which Psychology and Cosmology should be derivatives. If there were assumed a one Absolute existence, identical both with

Self and Not-self—a kind of Neutrum of Self and Not-self, and of which the two together constituted the life or manifestation—here Psychology might have a real ontological beginning. It remained, however, for Schelling and Hegel to work out this famous Identity doctrine, if, indeed, it did not belong to them, or to one of them, originally more than to Fichte. As Schelling first distinctly published the doctrine, and as he outlived Hegel for many years, it is with Schelling's name that the doctrine has been universally associated, and the place usually assigned to Hegel has been that of an Aristotle contemporary with this Plato in the most important part of his career, and subjecting all his views, the Identity doctrine included, to a vigorous logical grasp.* Taking the Identity doctrine, therefore, as Schelling's, and leaving Hegel out of account in the meantime, we can see how, in the Schellingian doctrine, the world was made aware of a form in which the possibility of an Ontology might be vindicated. The Absolute, according to this doctrine, is the one Infinite Existence or

* For some very interesting observations on the relations of Hegel to Schelling in respect of the Identity doctrine, and on the relations of both generally to Fichte, and of all three to Kant, see Mr. Stirling's "Secret of Hegel," vol. i. pp. 20—31. Mr. Stirling holds that the *outcome* of the German Philosophical movement was in Kant and Hegel, and that Fichte and Schelling, though interesting historically, may be neglected by the student of results.

Essence of which both Mind and Nature are the manifestations. The Absolute going forth expansively, or embodying itself in the finite or phænomenal, is Nature; the regressive or contractive movement of the Absolute out of the finite or phænomenal back into itself, is the sum-total of Mind or Consciousness. Being and Knowing are coincident; all that is known *is*, and nothing *is* that is not known; the universe of Knowledge and the universe of Existence are the same; Ontology is the self-consciousness of the Absolute. But how can individual men rise to such an ontology? By participation in the self-consciousness of that Absolute of which they are items! How is this possible? By an act of "intellectual intuition" the soul of man may swoon beyond the bounds of mere individual consciousness, and may behold and know the Eternal Essence of things! It is on this power in the reason of each of us to participate in the self-knowledge of the Absolute, and to know itself as a fibre in that Absolute, that the Universe proceeds and holds together. It is this certain intuition of Absolute Truth, and not any spasmodic action of the soul in the shape of a faith straining into a void, that has been, is, and ever will be, the sustenance of mankind, the basis of religion and of all great action. So, in brief terms, I interpret the ontological doctrine of Schelling.

Having thus expounded severally the three great differences, or sets of differences, that have been found appearing and re-appearing hitherto in the history of Philosophy—and having named them, for the sake of easier reference, the *Psychological Difference*, the *Cosmological Difference*, and the *Ontological Difference*—let me proceed to inquire how far, and in what forms, these differences have repeated themselves in our British Philosophy of the last thirty years. In this inquiry, as has been already explained, it is with Sir William Hamilton, Mr. Carlyle, and Mr. John Stuart Mill, that we must first concern ourselves:

I. *In respect of the Psychological Difference.* Here Mr. Carlyle and Sir William Hamilton obviously range themselves on one side, and Mr. Mill as obviously on the other.

Take Mr. Carlyle. "Our whole Metaphysics itself," he wrote in 1829, in that essay from which we quoted his complaint as to the miserable condition into which Philosophy had fallen in Britain, "our whole Metaphysics itself from Locke's time downwards has been physical—not a spiritual philosophy, but a material one. The singular estimation in which his Essay was so long held as a scientific work (an estimation grounded, indeed, on the estimable character of the man) will one day be thought a curious indication of the spirit of these times." This is surely an abjuration of Lockism. Again, in the same Essay, he writes, "To speak a little pedantically, there is a science of Dynamics in Man's fortunes and nature, as well as of Mechanics. There is a Science which treats of, and practically addresses, the primary, unmodified forces and energies of Man, the mysterious springs of Love, and Fear, and Wonder, of Enthusiasm, Poetry, and Religion, all which have a truly vital and *infinite* character, as well as a Science which practically addresses the *finite*, modified developments of these, when they take the shape of immediate 'motives,' as hope of reward, or as fear of punishment. Now it is certain that in former times the wise men, the enlightened lovers of their kind, who appeared generally as moralists, poets, and priests, did, without neglecting the Mechanical province, deal chiefly with the Dynamical." * This also is an assertion of the principle of Transcendentalism. Indeed, in a previous Essay, Mr. Carlyle had approvingly expounded the Transcendentalism of Kant's philosophy in opposition to the Empiricism of Locke and Hume. "The Germans," he had said, "take up the matter differently, and would assail Hume, not in his outworks, but in his citadel. They deny his first principle, that Sense

* Art. "Signs of the Times," in Edin. Rev. 1829; reprinted in Carlyle's *Miscellanies*.

is the only inlet of knowledge, that Experience is the primary ground of belief. Their pure truth, however, they seek, not historically and by experiment, in the universal persuasions of men, but by intuition, in the deepest and purest nature of Man."* But what need of proving by particular quotations that Mr. Carlyle then was, and since then has always continued to be, a champion of the doctrine of necessary or *à priori* truth or elements of truth? What else mean his well-known phrases "Eternal Justice," "the Eternal Veracities," and the like? In short, if words have any meaning, Mr. Carlyle, since Coleridge died, and with an energy of genius more vehement and tumultuous, has been the most conspicuous Transcendentalist, the most conspicuous anti-Lockist, anti-Benthamist, in the Literature of Britain.

What Mr. Carlyle has been implicitly, and for the mind of the nation at large, in this aspect, Sir William Hamilton has been explicitly, and for our philosophic scholars. He has been the founder of a philosophy which, though it offered itself primarily as a continuation and improvement of that previously known (and though old-fashioned) as the Scottish, and though it might be properly enough called "Scoto-German," is described most truly of all as the Hamiltonian. And

* Art. "State of German Literature," in Edin. Rev. 1827; reprinted in Carlyle's *Miscellanies*.

from first to last in this philosophy, and in almost every scrap of writing that came from Hamilton's pen, we mark the strength of his conviction that only on the theory of necessary ideas, *à priori* forms of thought, could philosophy establish itself, or the spirit of man find satisfaction. "A very able disquisition," he would say again and again, commenting upon some treatise or essay of the opposite school which he thought worthy of praise; "but I do not see how you can fabricate this notion (naming it), out of experience!" A reduction of what was to be taken as *necessary* in our beliefs to the smallest compass in which it could be expressed—an essence of the fewest and deepest propositions—was a task in the achievement of which he foresaw results that might have made Reid groan, and Kantists uncomfortable.* He did not live to accomplish the task. But the whole tenor of his labours was towards an assertion, purification, and redefinition of Transcendentalism; and, when he died, he left the flag of Transcendentalism waving anew over more than one citadel of the land.

It will be a dreary day for the world when disagreements cease, when there are not even fundamental differences. There is an old Wiltshire song, which has this remarkable stanza:—

* See *Dissertation* A. appended to Edition of Reid, p. 743: footnote.

"If all the world were of one Religion,
Many a living thing should die;
But I will never forget my true love,
Nor in any way his name deny."

Now, if there is any man among us who has pre-eminently helped to keep Britain from that danger of intellectual death to many which would arise from her being of one Religion in Philosophy, it is Mr. Mill. *He* has never forgotton his true love, the principle of Empiricism, nor in any way denied its name—though the name "Empiricism" is one which he would not himself choose, and for which he would probably substitute *Experientialism.* In stating the question between the two metaphysical schools in that essay on Coleridge which was so admirable an example in its time of the sympathetic appreciation of a system of opinions different from one's own,* Mr. Mill thought it right to record his own view, even when refraining from arguing for it. "It is," he said, "that the truth, on this much debated question, lies with the school of Locke and Bentham." And his writings before this, and in all his writings after this, the same assertion of the principle of his philosophical faith is continually made. But, indeed, not only is this principle continually

* Essay on Coleridge, London and Westminster Review, 1840; reprinted in Mill's *Dissertations.*

avowed in Mr. Mill's writings; it is the key to the nature of the writings themselves. Mr. Mill's *Logic* corresponds with what the science of Logic could alone be consistently with his fundamental psychological principle. It could not be, like the old Logic and Hamilton's Logic, a Science of the Necessary Laws of Thought, but only a Science of the method of quest after experimental truth or probability. So, in his fine Essay on *Liberty* the radical idea is that one can never be surer of anything, be it even the forty-seventh proposition of the first book of Euclid, than in proportion as the chances of contradiction are exhausted; and the high value set there upon human freedom, and even upon eccentricity of thought or action, seems to be grounded on the conviction that the human race can never know what it may attain to, in the shape either of knowlege or of power, until it has sent out a rush of the largest number of individual energies simultaneously, and with the least restraint from law or custom or mutual disparagement, on actual experiments and investigations in all directions. As for the Essay on *Utilitarianism*, it is expressly a restatement of Paley's and Bentham's theory of expediency as the sole possible foundation of morals, but with a suggestion of this higher and more exquisite definition of expediency, characteristic of Mr. Mill, that it means the largest possible amount of pleasure, and the least possible amount of pain, not to you or me, or this age, or all mankind only, but to the sum-total of sentient existence. In short, if I am not mistaken, Mr. Mill's writings prove that, if he thinks of any one particular mode of thought among his contemporaries as being more than any other chargeable with the total mass of obstruction, fallacy, and misery that yet rolls in the heart of society—as being more than any other the False God, or Baal, or Moloch, of the human mind—it is of the theory of necessary beliefs. One marks almost an impatience of manner in his writings whenever this word "necessary" comes across him. "Never name to me," he seems to say, "that brute of a word."

It required, indeed, that the cause of British Empiricism should have no ordinary standard-bearer. The learning and speculative profundity of a Hamilton, and the great spiritual energy of a Carlyle, were a formidable conjunction of opposite forces. Even numerically, in respect of the leaders, the odds were as two to one. And, curiously enough, this is about the numerical odds in which, if we take the whole list of our recent philosophical writers, British Transcendentalism has continued to stand to British Empiricism to the present day. It is difficult to be exact in such a matter, and I will not specialize at present; but the names of Whewell and Tennyson at once suggest themselves on the one side, and that of the late Mr. Buckle on the other.

II. *In respect of the Cosmological Differences.* To think we had laid sufficient hold of the movement of British philosophical thought during the last thirty years merely by the division of its representatives into two schools according to their difference in respect of Psychological Theory, would (it must be felt now, if it was not felt before) be the very greenness of innocence. Hamilton, Carlyle, Whewell, and Tennyson—we may bracket these men together and have a reason for it; but what would the men themselves say? Methinks I see strange mutual glances passing among them—in part, glances of mutual liking, but not all of that character. Nor, though the conjunction of Buckle and Mill might be less amiss, in respect of reputed affinity, would that conjunction be beyond criticism. In short, we must complicate matters by having recourse to the second means of distributing philosophers—the recognition of the differences of their cosmological conceptions. But here we are confronted with difficulty and chances of error. "Who told you my cosmological conception, pray?" is what many a man, and even many a writer, might say to a critic professing to fasten one upon him and to expound it. What a man generally keeps to himself is precisely his cosmological conception. In this country especially that which most men avoid, even when they are our public teachers and writers—that which they are compelled to avoid by the tyranny of a many-voiced multitude, whose own cosmological conception was made for them long ago, and might be hung up in the British Museum as a curiosity to-morrow—nay, worst of all, that which the cynicism of a *blasé* literature of wit, and mutual chaff, and a cultivated antipathy to the large or grand, compels them to avoid—is the attempt to present, in any approach to complete form, systematic or poetical, their real and total conception of the world. The more the pity! Never was there a great book in the world that did not flash out, and burn into the minds of its readers, some outline of its author's cosmological conception. Nor, under all the discouragements of our time, have our best and greatest forgotten the duty, nor their right hands, in performing it, the true and ancient cunning. What—and, here surely, if anywhere, we may name him—what of our laureate Tennyson? Or, again, of Mr. Carlyle? What is it that breaks through upon us from all Mr. Carlyle's writings, and seems to constitute, when we investigate through all the rest, their distinguishing peculiarity? What but a pervading, continually presented, cosmological conception of surpassing vastness, intense and stern at the centre, where the moral forces meet round a solid terrestrial core, but otherwise astronomically boundless? Nay, is it not his habit to have faith in this presentation again and again of a cosmological conception, constant or slightly varying, as better than formal philosophizing? Reconceive if you can, my cosmological conception, he seems to say; let it burst the obstructions and boundaries it meets with in your mind; and from the new mental heaven there will doubtless be a rain, as far as is necessary, of the right propositions!

Just because Mr. Carlyle's philosophy takes so much the form of the incessant presentation of his general cosmological conception that it refuses to argue about the conception itself, it is difficult to bring him into a place in any of those six philosophical systems which have been enumerated as resulting from the attempt to classify philosophers by attending to their points of attachment to different theories of the act of external perception. It might not be really impossible so to place him; but it would be difficult. Let us, therefore, take leave of him, and attend to the other two. In regard to them, from the nature of their writings, there is not the same difficulty.

Six philosophical systems, we said, have been recognised as arising out of the different known interpretations of the so-called act of external perception—*Nihilism* or *Non-Substantialism*, *Materialism*, *Natural Realism*, *Constructive Idealism*, *Pure Idealism*, and the *Identity System*. Of these six systems, I may now say, only the middle four seem to me purely cosmological. The two extreme systems,—*Nihilism* and *Absolutism*,—involve ontological considerations. They are not solely theories of the contents of the Cosmos, considered in itself, but also theories on the subject of the relatedness or non-relatedness of the Cosmos, whatever may be the conception of its contents, to an essence of things beyond. The middle four, however—*Materialism*, *Natural Realism*, *Constructive Idealism*, and *Pure Idealism*—are more strictly cosmological. Now, each of these four systems has had a footing in Britain, and the present question is, to which of them Sir William Hamilton and Mr. Mill respectively adhere.

Sir William Hamilton is a *Natural Realist*. He regarded it, indeed, as perhaps the chief distinction of his speculative philosophy that, in opposition to the tradition of all former modern philosophers, save one or two, it proclaimed the cosmological doctrine of Natural Realism to be the true one. His views on the subject are expressed in his *Edinburgh Review* articles—"The Philosophy of Perception" and "Idealism" (reprinted in his *Discussions*); also in his *Lectures on Metaphysics* (Lectures XV. XVI.); but they are to be gathered, with greatest abundance of illustration and detail, from his Notes, B, C, D and D*, appended to his edition of Reid. In these Notes he first expounds, as all-important to his purpose, the distinction between Presentative, Immediate, or Intuitive Knowledge, and the knowledge called Representative or Mediate. Presentative Knowledge is that in which the mind apprehends a thing directly, in itself, and as it were face to face; Representative Knowledge is that in which the mind apprehends a thing not directly, but through some sign, image, or suggestion distinct from the thing itself. Now, though the great mass of our accumulated knowledge is undeniably Representative—all our knowledge, for example, of the past and the distant—yet, in the centre of all, as the ever-welling momentary supply out of which all the rest is evolved or woven, there is a Presentative Knowledge in every act of present consciousness. More particularly in what is called the act of external perception we have a direct, immediate, face-to-face knowledge of objects in an external world. Most philosophers, Sir William proceeds to say, have denied this, and have maintained that our knowledge of an external world is only representative, or a bundle of inferences from certain signs in our own affections, which may, or may not, be in analogy with the things they represent. Reid alone had got hold of the doctrine of an immediate face-to-face cognition of external nature in every act of perception. But Reid's use of the doctrine had been vacillating, confused, and incomplete, insomuch that he had been misunderstood in all that depended upon it by his critics, and most of all by Brown. Hence, vindicating Reid, and at the same time avowing his own acceptance of Reid's doctrine, though he should be left in a minority of one in supporting it, Hamilton does all he can to put the doctrine in proper shape. "The developed doctrine of Real Presentationism, the basis of Natural Realism," he says, "asserts the consciousness or immediate perception of certain essential attributes of matter objectively existing; while it admits that other properties of body are unknown in themselves, and only inferred as causes to account for certain subjective affections of which we are cognizant in ourselves." The attributes of matter thus alleged to be immediately perceived as really and objectively existing are mainly those which since Locke's time had been generally known as the "primary qualities,"—to wit, solidity or extension, impenetrability, number or divisibility, size, figure, mobility, and position in space. In addition to these qualities Sir William discriminates two other classes —the "secundo-primary qualities" (such as gravity, cohesion, repulsion, &c.), in which he recognizes modifications of the primary by conjunction with a subjective element; and the "secondary qualities" proper (colour, sound, flavour, heat, &c.), which he allows to consist merely in determinations of the subjective sentiency.

Such is Sir William Hamilton's system of *Natural Dualism* or *Natural Realism.* In the course of his expositions of his own system he has some criticisms of the rival systems. If he were not a Natural Realist, then, he avows, he would be a Pure Idealist. "Natural Realism and Absolute Idealism," he says emphatically, "are the only systems worthy a philosopher." * On the other hand, the rival system which he liked least, and which he pronounced "the most inconsequent of all systems," was that half-way kind of Idealism which we have called Constructive Idealism. He admitted, nevertheless, that this was the system which had been "embraced in various forms by the immense majority of philosophers." † Now, as far as I have been able to ascertain, it is precisely to this system that Mr. Mill would confess his allegiance. I make the statement somewhat diffidently. It has seemed to me doubtful whether some of his views might not be susceptible of an interpretation

* Note C to Edition of Reid, p. 817, footnote.

† Art. Philosophy of Perception, *Discussions*, p. 55.

into Pure Idealism. On the whole, however, I am inclined to think that, if any of the existing cosmological systems might claim him, it is that of *Constructive Idealism.*

In his *Logic* there is a chapter devoted to an enumeration or classification of "the Things denoted by names." It results in the conclusion that there are four classes of nameable things—(1) "Feelings, or States of Consciousness;" (2) "The Minds which experience these feelings;" (3) "The Bodies, or external objects, which excite certain of these feelings;" and (4) "The Successions and Coexistences, the Likenesses and Unlikenesses, between feelings or States of Consciousness." This is so far a cosmological classification; but, from the paragraphs through which it is arrived at, it distinctly appears that it is not Mr. Mill's ultimate classification of the contents of the Cosmos as given in consciousness, but a classification deferring, partly at least, and for the practical purposes of Logic, to popular habits of speech and thought. In reading these paragraphs it is distinctly seen that, according to Mr. Mill, the one and only reality of the Cosmos for our knowledge consists in the existence of the first of the four classes of nameable things, or of the first compounded with the fourth. All that we really know, or are in any way aware of, is a series of feelings or states of consciousness, a stream or succession of sensations, thoughts, emotions, and volitions. When we speak either of Mind as a substance undergoing these successive states, or of Matter or Body as an external cause of some of them, we go beyond what we know. Thus, of Mind: "There is a something I call Myself, or by another form of expression, my mind, which I consider as distinct from these sensations, thoughts, &c.—a something which I conceive to be not the thoughts, but the being that has the thoughts, and which I can conceive as existing for ever in a state of quiescence without any thoughts at all. But what this being is, although it is myself, I have no knowledge further than the series of its states of consciousness." * So of Matter or Body: "A body, according to the received doctrine of modern metaphysicians," says Mr. Mill, "may be defined the external cause to which we ascribe our sensations. . . The sensations are all of which I am directly conscious; but I consider them as produced by something not only existing independently of my will, but external to my bodily organs and to my mind. This external something I call a Body. It may be asked, How came we to ascribe our sensations to any external cause? and is there sufficient ground for so ascribing them? It is known that there are metaphysicians who have raised a controversy on this

* Logic: 1st Edit. vol. i. p. 82.

point, maintaining the paradox that we are not warranted in referring our sensations to a cause such as we understand by the word Body, or to any cause whatever, unless, indeed, the First Cause. . . . A fixed law of connexion, making the sensations occur together, does not, say these philosophers, necessarily require what is called a *substratum* to support them. The conception of a substratum is but one of many possible forms in which that connexion presents itself to our imagination—a mode of, as it were, realizing the idea. If there be such a substratum, suppose it this instant annihilated by the fiat of Omnipotence, and let the sensations continue to occur in the same order, and how would the substratum be missed? By what signs should we be able to discover that its existence had terminated? Should we not have as much reason to believe that it still existed as we now have? and, if we should not then be warranted in believing it, how can we be so now? A body, therefore, according to these metaphysicians, is not anything intrinsically different from the sensations which the body is said to produce in us; it is, in short, a set of sensations joined together according to a fixed law. . . . These ingenious speculations have at no time in the history of philosophy made many proselytes; but the controversies to which they have given rise, and the doctrines which have been developed in the attempt to find a conclusive answer to them, have been fruitful of important consequences to the Science of Mind. . . . It was soon acknowledged by all who reflected on the subject, that the existence of matter could not be proved by extrinsic evidence. The answer, therefore, now usually made to Berkeley and his followers is, that the belief is intuitive—that mankind, in all ages, have felt themselves compelled, by a necessity of their nature, to refer their sensations to an external cause; that even those who deny it in theory yield to the necessity in practice, and, in speech, thought, and feeling do, equally with the vulgar, acknowledge their sensations to be the effects of something external to them. . . . But, though the extreme doctrine of the Idealist metaphysicians, that objects are nothing but our sensations and the laws which connect them, has appeared to few subsequent thinkers to be worthy of assent, the only point of much real importance is one on which these metaphysicians are now very generally considered to have made out their case—viz.: that *all we know* of objects is the sensations which they give us, and the order of the occurrence of these sensations. . . . There is not the slightest reason for believing that what we call the sensible qualities of an object are a type of anything inherent in itself, or bearing any affinity to its own nature. A cause does not, as such, resemble its effects; an east wind is not like the feeling of cold, nor is heat like the steam of boiling water: why then should matter resemble our sensations? why should the inmost nature of fire or water resemble the impressions made by these objects upon our senses? And, if not on the principle of resemblance, on what other principle can the manner in which objects affect us through the senses afford us any insight into the inherent nature of these objects? It may therefore safely be laid down as a truth, both obvious in itself, and admitted by all whom it is at present necessary to take into consideration, that of the outward world we know and can know absolutely nothing except the sensations which we experience from it." *

Now, so far as these quotations indicate Mr Mill's cosmological system, it is certainly not the *Natural Realism* of Reid and Sir William Hamilton. But, when we inquire with which of the other systems Mr. Mill's views are to be identified, the atmosphere does not seem so clear. There is evident, indeed, a broad general preference for the idealistic manner of thought. The sole cosmical certainty for us, Mr. Mill avows, is a certain succession of ideas, or states of consciousness; this is the one phænomenon which we cannot transcend in knowlege, do what we will; all else is faith, hypothesis, or inference. Now this,

* Logic: 1st Edit. vol. i. pp. 74—81.

at first sight, looks like *Pure Idealism*. It goes beyond even the Idealism of Berkeley, which only abolished Matter or Body as an Independent cosmical factor, and retained Mind; and it approaches the extreme Idealism of Hume and Fichte, which, by abrogating all knowledge of a substance of Mind as well as all knowledge of a substance of Matter, left nothing between one and *Nihilism* or *Non-Substantiation*, save an act of ontological faith, which one might experience or not, or wish to experience or not. But Mr. Mill's language seems to show that, more willingly and easily than Hume, if not with such vehemence and passion as Fichte, he would allow as much of ontological faith in Philosophy as would keep it from the Nihilistic conception of the Cosmos as a mere baseless succession of ideas. True, all that we really know is a succession of ideas or states of consciousness, and our imagination either of a substance of Mind undergoing these, or of an external world of Matter implicated in some of them, may be purely illusive. But, as all mankind proceed on the imagination, and can no more shake themselves clear from it than they can leap off their own shadows, Philosophy must risk the illusion, especially as the character of *orderliness* in the succession of ideas conveys to Philosophy itself (legitimately or illegitimately?) a notion of ulterior law. In short, some mystery, some hypothesis of an unknown, must be allowed in Philosophy, and the question is, how much? Allow the minimum, and we are brought back to *Pure Idealism*, recovering itself from Nihilism, and positing in the Cosmos at least a something nameable as Mind, an unknown something that feels and thinks. Mr. Mill is willing, however, to go farther, and, always with the proviso that we are talking in the dark, to allow another unknown something in the Cosmos, external to the mind, and which is the determining cause of some of the mind's feelings. Accordingly he sums up thus: "As Body is the mysterious something which excites the mind to feel, so mind is the mysterious something which feels and thinks." Again, "As Body is the unsentient cause to which we are naturally prompted to refer a certain portion of our feelings, so Mind may be described as the sentient subject (in the German sense of the term) of all feelings—that which has or feels them. But of the nature of either body or mind, further than the feelings which the former excites, and which the latter experiences, we do not, according to the best existing doctrine, know any thing." * Of Body, indeed, we may assume (so Mr. Mill has already argued) that we know something negatively. Whatever it is, it can hardly be, in any way or to any degree, that which we are in the constant habit

* Logic: 1st Edit. i. pp. 81, 82.

of supposing it to be. When we speak of solidity, impenetrability, size, figure, &c., as primary qualities of bodies, and of colour, roughness, hardness, sourness, &c., as secondary qualities of the same bodies, we but skeletonize an unknown and unknowable cause in the form of some of its effects, and then clothe the skeleton with a garment of others of its effects. And so, Mr. Mill's cosmological doctrine, as he seems willing that it should stand, after sufficient caveats and explanations, seems to be that of *Constructive Idealism.**

* Of attachment on Mr. Mill's part to the *Identity-system* there is no hint; and the only other of the six systems to which his views are not adjusted in the text is *Materialism.* Now it is quite conceivable that a *Constructive Idealism* such as has been described might resolve itself scientifically into *Materialism.* Might not Science, starting with the conception of a *present* Cosmos consisting of a sentient something called Mind and an unsentient something else called Matter, and regarding both as apprehensible only in the successive states of the sentient something, reach the conclusion, through the manipulation of these states themselves, that the unsentient is the more ancient of the two, and that the sentient, which is thus finding out its own ancestry, is but a development of the unsentient? Such a suicide of Constructive Idealism, or translation of itself into Materialism, is, as I have hinted in a previous footnote, so far from impossible that it is the commonest of processes in the present state of Philosophy. The reason why I note the fact again here is not that Mr. Mill is ever found forswearing his Idealism, but because the fact is interesting in connexion with his great liking for the speculations of other philosophers who, without denying that a succession of states of consciousness is the sole known reality of the Cosmos, are yet conspicuous for the resoluteness with which they leave that contemplation behind, and assume a material Cosmos of good thumping realities, mineral and other, as having existed for ages before it had bred nerve or learnt any trick of self-sentiency.

III. *In respect of the Ontological Difference.*—So far as we have gone, the result is that, compounding the Psychological doctrine with the Cosmological in the case of each of the two philosophers, and throwing out what alone seems to be doubtful in Mr. Mill's case (to wit, whether under the latter doctrine he is a Pure Idealist or only a Constructive Idealist), we may define Sir William Hamilton's philosophy as a system of *Transcendental Natural Realism* or *Dualistic Transcendentalism*, and Mr. Mill's as a system of *Empirical Idealism* or *Idealistic Empiricism*. There remains to be applied to each of the philosophers, however, the third of the traditional differences—that which we have called the Ontological. Here, at first sight, the two philosophers seem to meet and shake hands. The agreement, however, even here, is more apparent than real.

There are no portions of Sir William Hamilton's writings better known than those in which he proclaimed his conviction of the utter impossibility of an Ontology. The very first of his contributions to the *Edinburgh Review* was his now famous Article "On the Philosophy of the Unconditioned," criticising more particularly Cousin's doctrine of the Infinito-Absolute. In all his subsequent writings he assumes this article as lying in the background, to be referred to, if necessary, for the correct interpretation of whatever new exposition he may be engaged in; and on several occasions—as, for example, in the eighth and ninth of his Lectures on Metaphysics—he recurs to the topic for a fresh treatment of it. The result has been that there is no doctrine more strongly identified at the present day with Sir William Hamilton's name than the doctrine which he expressed most generally by calling it "The Relativity of Human Knowledge."

Thousandfold as might be the differences of system among philosophers, and of vast importance as might be not a few of these differences, yet all philosophers, Sir William Hamilton held, were bound, if they really understood what they were talking about, to agree in one proposition—to wit, that our knowledge is, and can be, only of the relative or phænomenal. This, which he called "the great axiom," he asserted in many varieties of form and with many varieties of illustration. "*Omne quod cognoscitur*," he says, quoting with approbation the celebrated maxim of Boethius, "*non secundum sui vim, sed secundum cognoscentium potius comprehenditur facultatem:*" "All that is known is comprehended, not according to the force of itself, but according rather to the faculty of those knowing." Hence, not only is human knowledge relative, but, even in its quality as relative, it may be far inferior to such relative knowledge as might be attainable through an extension of our faculties, or as may be even now in the possession of beings with faculties more extended than ours. Just as to a man who has been blind from his birth the phænomenal world or Cosmos of his conceptions cannot be the same as that figured forth in the conceptions of his seeing fellow-creatures, but must lack all those attributes which depend on the direct co-operation of Sight with the other senses, so, if a new sense or two were added to the present normal number in man, that which is now the phænomenal world for all of us might, for all we know, burst into something amazingly wider and different in consequence of the additional revelations through these new senses.

"The universe may be conceived as a polygon of a thousand, or a hundred thousand sides or facets—and each of these sides or facets may be conceived as representing one special mode of existence. Now, of these thousand sides or modes all may be equally essential, but three or four only may be turned towards us or be analogous to our organs. One side or facet of the Universe, as holding a relation to the organ of sight, is the mode of luminous or visible existence; another, as proportional to the organ of hearing, is the mode of sonorous or audible existence; and so on."* But, even were our organs or senses to be made co-numerous with the modes of existence, our knowledge

* Lectures on Metaphysics, p. 142.

would still be only of the phænomenal, though of a phænomenal totality far more multiplex than the present. Had we faculties equal in number to all the possible modes of existence, whether of mind or matter, still would our knowledge of mind or matter be only relative." * In every way, therefore, an Ontology, or knowledge of things in themselves, of Noumena or Self-subsisting Actualities, as distinct from Phænomena, must be declared impossible. More expressly, in human Philosophy, must Ontology, or speculation of the Absolute, be *ab initio* given up. "As the conditionally limited (which we may briefly call the *conditioned*) is the only possible object of knowledge and of positive thought, thought necessarily supposes conditions. *To think* is *to condition;* and conditional limitation is the fundamental law of the possibility of thought. For, as the greyhound cannot outstrip his shadow, nor (by a more appropriate simile) the eagle outsoar the atmosphere in which he floats, and by which alone he may be supported, so the mind cannot transcend that sphere of limitation within and through which exclusively the possibility of thought is realized." † All Science, in short, is the science of the phænomenal, or conditioned, or relative, and Philosophy is the science of this Science.

* Lectures on Metaphysics, p. 145.

† Art. "Philosophy of the Unconditioned:" *Discussions*, p. 14.

In expounding so emphatically this great doctrine of the Relativity of Knowledge, Sir William Hamilton professed only to be bringing out into distinctness a proposition which philosophers of all schools and times, with hardly an exception, had announced or assumed. "This is, indeed, a truth," he said, "in the admission of which philosophers, in general, have been singularly harmonious, and the praise that has been lavished on Dr. Reid for this observation is wholly unmerited. In fact, I am hardly aware of the philosopher who has not proceeded on the supposition, that there are few who have not explicitly enounced the observation. It is only since Reid's death that certain speculators have arisen who have obtained celebrity by their attempt to found philosophy on an immediate knowledge of the Absolute or Unconditioned." * The speculators here referred to are the post-Kantian philosophers of Germany, Schelling and Hegel, and their French disciples, more especially Cousin. It is against the attempts of these modern philosophers to establish an Ontology as a development or consummation of Philosophy, that Sir William's article "On the Philosophy of the Unconditioned" is from first to last directed. Cousin, as having made the most elaborate attempt to bring Ontology within the domain of reason, bears the brunt

* Lectures on Metaphysics, vol. I. pp. 138, 139

of the attack. Defining Cousin's opinion to be that "the Unconditioned or Absolute is cognizable and conceivable by consciousness and reflection, under relation, difference, and plurality," Sir William argues that it is self-contradictory and in fact consists in calling Absolute that which is at the same time spoken of in terms which are meaningless except as implying relativity. More briefly Schelling's opinion is set aside—that opinion being thus defined: "The Unconditioned is cognizable, but not conceivable; it can be known by a sinking back into identity with the Absolute, but is incomprehensible by consciousness and reflection, which are only of the relative and the different." Of this theory of Schelling's, and of that act of Intellectual Intuition by which he supposed the cognition of the Absolute to be possible, Sir William speaks all but derisively. "Out of Laputa or the Empire," he says, "it would be idle to enter into an articulate refutation of a theory which founds Philosophy on the annihilation of consciousness and the identification of the unconscious philosopher with God." But even Kant, whose sobriety had kept him far on this side of any such dreamy assertion, and one of whose great services to the world had been that he had most emphatically proclaimed or re-proclaimed the proposition that all human knowledge can only be of the Phænomenal or Relative—even he, according to Sir William, had inadvertently left in his Philosophy a stump of that Ontology of which he believed himself to have cleared the rational world. Kant's statement had been, according to Sir William's summary of it, that the Unconditioned or Absolute "is not an object of knowledge, but its notion, as a regulative principle of the mind itself, *is more than a mere negation of the Conditioned.*" In other words, though the Supernatural, as an objective reality, was beyond all cognisance or conception, and could be nothing more to Philosophy than a name for Void Unknowableness, or the cessation of all power of apprehension or predication, yet the psychological fact of a straining, in man's spirit, towards this vacuum, as if towards objects which might or might not be there, was to have some allowance made for it in positive speculation. Not even this, however, would Sir William allow; and accordingly, his own doctrine in respect of the Philosophy of the Absolute outgoes even Kant's. "The Unconditioned is incognizable and inconceivable, its notion being only negative of the conditioned, which last can alone be positively known or conceived." * Such, in contrast with the diverse opinions of Kant, Schelling, and Cousin, is Sir William Hamilton's statement of his own opinion on the question of the Absolute. To the Ontology of Plato's

* Art. "Philosophy of the Unconditioned:" *Discussions*," p. 12.

philosophy, or of Spinoza's, or of the Oriental systems, little reference is made in the course of the discussion.

How is Sir William Hamilton's ontological doctrine, if we may so call a doctrine which simply repudiated Ontology, to be reconciled with those parts of his Philosophy which we have had already before us —*i. e.* with the transcendentalism of his Psychological theory, and with the Natural Realism of his cosmological conception? Here I am not sure but he would have avoided certain chances of misapprehension if he had persistently employed some such distinct triplicity of terms, in describing the main divisions of philosophical inquiry, as that which we have ventured to think desirable. Thus, at first sight, it seems difficult to reconcile his strongly asserted principle that all our knowledge can only be of the relative or phænomenal, and can never reach substances or things in themselves, with his resolute Natural Realism. Has he not spoken, for example, of a direct, immediate presentative, or face-to-face knowledge of the external world of matter as given in every act of consciousness? Has he not even spoken of solidity, figure, size, and other so-called "primary qualities" of matter, as being qualities to be attributed to natural objects, considered in themselves, or in their own proper nature, and as herein distinguishable from the so-called "secondary" or "secundo-primary" qualities, which have their origination more or less within the sentiency? Does he not here seem to imply that our knowledge of matter is, to a considerably large extent, real and not phænomenal—a knowledge of the very thing itself? Sir William seems to have been aware that there might be this apparent inconsistency between those portions of his writings in which he expounded his disbelief in the possibility of an Ontology. He several times incidentally guards himself by anticipation against the objection. Thus, "I have frequently asserted that in perception we are conscious of the external object immediately and in itself. This is the doctrine of Natural Realism. But, in saying that a thing is known in itself, I do not mean that this object is known in its absolute existence—that is, out of relation to us. This is impossible; for our knowledge is only of the relative. To know a thing in itself or immediately is an expression I use merely in contrast to the knowledge of a thing in a representation "or mediately," * Perhaps it might have been well if Sir William had more strongly and repeatedly discriminated that sense of the phrase "knowledge of a thing in itself" in which he maintained that we possess such knowledge, and that other sense of the phrase in which he denied such knowledge to be possible. He might have done so by declaring that in

* Edition of Reid, p. 866, footnote.

the former case he was speaking *cosmologically*, in the latter *ontologically*. His meaning, at all events, may be explained as follows: *Cosmologically*, or in respect of that conception of the phænomenal Cosmos which is to be taken as the ultimate revelation of consciousness, I am a Natural Realist; that is, I believe the ultimate and universal fact of consciousness, as given in every act of external perception, to be the antithesis of two independent but mutually-related factors—an Ego or Percipient, and a Non-Ego or Percept. Firmly to distinguish between these two, so that neither may be merged in the other, I hold to be of extreme importance in view of various philosophical consequences. Now, though, on analysis, I find certain of the qualities popularly attributed to material objects to be only affections of the sentient Ego somehow occasioned by the objects, yet there are others of the qualities of matter—the so-called primary qualities—which I consider to belong really to the external material objects apart from the perceiving mind. In respect of these I say that we have a direct and immediate knowledge of matter as it is in itself. But, in talking so, I am still talking only *cosmologically*—*i. e.* I am only settling accounts between the two cosmical factors. When I proceed to talk *ontologically*, my language must be different. From this point of view, both the factors are phænomenal; that antithesis of the two which I hold to be revealed in every act of perception is but a phænomenon; consciousness itself is but a phænomenon; the Cosmos is a stupendous phænomenon, with a character of duality. By my constitution I feel myself constrained to believe that these phænomena, are phænomenal of a Somewhat; but, when you ask me of *what* they are phænomenal, I can only say "of an Unknown." Here I confront an impenetrable mystery, for my knowledge is and can be only of the relative. Thus I who, talking cosmologically, maintained that we have to some extent a knowledge of matter "as it is in itself," meaning thereby only to partition rightly between the phænomenal Percipient and the phænomenal Percept, must now, while talking ontologically, declare all knowledge of Mind in itself, or of Matter in itself, or of the cause of their phænomenal antithesis, to be equally impossible. Rightly to characterize the Phænomenal is the business of philosophy, and a sufficiently important and difficult business; but beyond the Phænomenal all possible philosophy sums itself up in one word—mystery, incogitability, inconceivability, nescience.

Such I believe to be a fair statement of Sir William Hamilton's ontological, or rather anti-ontological doctrine, in connexion with his cosmological system of Natural Realism. Without discussing objections that may present themselves—the objection, for example, which some might feel, of the strangeness of such a notion of the phænomenal as would bind us to think of Matter as a multiplex phænomenon that would persist the same in space, multiplex on its own account, even were all created sentiency abolished to which it could be phænomenal—let us attend to Sir William Hamilton's declarations of his views on questions of Theology.

Sir William Hamilton was a Theist, a Supernaturalist—no philosopher of modern times more strenuously, more passionately so. Not only did he answer with a passionate affirmative the first question of all Ontology, "*Is* there a Supernatural, or an Absolute beyond the Phænomenal, and on which the Phænomenal depends?" he went on, not a whit the less vehemently because of his speculative doctrine of the utter unknowableness of the Absolute, to assume for himself, and to avow as assumed by him, certain definite beliefs as to this Absolute in relation to the Universe and Mankind. It might be improper to refer at any length to what is known in this connexion of Sir William Hamilton personally. Suffice it to declare that this thinker of most severe and catholic reason—to whom all speculation was welcome if only it was sincere and able, who defended philosophic scepticism and wished there were more of it, who boldly upheld the fame of Hume as a good man and a great philosopher, and whose respect for the clergy was avowedly far from great—was himself liable to fits of theistic fervour such as the Church seldom hears of in a modern bishop. There are writings of his also which prove his interest, and something more than his scholarly interest, in Christian Theology. He found noble men, and spirits with whom he could sympathize, in the old theologians, from Tertullian and St. Augustine downwards. He had a special admiration of Calvin, and he would have laughed to scorn that wretched appreciation of this great ecclesiastic which ignorance, namby-pambyism, and the power of modern theology, have of late joined to make current. But let us not go beyond his purely philosophical writings. Even there we shall find expressions predicating, in Sir William's own name, certain attributes of that ultra phænomenal Existence of which he protests that, in the name of reason, nothing whatever can be predicated. To aver such an existence at all, to assume that the Phænomenal Universe is not all that exists, is already the planting of one huge predication in the region into which it was declared the mood of predication could not rationally go. It is the conversion of what was declared to be a zero into a vast, if vague, positive. But the apparent contradiction does not stop here. "To suppose their falsehood," says Sir William in one place, where he is speaking of these primary beliefs, or elements, or consciousness, for which, as a Transcendentalist in Psychology, he contends, "is to suppose that we are created capable of intelligence in order to be made the victims of a delusion,—that God is a deceiver, and the root of our nature a lie. But such a supposition, if gratuitous, is manifestly illegitimate." * Again, speaking of the Constructive Idealists (called by him the Cosmothetic Idealists), he says, "The Deity on their hypothesis is a deceiver; for that hypothesis assumes that our natural consciousness deludes us in the belief that external objects are immediately, and in themselves, perceived. Either, therefore, maintaining the veracity of God, they must surrender their hypothesis; or, maintaining their hypothesis, they must surrender the veracity of God." † Nothing is more characteristic of Sir William Hamilton than the occurrence of such hot theistic phrases in his purely speculative discussions. They never occur irrelevantly and certainly never in the form of those disgusting *petitiones principii* which are so rife in the argumentations of clerical and other writers, who in their virulent eagerness to blaspheme an opponent whom they

* "On the Philosophy of Common Sense." Note A: Edition of Reid, p. 743.

† *Ibid.* p. 751.

cannot answer, clutch at the word Atheist and its cognates as a street blackguard does at stones or mud. Their occurrence is very differently significant. It is, I think, nobly, and at the same time puzzlingly, significant. For are not these phrases most intensely and definitely ontological, and has not Sir William forsworn Ontology? What is the explanation? How can one be consistent who first maintains that nothing can be predicated speculatively of the Absolute, and then proceeds straightway not only to predicate existence of the Absolute, but to speak as if the human virtue of veracity must also be predicated of the same?

From Sir William here we have substantially the same answer as from Kant, Fichte, and others. *Faith* is the word that sums up the answer. "The sphere of our belief," says Sir William Hamilton, "is much more extensive than the sphere of our knowledge; and therefore when I deny that the infinite can by us be *known*, I am far from denying that by us it is, must, and ought to be, *believed*." * Now I am pretty sure that I express the general feeling of all who are acquainted with Sir William Hamilton's writings when I say that, of all the gaps which they leave in the interpretation of his entire system, there is none which it would have been so interesting to see filled

* Letter to Mr. Henry Calderwood, appended to Lectures on Metaphysics, vol. ii.

up by himself as that which the above extract brings to mind. A full exposition of Sir William Hamilton's views of Faith in its connexion with Philosophy would have supplied the missing keystone to the total arch. How would he have discriminated Belief from Knowledge? How would he have distinguished between that faith in the Infinite the necessity and obligation of which he so strongly upheld and either of those metaphysical doctrines which he disowned—Kant's supposition of "the notion of the Unconditioned as being, in its character of a regulative principle of the mind itself, more than a mere negation of the Conditioned," or Schelling's doctrine of an "intellectual intuition of the Absolute"? One can divine, or infer from expositions of his disciples, what might have been the nature of his replies; but the absence of a full exposition from himself is felt as a serious blank. Here, in the shape of a passing note on the word BELIEF or FAITH as one of the terms of the philosophic vocabulary, is perhaps the most express statement on the subject which he has left;—"BELIEF or FAITH (πίστις, *Fides*, *Croyance*, *Foi*, *Glaube*, &c.), simply or with one or other of the epithets, *natural*, *primary*, *instinctive*, &c., and some other expressions of a similar import, as *Conviction*, *Assent*, *Trust*, *Adhesion*, *Holding for true or real*, &c. (Συγκατάθεσις, *Assensus*, *Fuerwahr-und-wirklichhalten*

&c.), have, though not unobjectionable, found favour with a great number of philosophers, as terms whereby to designate the original warrants of cognition. Among these may be mentioned Aristotle, Lucretius, Alexander, Clement of Alexandria, Proclus, Algazel, Luther, Hume, Reid, Beattie, Hemsterhuis, Kant, Heidenreich, Fichte, Jacobi, Bouterweck, Köppen, Ancillon, Hermes, Biunde, Esser, Elvanich, &c., &c. Nor can any valid objection be taken to the expression. St. Austin accurately says, 'We *know* what rests upon *reason; we believe* what rests upon *authority.*' But reason itself must rest at last upon authority; for the original data of reason do not rest on reason, but are necessarily accepted by reason on the authority of what is beyond itself. These data are, therefore, in rigid propriety, Beliefs or Trusts. Thus it is that, in the last resort, we must, perforce, philosophically admit that belief is the primary condition of reason, and not reason the ultimate ground of belief. We are compelled to surrender the proud *Intellige ut credas* of Abelard, to content ourselves with the humble *Crede ut intelligas* of Anselm." * The briefer definition of Faith by the Apostle † would probably have been accepted by Sir William as conveying, quite as unexceptionable as any words of his own, his whole intended meaning:—"Now faith is the sub-

* Edition of Reid, p. 760.

† Heb. xi. 1—3.

stance of things hoped for, the evidence of things not seen (ἔστι δὲ πίστις ἐλπιζομένων ὑπόστασις, πραγμάτων ἔλεγχος οὐ βλεπομένων). For by it the elders obtained a good report. Through faith we understand that the worlds were framed by the word of God, so that things which are seen were not made of things which do appear (εἰς τὸ μὴ ἐκ φαινομένων τὰ βλεπόμενα γεγονέναι)."

In respect of that difference among philosophers, therefore, which we have named the Ontological Difference, Sir William Hamilton may, on the whole, be described as a philosopher who, while denying speculatively in the strongest terms the possibility of an Ontology, was himself endowed in an almost inordinate degree with the ontological feeling or passion. Let us now turn to Mr. Mill.

Fortunately, while these pages have been passing through the press, there has been published an essay of Mr. Mill's, in which, while characterizing another philosopher with whom he has a general and admiring sympathy, he has digested, in a more summary and exact form than it would be easy for a reader of his earlier works to do, his views on the metaphysical questions at present concerning us.* I avail myself the more readily of this essay, because, though M. Comte is the philosopher criticised in it, the language

* Art., *The Positive Philosophy of Auguste Comte* (signed J. S. M.), in the Westminster Review, April, 1865.

in the passages which I shall quote is evidently adjusted to the state of the controversy with Sir William Hamilton:—Mr. Mill hardly likes Comte's terms "Positive" and "Positivism" as names expressing the character of his Philosophy. Thinking that the essential principle of this philosophy is its thorough adhesion to the Empirical or Experiential theory in Psychology, as opposed to the theory of Transcendentalism, he hints that, in its subjective aspect, it might be more intelligibly described as the *Experiential* Philosophy, or the Philosophy of *Experientialism*, and that in its objective aspect, the synonyms for it might be the *Phænomenal* Philosophy, or the Philosophy of *Phænomenalism*. The fundamental maxim of the Philosophy, at all events, is that all we know or can know anything about is phænomena. "We have no knowledge of anything but Phænomena; and our knowledge of phænomena is relative, not absolute. We know not the essence, nor the real mode of production, of any fact, but only its relations to other facts in the way of succession or of similitude. These relations are constant—that is, always the same in the same circumstances. The constant resemblances which link phænomena together, and the constant sequences which unite them as antecedent and consequent, are termed their laws. The laws of phænomena are all we know respecting them.

Their essential nature and their ultimate causes, either efficient or final, are unknown and inscrutable to us." This conception of human knowledge, Mr. Mill goes on to say, does not belong originally to Comte, or to any thinker in particular. It has been the growing conception of the scientific mind of Europe from the time of Bacon, Descartes, and Galileo. These thinkers had it, but, almost inevitably in their circumstances, not in its full clearness. "It was, however, correctly apprehended by Newton. But it was probably first conceived in its entire generality by Hume." Hume, indeed, carried it to the uttermost, "maintaining not merely that the only causes of Phænomena which can be known to us are other phænomena, their invariable antecedents, but that there is no other kind of causes: cause, as he interprets it, *means* invariable antecedent. This is the only part of Hume's doctrine which was contested by his great adversary, Kant. . . . Among the direct successors of Hume, the writer who has best stated and defended Comte's fundamental doctrine is Dr. Thomas Brown. The doctrine and spirit of Brown's Philosophy are entirely Positivist, and no better introduction to Positivism than the early part of his Lectures has yet been produced. Of living thinkers we do not speak; but the same great truth formed the groundwork of all the speculative philosophy of Bentham, and pre-eminently of James Mill. Sir William Hamilton's famous doctrine of the Relativity of Human Knowledge has guided many to it, though we cannot credit Sir William Hamilton himself with having understood the principle, or been willing to assent to it if he had."

Let us attend to the last sentence. Mr. Mill accepts Sir William Hamilton's doctrine that human knowledge can only be of the Relative or Phænomenal and not of the Absolute; but he holds this doctrine with a difference. With *what* difference? Here again the habit of clearly distinguishing between the cosmological part of a philosopher's creed and the ontological part will be found convenient. Sir William Hamilton, as I have already explained, holds the ontological or anti-ontological doctrine of the Relativity of Human Knowledge as it may be held by one who is, cosmologically, a Natural Realist; Mr. Mill, if I mistake not, holds the same doctrine as it may be held by one who is, cosmologically, a Constructive Idealist. This seems confirmed by the fact that the philosophers whom Mr. Mill cites as having, before Comte, held the doctrine of Relativity in what he thinks the true form—to wit, Newton, Kant, Thomas Brown, Bentham, and James Mill—were all, like himself, Constructive Idealists. For Hume, it will be noted, is represented by Mr. Mill as standing by himself in a peculiar position, far out beyond this group, in respect of *his* form of the Relativity Doctrine; and Hume was, cosmologically, a Nihilist or Non-Substantialist. Evidently, therefore, the clue to the difference of Mr. Mill's form of the Relativity Doctrine from Sir William Hamilton's is to be found in the prior difference of their cosmological conceptions.

The matter may be easily brought out. Sir William Hamilton and Mr. Mill agree in the statement that all our knowledge is of the phænomenal only, but with a prior difference of opinion as to what is to be considered the true sphere or central fact of the Phænomenal. Sir William considers that the central fact of the Phænomenal is a dualism or antithesis of two series of phænomena, given immediately in consciousness, the one constituting, if we let ourselves think a substance or substratum for it, the Ego or Mind, the other, if we give ourselves a similar liberty, the External World or Matter. The whole conception of the phænomenal Cosmos is the development, by memory, imagination, and science, of this radical belief of the consciousness. It is *this* Phænomenal Cosmos that is to be figured as hung, so far as speculation is concerned, in an infinity of the Unknowable; it is round the perimeter of *this* Phænomenal Cosmos that the ontological beats everlastingly, and we seem to hear the roar of its obdurate silence. With Mr.

Mill, on the other hand, the radical fact of the phænomenal is not a dualism at all, but simply a stream, a flow, a succession of feelings, sensations, or states of consciousness. Unwind the wrappages of the Cosmos so as to get at the one physical fact of which they are all self-swathings, and to this and this alone we must come. All knowledge, all belief, all known existence, has been generated out of this succession of sensations or states of consciousness, registering its own interrelations of recurrence, co-existence, and similitude. The paramount fact in the result certainly is the universal persuasion of men of their own existence as beings distinct from an external world around them. But this is a leap beyond the original datum. Of a substance or substratum of Mind, or a substance or substratum of Matter, underlying the phænomenal series of feelings or sensations —nay even of a phænomenon Mind *per se* or a phænomenon Matter *per se*—we do, and can, know nothing. In speaking of such *substrata*, or such phænomena *per se*, and much more in averring their ultimate real or even phænomenal distinctness, we make a postulate or assumption, which, so far as we know, may be quite illusive. The radical datum of speculative Philosophy is not "*Cogito*," nor is it "*Est cogitabile*," but only "*Sunt cogitationes*." Here, if I do not misrepresent Mr. Mill, he accepts, for the moment at least, Hume's utmost sceptical analysis of existence. But he is not by any means anxious, as we have seen, for any purpose of philosophy, to remain in Hume's Non-substantialism or Nihilism. He is willing to be a substantialist so far as to allow the existence of a substance called Mind, which is the seat or subject of the phænomenal *cogitationes*, provided always it is granted that this substance is unknown and unknowable, and that, though a substance as regards the *cogitationes* which are then thought of as its modifications, it is itself only a phænomenon. This brings him up to Pure Idealism, so that he may exchange the proposition "*Sunt cogitationes*" for the proposition "*Cogito*," or, with reference to the multiplicity of phænomenal sentiencies, "*Cogitamus*," or "*Sunt cogitantes*." But he is willing, as we have farther seen, to go beyond even this, and, by allowing not only a thinking or feeling subject, but also an independent external cause of sensations in such a subject (always an unknown cause, however, and only phænomenal even were it known), to rank himself, with the majority of philosophers, among the Constructive Idealists. On the whole, this is the system which he practically prefers. *Sunt cogitationes; immo, si placet, sunt cogitantes; sunt etiam fortasse cogitabilia extra cogitantes; hæc tamen cogitabilia, si quomodo extant, nihil certe cogitationibus ipsis consimilia sunt existimanda*

—so we may formulize the creed of Constructive Idealism as entertained by Mr. Mill. Now, at whichever point of the creed we stop, it is evident that the phænomenal totality which it orbs forth as hung in an unknown and unknowable infinite is not the same as the phænomenal totality in Sir William Hamilton's system of Natural Realism. If we stop at the *cogitationes*, we plunge at once from them, as from a curdling consistency of phænomenal thought-phantasms into Ontology, or (Ontology being impossible) into Nescience. If we go as far as the *cogitantes*, we have, as the phænomenal Cosmos, Minds or Thinking Beings, and all the evolution of their thoughts, and from that comparative solidity we take the same plunge into Nescience. If we add to the phænomenal world, as Mr. Mill is willing to do, the *cogitabilia extra cogitantes*, we so far complicate the vision to which we belong, and have an option of another phænomenal point from which to plunge into Nescience. But, even on this last supposition—accompanied as it is by the injunction not to think that the external objects or causes of sensation which act upon consciousness are at all such as consciousness represents them—there is still a difference between the radical phænomenal totality of Constructive Idealism and that of Natural Realism. The Cosmos, in the scheme of the Constructive Idealists, grapples the Absolute, if we may so say, by one available anchor (Mind seeking its cause), and would grapple it by another if it knew where to find that other (the unknown external cause of sensation, for which also, were it realized, a cause would have to be sought); the Cosmos, in the scheme of the Natural Realist, grapples the Absolute by two anchors, considered equally available—Mind, and that Material Nature which Mind knows face to face as phænomenally existing out of itself.

Seeing it is confessed by both parties that the grappling is hopeless—that this is a case in which all anchors and all chains melt the moment they touch the element into which they would insert themselves—the difference may seem unimportant. But it did not seem unimportant to Sir William Hamilton; nor does it to Mr. Mill. The essential battle between these two philosophers, indeed, reduces itself to the battle cosmological—to the controversy as to what the phænomenal totality readily is and consists of. As to the impossibility of transcending the phænomenal speculatively they both agree. And yet with this *speculative* agreement there is a *sentimental* diversity.

Newton, Kant, Thomas Brown, Bentham, James Mill, and Comte are collectively cited by Mr. John Stuart Mill as philosophers who had realized the doctrine of the Relativity of Knowledge in what he considers its correct form—that is, as I interpret, had appended the doctrine to a cosmological system of Constructive Idealism, and not to any such cosmological system as the Hamiltonian one of Natural Realism. Now it requires but the vaguest recollection of these philosophers severally to see that, though thus grouped together as all in the right speculatively on the Relativity question, they differed enormously in respect of the state of sentiment with which they confronted the Unknowability to which they confessed in common. Newton was a Theist and Theologian; Kant was a Theist; Thomas Brown was a Theist; of the others it may certainly be said that, though they never denied real or Noumenal existence or causes beyond the Phænomenal world, they were not theologically inclined. Here, then, is a difference, and one of immense moment practically, among some who have been cited as all in the right speculatively on the great doctrine of the Relativity of Knowledge, or the impossibility of an Ontology. How is this? Is it that they were not all *equally* in the right in their apprehension of the doctrine, that there adhered to some of them inconsistencies which they had not got rid of, chips of the ancient egg-shell? This is not the explanation which Mr. Mill suggests. His explanation is that Theism, and Theology, under certain conditions, still are, and ought to be allowed to remain, "open questions" in the most advanced school of Philosophy. Referring to M. Comte, and to his avowed opinion that, when properly converted to the positive mode of thought, "mankind would cease to refer the constitution of Nature to an intelligent will, or to believe at all in a Creator and Supreme Governor of the world," Mr. Mill takes occasion to protest that this was unnecessarily encumbering the true doctrine of Positivism, or the Relativity of Knowledge, with a religious prejudice. "It is one of M. Comte's mistakes," he says, "that he never allows of open questions." And he thus states his own views of the whole matter:—"The positive mode of thought is not necessarily a denial of the supernatural; it merely throws back that question to the origin of things. If the universe had a beginning, its beginning, by the very conditions of the case, was supernatural; the laws of nature cannot account for their origin. The Positive philosopher is free to form his opinion on this subject according to the weight he attaches to the analogies which are called marks of design, and to the general traditions of the human race. The value of these evidences is indeed a question for Positive philosophy, but it is not one on which Positive philosophers must necessarily be agreed. . . . Positive philosophy maintains that, within the existing order of the Universe, or rather of the part of it known to us, the direct determining cause of every phænomenon is not supernatural but natural. It is compatible with this to believe that the universe was created and even that it is continuously governed by an Intelligence, provided we admit that the intelligent Governor adheres to fixed laws, which are only modified or counteracted by other laws of the same dispensation, and are never either capriciously or providentially departed from." This is as explicit a statement as is to be found in Mr. Mill's writings of his notion of the amount of ontological sentiment that may properly mingle with philosophy; nor do I find any ontological passion in his own procedure as a philosopher that is at all in excess of this. Herein, I repeat, there is a contrast between him and Sir William Hamilton, even where, at first sight, they seem most nearly to agree.

We may now end this chapter. The result, historically, is that, during the greater portion of the last thirty years, the most prominent rival leaders in formal or systematic British speculation have been two philosophers, one of whom may be described as a Transcendental Natural Realist, forswearing speculative Ontology, but with much of the ontological passion in his temper, and the other as an Empirical

Idealist, also repudiating Ontology, but doing so with the ease of one in whom the ontological feeling was at any rate suppressed or languid. *Transcendental Natural Realism* in Hamilton, announcing itself as anti-ontological, but with strong theological sympathies, and *Empirical Constructive Idealism* in Mill, also announcing itself as anti-ontological, but consenting to leave the main theological questions open on certain pretty strict conditions—such, it seems to me, were the two philosophical Angels that began to contend formally for the soul of Britain about thirty years ago, and that are still contending for as much of it as has not in the meantime transported itself beyond the reach of either. Whether any has done so, and how much, and where it has gone, are matters that remain to be seen.

CHAPTER III.

EFFECTS OF RECENT SCIENTIFIC CONCEPTIONS ON PHILOSOPHY.

However earnestly we may contend for such a notion of Philosophy as shall keep up the tradition of it as something more than Science, yet the perpetual liability of Philosophy to modifications at the hands of Science is a fact obvious to all. Not a new scientific discovery can be made, not a new scientific conception can get abroad, but it exercises a disturbing influence on the previous system of thought, antiquating something, disintegrating something, compelling some re-adjustment of the parts to each other, some trepidation of the axis of the whole. Sometimes the action is almost revolutionary. What a derangement in men's ideas about everything whatsoever, what a compulsion to new modes of thinking and to new habits of speech, must have been caused by the propagation of the Copernican Astronomy! What a wrench to all one's habits of thought, to be taught that the little ball which carries us rotates on itself, and is one of a small company of celestial bodies that perform their periodical wanderings round the sun, in lieu of the older astronomical faith, according to which the earth was fixed in the centre, and the limitless azure with its fires was one vast spectacular sphere, composed of ten successive and independent spherical transparencies, made to wheel round the earth diurnally for her solitary pleasure! Man's thoughts, even about himself and his destinies, could not but be changed in some respects by this compulsion of his imagination to a totally new way of fancying physical immensity and our earth's share in its proceedings. True, the great spiritualities and moralities that the human race held within it, and that constituted a million-fold more truly the real substance of its life than all its accompanying theories and imaginations of things physical—these survived intact and uninterrupted. We read the old poets now, the old historians, the old moralists, with no acquired sense that they, or their themes, or their teachings at the deepest, are appreciably removed from us because of their pre-Copernicanism. It hardly occurs to us to remember that they *were* pre-Copernicans. What does it matter, in respect of the power over our hearts and spirits as we read, what astronomical system we may fancy we detect in the Book of Job? And yet not the less true is it that even the spiritualities and moralities that constitute the essence of philosophy *are* tremulous to our imaginations of physical nature, and are ever re-adjusting the expressions of themselves to the new conceptions which Science makes imperative. It would be possible to point out in our greatest old poets, including Shakespeare, not only pervading peculiarities of phraseology, but even fashions of speculative thought, which might be debited to their pre-Copernicanism.* And so throughout the whole history, and especially the recent history, of Philosophy. It is not every day, indeed, nor every century, that there occurs such a vast compulsory shifting of the very axis of men's conceptions of the physical universe as that which our ancestors had so reluctantly to submit to only a century or two ago. But every generation, every year brings with it a quantum of new scientific conceptions, new scientific truths. They creep in upon us on all sides. Is Philosophy to stand in the midst of them haughtily and superciliously, taking no notice? She cannot do so

* Although Copernicus died in 1543, it was not till the end of the seventeenth century that Copernicanism was the established belief even of educated European minds. If it was the Roman Inquisition that condemned Galileo, there were probably fewer persons at the time in Britain than in Italy who thought Galileo's opinion right. We are apt now to forget this.

and live. Whether she knows it or not, these are her appointed food. She must eat them up or perish. They do not constitute her vitality, any more than the food that men eat constitutes the life that is in them; but, just as men, in order merely to continue alive, must refresh themselves continually with food, so Philosophy, that she may not fall down emaciated and dead by the wayside, must not only not hold aloof from Science, but must regard what Science brings as her daily and delicious nutriment. Whatever definition of Philosophy we adopt—whether we call it simply and beautifully with Plato in one passage "a meditation of Death," or adopt some of the more laboured definitions that have been given expressly to indicate its relations to Science—it is equally certain that a philosophy that should be out of accord with any ascertained scientific truth or tendency to truth, or that should not in some efficient manner harmonize for the reason all the conceptions and informations of contemporary science, would be of no use for educated intelligences, and would exist as a refuge for others only by sufferance. Shall Philosophy pretend to regulate the human spirit, and not know what is passing within it—to supervise and direct man's thinkings, and not know what they are? We can all admire, indeed, and understand, the feeling of Wordsworth when he says:

"Great God! I'd rather be
A Pagan suckled in a creed outworn,
So might I, standing on this pleasant lea,
Have glimpses that would make me less forlorn,
Have sight of Proteus rising from the sea,
Or hear old Triton blow his wreathèd horn."

We can feel with the poet in this passionate outburst. But *need* we be suckled in an "outworn creed" to hope for these glorious glimpses? Those mysterious sights and sounds that took the lightsome Greek with such quick awe and ravishment by the shore of some ancient bit of blue Ægean bay, rise they not yet, are they not to be heard yet, the same Proteus, the same horn of Triton, by the shore of a greyer and grander ocean? And what though the glimpses should not all be pleasant? What though they should make some of us, for a moment or so, consciously *more* forlorn! Is there not good in such sorrow itself?

In no age so conspicuously as in our own has there been a crowding in of new scientific conceptions of all kinds to exercise a perturbing influence on Speculative Philosophy. They have come in almost too fast for Philosophy's powers of reception. She has visibly reeled amid their shocks, and has not yet recovered her equilibrium. Within those years alone which we are engaged in surveying there have been developments of native British science, not to speak of influxes of scientific ideas, hints, and probabilities from without, in the midst of which British Philosophy has looked about her scared and bewildered, and has felt that some of her oldest statements about herself, and some of the most important terms in her vocabulary, require re-explication. I think that I can even mark the precise year 1848 as a point whence the appearance of an unusual amount of unsteadying thought may be dated—as if, in that year of simultaneous European irritability, not only were the nations agitated politically, as the newspapers saw, but conceptions of an intellectual kind that had long been forming themselves underneath in the depths were shaken up to the surface in scientific journals and books. There are several vital points on which no one can now think, even were he receiving four thousand a year for doing so, as he might very creditably have thought seventeen years ago. There have been during that period, in consequence of revelations by scientific research in this direction and in that, some most notable enlargements of our views of physical nature and of history—enlargements even to the breaking down of what had formerly been a wall in the minds of most, and the substitution on that side of a sheer vista of open space. But there is no need of dating from 1848, or from any other year in particular. In all that we have recently seen of the kind there has been but the prolongation of an action from Science upon Philosophy that had been going on for a considerable time before 1848. It had been going on before British Philosophy had assumed what I will now venture to call its *penultimate* shape, or opposition of shapes—to wit, that shape, or opposition of shapes, which it began to assume about thirty years ago, when Hamilton and Mill presented themselves as the likeliest chiefs of formally opposed systems.

It is nine years since Sir William Hamilton died; and, with hardly an exception, all his philosophical remains, as they are now before the world, had left his pen ten years before that—or more than nineteen years ago.* Assume that there was—as his openmindedness and his insatiable appetite for all kinds of knowledge make it likely that there was—the most perfect adjustment in his own mind of his philosophical system at that time to the surrounding medium of the best and widest scientific conceptions. Still, is it not possible that, in the lapse of time, his system, or some portion of it, may have lost its *bite* upon the British mind? May it not be different questions that the intellect of the age is now refer-

* His Lectures on Metaphysics and Logic, though posthumously published, had been in manuscript substantially as they are before 1838.

ring to Philosophy, or, if the same questions, may not the forms of them be changed? As regards Mr. Mill the case is, happily, different. He is still among us to hear what new questions are asked, or what new forms old questions assume, and to further Philosophy by his answers. His Philosophy is not yet completed. Indeed, it has been the characteristic of his writings hitherto that they rather avow and assume the metaphysical principles of his system, and proceed to rich and interesting applications of them, than fundamentally discuss them. Hence, up to the present moment, and waiting what to-morrow may bring forth,* I am still inclined to hold that the state of British Philosophy, as represented by Mill in contrast with Hamilton, in respect of the questions selected in last chapter as most important, cannot be considered the ultimate state, but only the penultimate. Neither Hamilton's writings, nor Mill's, nor both together, present these questions in the exact form in which, so far as I see, it would be now necessary to put them.

* Written in anticipation of Mr. Mill's *Examination of Sir William Hamilton's Philosophy*, which had been announced, but had not appeared, when this part of the text of these pages was in type. What reference to this work seems necessary for the purposes of these pages will be made farther on. My references to Mr. Mill in the present and previous parts of the text are to be considered independent of that work, or such as, after my first perusal of that work, I have thought fit to let stand, as true for the period referred to.

Let us take the state of the controversy between the two opposed psychological theories of Empiricism and Transcendentalism, as it is exhibited in Mill's writings, and Hamilton's. I do not think that what is exhibited there is the exact present state of the controversy. Believing that Transcendentalism and Empiricism are still locked in each other's grips and struggling with each other as of old, I do not think that they are now gripping each other and struggling precisely as we see them in the writings of Hamilton and Mill. Nay, more, it seems to me that, of the two writers, Mill is, in this respect, the farther back.

Whatever Mr. Mill may think of the value to general philosophy of Berkeley's prosecution of Locke's doctrine into Idealism, and of Hume's more exhaustive thinking out of the same into universal Scepticism, he seems, like previous English thinkers, to have regarded these early metaphysical demonstrations in the path of Lockism only as air-clearing explosions, after which there was nothing to do but to pursue the path all the same. Be it, as Hume has shown, that all that Man is presented with is a mere vision or phænomenal aggregate of mental co-existences and sequences floating in a void, still, as this is the only universe of Knowledge that man has got, and as it is mightily real for *him*, he must have a philosophy for it! Now, all the more, rather than all the less, for this shutting up of the human mind conclusively in a phænomenal world of co-existences and sequences with which to have commerce, that philosophy must be Lockism! Experience is the only rule for such a Universe at any rate, whatever might be the rule for others! In this spirit, and with very much this appreciation of Hume's speculative services to Philosophy, Hartley and Priestley proceeded straightforward from Locke. Now Mr. Mill seems, as regards his fundamental psychological theory, to proceed straight from Locke too. He speaks with esteem of Hartley and Priestley, and more especially of Hartley. "With respect," he says, "to those of Locke's doctrines which are properly metaphysical, however the sceptical part of them may have been followed up by others, and carried beyond the point at which he stopped, the only one of his successors who attempted and achieved any considerable improvement and extension of the analytical part, and thereby added anything to the explanation of the human mind on Locke's principles, was Hartley." * This certainly implies a belief on Mr. Mill's part that Locke's principle of experience was susceptible of farther scientific development, and that Hartley contributed to that development by bringing his physiological method to the aid of psychology—*i. e.* by his study-

* Essay on Coleridge: *Dissertations*, vol. i.

ing the radical mental phænomenon, sensation, in and through its physical equivalent or concomitant of nerve-vibration. But Mr. Mill, for himself, seems to have abandoned that method, with only his good wishes. He seems, for himself, rather to avoid that mode of speech or of thought respecting the mind which would refer the origin of our ideas, habits, knowledge, and beliefs to infinite numbers of past nerve-vibrations treasured up in the organism, there associated in all varieties of simple and compound combination, and recoverable on stimulus or demand. He prefers, in the main, the older language of the pure psychologists, who speak of Experience simply as Experience, and begin their cognizance of mental actions when they may be observed as phænomena, occurring, so to speak, within an inner chamber called Mind or Consciousness, through whatever nervous labyrinths they came there, or by whatever nervous mechanism they were generated. I am not sure but there is involved in this, among other things, a protest on Mr. Mill's part against the resolution of Empiricism into Sensationalism. If he would let the word Empiricism itself stand, as, though objectionable, yet so far an established name in the Schools for Philosophy on Locke's principle, he would certainly disown Sensationalism as an odious nickname even for this Empiricism. Thus he rejects, almost with loathing, the philosophy of Condillac and his school. He considers that philosophy an unwarrantable degradation of the philosophy of Locke, and believes that it did more than anything else to bring Locke's name into disrepute. In what form, he asks, did Locke's philosophy present itself to European critics towards the end of the last century and the beginning of the present? "In that," he says, "of the shallowest set of doctrines which perhaps were ever passed off upon a cultivated age as a complete psychological system—the ideology of Condillac and his school; a system which affected to revolve all the phænomena of the human mind into sensation by a process which eventually consisted in merely *calling* all states of mind, however heterogeneous, by that name; a philosophy now acknowledged to consist solely of a set of verbal generalizations, explaining nothing, distinguishing nothing, leading to nothing." * From this passage it appears that, with whatever kindliness Mr. Mill, when it was written, looked upon the English Hartley's psychological inroad upon psychology, he viewed with anything but liking the French Condillac's extended reduction of Psychology under Physiology by the generalization that all our thoughts, powers, and feelings are but transformed sensation.

The upshot then is that Mr. Mill's statement of

* Essay on Coleridge, 1840, reprinted in Mill's *Dissertations.*

his fundamental psychological theory does not differ much from Locke's. "We see no ground for believing," he says, "that anything can be the object of our knowledge except our experience, and what can be inferred from our experience by the analogies of experience itself; nor that there is any idea, feeling, or power in the human mind which, in order to account for it, requires that its origin should be referred to any other source." * And again, "Not only what man knows, but what he can conceive, depends upon what he has experienced"—where Mr. Mill must mean "*wholly* depends." † Other passages might be cited, but, so far as I remember, with no essential change in the wording of the principle.

Now it seems to me that Mr. Mill, starting with his principle in a form so little differing in appearance from Locke's, has to run the gauntlet over again of all those objections which were levelled at Locke's, and from which it certainly did not escape unscathed. In the end (he will be told, whether justly or not) his "Experience" *must* mean "Sensation" and nothing more; for any allowance for the mind's consciousness of its proceedings with the matter given it in sensation, whether under Locke's name of Reflection, or any other, is, it will be reiterated, either a surrender of the principle, or an addition which turns out

* Essay on Coleridge. † Logic, II. 109, 110.

meaningless, inasmuch as blank conscious retention of a deposit adds nothing to the deposit. Then, farther, this reduction of the mind aboriginally to a pure passivity to sensation, a mere receiving-surface for matter of experience, is liable to all the old objections afresh. Leibnitz again starts up with his irrefragable "*nisi intellectus ipse.*" The mind must be more than a pure passivity or receiving-surface; it must be an organism of some kind, treating what is put upon it or into it in some manner or manners dependent on its structure. The *à priori* nature of the *intellectus ipse* must, from the first, be a co-efficient with matter of experience in the production of thought or knowledge. On the whole, Condillac's theory, which Mr. Mill speaks of with so much dislike, would seem at this point to be the most natural resting-ground for Mr. Mill himself as we can conceive him so pursued by Transcendentalist critics. Condillac does furnish a way of looking at the thing by which the *à priori* element, the co-efficiency of anything in the shape of an endowed *intellectus ipse*, might be reduced to a *minimum*. All the so-called feelings and powers of the mind are, according to him, conceivable as so much past sensation transformed, indurated, or concreted, by repetition and association, into faculty or organ. Give him, therefore, the smallest speck of sentiency to begin with, and the rest would require but suitable food for this sentiency, and time for its accumulated sensations to transform themselves into the various habits or faculties of organized mind. But here arises Kant to confront even Condillac, and to maintain that his theory is but a delusive resting-ground. Sentiency itself, Kant declares, involves an *à priori* element; there can be no sentiency, any more than there can be thinking or intellection, except according to innate forms, or laws, of the sentient subject. Nothing is gained then by going with Condillac. In for a pennyworth of the *à priori* element, you may as well go in for a pound's worth! And so Kant, not because he desired any such hap-hazard plunge into Transcendentalism in mere despite, but really because he aimed at as rigid an economy as possible of that *à priori* element, some considerable amount of which seemed requisite to account for the facts of Experience, hung up his famous definition or schema of the Mind of Man, as a something feeling in Space and Time, thinking according to Quantity, Quality, Relation, and Modality, and carrying in it intuitions of such suprasensuous objects as God, the Soul, and the Universe. Kant was cognisant of all that the Physiology of his time had done or proposed to do for the relief or help of Psychology; and, though his own method was the psychological, he would doubtless have been willing enough, for some purposes, to think of Man after the manner of the physiologists. "Give me an organism," he might have said, "having the potencies and functions enumerated in my Schema, and, whatever is the look of it, or however it came to be, I will call *that* Man or Human Reason." But it was a Soul, a Spirituality, an Invisibility, an unbounded dynamical Something, possessing these potencies and functions, and not a Brain and Body, that he recommended Philosophy to think of as the real organism.

The question at the end of last century thus really was whether Kant's notion of Mind or Condillac's should prevail, whether Man should be regarded by Philosophy psychologically or physiologically, whether the *Anima* should be studied in itself as heretofore or only through the *Animal.* Rightly or wrongly, the latter—the study of mind only physiologically, of Man as an animal organism—was that to which Lockism, partly in England itself, and more generally in France, had led. The reduction of Locke's "experience" simply to "sensations" had fastened attention on sensibility as the radical or initial property of the *Anima*, out of the action of which all else might be shown to result as product or accretion; and sensibility was precisely that in the *Anima* the study of which, if undertaken on its account, would have compelled attention to the bodily and especially the nervous organization of the *Animal.* But, in truth, it was not so much that Psychology had called in Physiology; it was that Physiology came in upon Psychology in its own natural course as a conquering power. Physiology had come into conscious existence as a science. All things that had life were her objects. Looking at all other animals, and connecting the phænomena of life in them unmistakeably with definite organic arrangements and actions of these arrangements, was she to refrain from extending her researches and comparisons to Man, simply because he was called Man? Really converted into a Psychology in respect of some portions of her investigations of the lower animals, she merged, in her study of Man, at that extreme, into what had always been considered Psychology proper. Nay, it was only over modesty, or hypocrisy, if she did not proclaim what was the fact, that the special Psychology then particularly in demand among French psychologists themselves—to wit, the science of the phænomena of sensibility—it was for her to furnish. "For the sake of economy of labour," the Physiologists might then have said to the Psychologists, "let there be a separation of our jurisdictions. Leave *us* in possession of this circular fringe or frontier of sensibility, which you have been so particularly cultivating, but which belongs now to us, and which we promise to do our best with. *You* retire into the interior, whither we will duly send you as much authentic material as we can for your especially psychological problem. That problem is, as you yourselves own, the transformation of sensation into feeling, habit, faculty, desire, will, conscience, and the like; a very beautiful problem it is, and worthy of your known abilities; do your very best with it. We will not absolutely swear never to follow you into the interior and undertake that problem too; but, in the meantime, we do not know the extent of our resources—so, till you hear from us again, let the circular fringe outside be Physiology, and the concentric interior Psychology."

Matters, I say, were in this state between the lineal heirs of Locke's Psychology in Europe, or those who assume to be such, and the pioneers of a noble new science of Animal Physiology, the hour of whose appearance in the world had arrived. There were in Europe, to be sure, the German Philosophy of Kant, and, in a much smaller and more local way of business, the Scottish Philosophy of Reid. But both of these, though they were not indifferent to the advances of Physiology for reasons affecting themselves, rather stood aloof from the negotiations going on, with such an excess of power on one side, between Physiology and what they considered their fallen and bankrupt relative. She had brought the crisis upon herself, and must get through it as she could! Hence, for a time, what continued Psychology we see in France, and all that portion of the continent which obeyed French influence, is not so much Psychology in the old sense as Physiology carrying on the business in the name of Psychology. In the hands of CABANIS (1757—1808) and others, Condillac's Ideology became more and more merged in Physiology, until it was a positive relief to all concerned to see the pretension of a distinction between Physiology and Psychology put an end to, and the affairs of the expiring firm finally wound up. This was done by the physiologist GALL (1757—1828), whose system of Cranioscopy, publishing itself under the name of Phrenology, took such rapid possession of every country, and had, and still has, such recommendations for the popular intelligence everywhere as a science of Mind made easy. Gall's real merits, it is now acknowledged by those physiologists who retain least of his system, were very great. He gave a stimulus to researches in the anatomy and physiology of the brain; and some of his leading conclusions were of provisional, if not of permanent, value. At all events, Phrenology, the influence of which was sufficiently powerful among ourselves, gave the *coup de grace* to the lingering remnant of what had once been Locke's Philosophy in France.

The Philosophy that offered itself at this moment

to fill the vacancy, and to satisfy any reawakened desires of the French mind which Phrenology or Physiology at large might not be meeting, was one which grounded its claims expressly on its repudiation of the essential principle of Lockism in all its forms back to Locke himself and beyond. We have all heard of that Philosophy—the Modern "Spiritualism" or "Eclecticism" of France. It began to be heard of towards the end of the First Empire, and it was at its most brilliant epoch in the reign of Louis-Philippe. M. ROYER-COLLARD, the father of the new School (1763—1845), avowedly drew his ideas from the Scottish Philosophy of Reid, and professed to import that philosophy into France in a form adapted to the mind of the nation as corrupted and debilitated by its course of Condillac and Cabanis. Fresh elements were added by M. MAINE-DE-BIRAN (1766—1824), COUSIN (*nat.* 1792), and JOUFFROY (1796—1842), until at length there was formed the system of views, compounded of Scottish psychology, fine native French speculations, and an overwhelming intermixture of ideas from the German Philosophy of Kant and his successors, of which Cousin continued to be the acknowledged head.

The School of French Scotto-Germanism had certainly an energetic life, and its place in French History is a marked one. Apparently, however, it rather floated in the middle of the nation, as a splendid factitious philosophy of a few associated minds, than expressed the real workings going on at large in French thought. Around it and underneath it, we can now see, the real French mind, still full of speculative life, but no longer detained by a Psychology as before, and having plenty of time after all the necessary attention to Phrenology or to Physiology generally, was tumbling about in all sorts of speculations as to the construction of Society and the theory of Politics. "Satan finds some mischief still for un-psychological hands to do," is the phrase in which the prejudice of some would express its opinion of the cause and drift of these speculations of an unusual order. But a more sympathetic criticism will recognise in such phænomena of the French intellectual world as Saint-Simonianism and Fourierism not only facts pregnant of much that was to come, but also the instinctive perception of Philosophy where her work lay if pure Psychology were really obsolete or were to be overpassed. And this new notion of Philosophy respecting her future work found, in a man utterly out of the school of Cousin, and whose training had been in Saint-Simonianism and in all the sciences from Mathematics to Physiology, a most competent exponent.

All the world has heard of AUGUSTE COMTE (1797—1857). And what was Comte's proclamation? It was that what had hitherto been known as Empiricism was to transmute itself for ever into *Positivism* or the *Positive Philosophy*, the principle of which was to be the utter rejection both of Theology and of Metaphysics, not only as fruitless, but as absolutely outgrown modes of thinking, and the exclusive study of positive physical laws in all departments with a special view to generalisations that might bear on the social well-being. Arranging the sciences in this order—Mathematics, Astronomy, General Physics, Chemistry, Biology, and Sociology—he announced Sociology or the Social Science as that ultimate and all-absorbing science of the world which it had been reserved for him to describe, name, and inaugurate. Philosophy in future was to be simply Sociology; which, however, implied a study of all the preceding five sciences in their social bearings. Such was his own *Cours de Philosophie Positive*, published in 1830–42. It was a series of treatises on the methods and generalities of Mathematics, Astronomy, Physics, Chemistry, and Biology (*i. e.* Vegetable and Animal Physiology), ending in a bulkier treatise on the Science of History and Politics. He gave no separate place whatever to Psychology or the Science of Mind. He nipped it into nothing between the two great sciences of Biology and Sociology. He did this deliberately, and made his doing so a characteristic merit of his system. Whatever of study or speculation respecting Man was not provided for, and did not really find its only possible gratification, in Sociology, or the science of men's actions in society, could only offer itself as that fragment or highest reach of Biology which took account of the phænomena and functions of nerve and brain in the human subject. Thought, radically, of all kinds, was *cerebration;* and only as cerebration could it be hopefully studied, except as it translated itself into the grander tide of social feeling and activity.

Thus, at last, Kantism was confronted with its fully developed European antagonist in Comtism. Previous physiological psychologists, including phrenologists, had generally shrunk from the extreme to which their opponents said they were committed. They had kept up the time-honoured distinction between Mind and Body; they had used language implying a recognition of some unknown *Anima,* or vital principle, concealed behind the animal organism; some of them had been even anxious to vindicate their belief in the immateriality or transcendental nature of this principle. But Comte ended all that shilly-shallying. Mind, he said, is the name for the functions of Brain and Nerve; Mind *is* Brain and Nerve. This destroyed, that ceases. You may fancy Mind or Consciousnesss, if you like, as an inner chamber, in which thoughts come and go like phantoms, or as a vast transparent space, without roof, without walls, without bounds, in which the very stars and celestial systems seem to wheel and make Pythagorean music; but that very fancy, I tell you, is the whimsical result of the arrangements and actions of an intricate flesh-and-blood organism of definite size and form. You may call mind a Spirituality, an Invisibility, a Dynamical Something, if you like. A Dynamical Something it certainly is; an Invisibility, in a sense, it is, but much as the power of a galvanic pile is an invisibility; but a Spirituality, as I know you to have understood that word, it is *not*, and never was.—Thus, I say, was Kantism at last confronted with its direct European antagonist.

Now the Transcendentalism of Sir William Hamilton is a Transcendentalism which had adjusted itself, to its author's own satisfaction at least, with all that had turned up in this long course of conflicting speculation, as far, at any rate, as to Kant, his immediate German successors, and the allied school of Cousin. He had not, I think, attended so much to Comte as he would have done had he foreseen the extent to which Comtism was to diffuse itself out of France. But he had attended closely to the movements of the physiological psychologists prior to their change of name into Phrenologists, and he had ventured his neck into the camp of the Phrenologists themselves that he might spy out their strength or their weakness. His Transcendentalism, therefore, was in a state of formation fit, as he conceived, to meet the enemy's latest line of battle. It is in this respect that Mr. Mill's Empiricism, as it is to be gathered from those of his writings mentioned in our conspectus, does not seem to me to be equally adjusted to the most recent exigencies of the question. That Mr. Mill was likely to have been as intimately acquainted as any of his countrymen with the history and varieties of philosophical opinion in the different nations of Europe, from Locke's time downwards, may be at once assumed. In extent and minuteness of acquaintance with French thought, at least, he can have had few competitors. Was it not he that introduced Comte, now some three-and-twenty years ago, to this country, and so opened up, in the English-speaking part of the world, a wider realm for that extraordinary French thinker than was prophesied by any recognition he was receiving in France? But, while it would be preposterous to imagine that Mr. Mill had not, in his own mind, disposed his Empiricism in accordance with the exact state of the ground and the likelihoods of the battle—that he had not seen even to its outposts and pickets—it must be confessed, I think, that he kept his dispositions secret. British Empiricism, as commanded by him, did not seem to have itself so well in hand, or to know the ground so well, as did British Transcendentalism, commanded by Hamilton.

Thus, was it not always, or generally, the pre-Kantian forms of Transcendentalism that Mr. Mill attacked—those forms which, asserting the doctrine of innate or *à priori* elements of knowledge, usually produced a number of uncouth-looking propositions, expressing the private convictions, or hereditary and professional tenets, of some individual or class, and called *them* the necessary beliefs of mankind? But, in doing so, was he not attacking fortresses evacuated by the enemy long ago, and left, if with anything in them, only with victuals and a guard of pensioners? It was the Kantian doctrine of *à priori* "forms"—of the very structure of the mind as a co-efficient *à priori* in the production of Knowledge—that had become the real position of Transcendentalism. How did Mr. Mill propose to attack this position? One observed in him not so much an indisposition to attack it as a seeming non-apprehension of its existence or whereabouts. If there was one thing that was missed more than any other throughout Mill's writings by those who would impartially see it out between him and the Transcendentalists, it was an adequate recognition and appreciation of their all-important distinction between "Form" and "Matter."

All the more because Mr. Mill was bound by his principles not to accept the distinction, but to war it down, one would have liked to see him stating it to himself, and keeping it before him, in the exact meaning given to it by his opponents.

But it was not only in the mode and direction of his outgoings against Transcendentalism that one missed satisfactory assurance that Mr. Mill had the exact state of the controversy in his view. When one looked again at his own position, so little changed in appearance since Locke's time, one could not see its superior tenability in the new conditions of the campaign.

In protesting against Comte's abolition of Psychology, as an intermediate science between Biology and Sociology, Mr. Mill did what it was perfectly competent for him to do, even while generously introducing Comte, and certifying to Englishmen the great importance and value of Comte's main system of speculation. By doing so Mr. Mill consulted the best interests of whatever might be common between his own philosophy and Comte's. He even supplied a deficiency in Comtism which must have been felt by Comtists themselves, though the master was resolute that it was no deficiency. It was quite competent for Mr. Mill to maintain, as he did so interestingly in his *Logic*, that there might still be, and ought to be, a science which, assuming the genesis of all the phænomena of Consciousness in an organism, should watch these phænomena on their own account as flitting through an imagined hall or chamber of Consciousness, should register their co-existences and sequences, and should arrive in the inductive way at generalizations of the laws of mind. And not only was it competent for him to do this; it was consistent also with a certain fine anxiety, which he had already shown, that what he believed to be Truth should never waive her rights to any power she might fairly possess over men's feelings of the becoming, the venerable, the grand, or the beautiful. We have seen his repugnance to the incessant driving-up, by Condillac and his school, of all the feelings and powers of mind into transformed sensation. This was, he said, essentially only to ignore all the multiplicity and variety of the mind's states and faculties, and to *call* all of them by the name of lowest and least agreeable associations. Was *that* so mighty a service to Philosophy? If there were candour in it, was it not only such candour as we meet with in men whose notions of being truthful is that it is to be as brutally offensive as possible? Because a rose or a lily may truly enough be spoken of as earth transformed, is that any reason for never saying rose, or lily, or stalk, or calyx? Is not the rosiness of the rose as lovely, hangs not the lily as whitely graceful, for him who knows them to be resolvable as for him who does not? And so, we doubt not, Mr. Mill felt when he refused to let Psychology be nipped out of existence, as Comte proposed, between a Biology and a Sociology. No good could be got by it, but much the reverse! Why give up such words as Soul, Spirit, Heart, Conscience, Love, with all their noble associations? Transcendentalists were too apt already to assume that they alone had a theoretical right to these words, and to the esteem and veneration engendered by them. As if, forsooth, the full rosiness even of this rose of roses, the impassioned Soul of Man, could not be known to the Empiricist! Now, as M. Comte agreed with all this—none more so; none with a richer retention, in his own case, of phrases from the vocabulary of popular and chivalrous emotion—why, by the obstinate omission of a special Science of Mind, give the Transcendentalists a cause of triumph? Was it such a stroke into the citadel of Truth to insist on translating thought into cerebration? Why not speak of thought, too, like other people, and show that Empiricism has as high and various a cognisance of all that is called thought as Transcendentalism can have?

Still the real question recurs—What *is* Mind to be called on the last analysis of it? What does the science of the rose arrive at ultimately as the beginning, principle, or root of its utmost rosiness? Had not the rose itself a start given it *à priori* in a certain germ, a potentiality of being a rose and nothing else? Could the rose be fabricated out of the mere experience of a preceding nothing in any set of conditions? Why, in such a case, the emergence, should a flower emerge at all, of a rose rather than a lily or any other flower? The immediate answer to these questions we can all divine. Well, is it the same answer that will be given by the Empiricist if we push him to a precise explication of what he means when he declares that there is not a particle of *à priori* composition in the mind of Man? When Mr. Mill says that "there is not any idea, feeling, or power, in the human mind which, in order to account for it, requires that its origin should be referred to any other source than Experience," what does he mean? He, of course, allows that, if we consider a full-grown individual man acting or deliberating at any particular moment, we do find in him an immense deal that, with reference to that moment, is decidedly of *à priori* origin. The man carries in him all his prior experience concreted and organized into knowledge, habit, tendency, faculty, character; and it is with the strength and according to the forms and ideas of this peculiar *à priori* mass of endowment that he apprehends and deals with the conditions of the new moment. Of course, therefore, in the statement that there is no *à priori* idea, or feeling or power in the human mind, it is intended that there shall be a regress to some point which shall be taken as the commencement of the human mind. But what shall be taken as that point? Shall a point be taken for each man individually, and shall it be when he began to exist? Shall it be maintained that every man, intellectually and morally, is wholly built up of his own experience from that point onward, and that, with reference to his individual life as a whole, there is nothing in his mind of *à priori* derivation? This would be to render it impossible to conceive why he should have existed as a man at all. That which did not start as some *à priori* potentiality of being a man and nothing else might as easily have been anything else, or have remained nothing. Or, if we were to try to suppose an *à priori* potentiality of being a man without any farther *à priori* outfit to be one kind of man rather than another (which, however, would yield the point), would not this be to deny heredity, the connexion of each individual physiologically with the past, the transmission of qualities? But, differ as people may as to the relative importance of these two things to a man's character—his inherited capability, and the education given him by circumstances—few, worth taking account of, now deny that there is in every man an inherited element. Comte certainly did not deny it. The Phrenologists resolutely asserted it, and offered their system as the means of taking account of transmitted qualities in the business of education. Our regress, therefore, in order to reach the point where Empiricism begins its reckoning, must be farther back yet. Let it be said that there *is* something of *à priori* or ante-natal derivation in each mind, but that, as this may be referred to past experience in the persons of parents and other ancestors, the principle of the all-sufficiency of experience is not abandoned. Shall the human race then be taken as a whole, and shall the allegation be that as regards Man or Humanity in the generalized sense, no idea, or feeling, or power is *à priori*, but all consists merely of organized and diversely-distributed Experience? But for a certain haziness in the language used in the controversy—the signification of the word "Man" alternating without warning between some single individual thought of and Humanity at large—we should probably have known that this was meant, and recent Empiricists would have escaped being charged with a form of their thesis which the farthest-sighted of them never would have undertaken to maintain.

If, however, up to this point, recent British Transcendentalism seems to have been more careful than recent British Empiricism to conform its enunciations of itself to the new conceptions which Science was bringing in, and to assert its entire durability in the midst of these conceptions, we now reach a point beyond which both Transcendentalism and Empiricism are seen as if carried out to sea, and equally swimming for their lives in strange waters.

The influx upon Philosophy of new and disorganizing scientific conceptions has never been greater than during the seventeen years since 1848. Scientific conceptions unknown to the physiologists of the earlier part of this century, unknown to the phrenologists, and not to be found even in the *Cours de Philosophiei Postive* of M. Comte,—scientific conceptions, I say, till recently unheard of, or existing only in the form of certain vague drifts and conjectures of the scientific mind—have of late years poured in upon us in full flood. Dykes have been burst; boundaries removed; we hardly know the old landmarks. Now, upon none of our previous modes of thought, whether among philosophers or among people at large, has the aggregate influence of these new conceptions been greater than precisely upon that notion of Man or Humanity as a whole over which, as we have said, there might have been a general opinion among the bystanders that the battle of Empiricism and Transcendentalism might at last be fought out. Lo! ere the battle could be begun, the very notion over which it was to be fought is dissolved, agitated out of definite shape, or rolled away, on one side of it, into an edgeless mist! No flag-staff, we are now told, can we plant at any one spot, however far back, in earthly time, and say that at that point Humanity is to be considered as beginning—that all before was a world prehuman, but all after is a history with Man in it. In the first place, what of all those recent speculations as to the Antiquity of the Human Species? It is not for me here to discuss these speculations, or even to enumerate them in their mutual relations; but to be speaking of Recent British Philosophy, and not to recognise the vast question of Science so raised as bearing upon British Philosophy, and as compelling her in some way or other to new explications of herself, would be a piece of hypocritical cowardliness. How our popular system of Chronology is faring, or may ultimately fare, at the hands of the new Archæologists, let Time (which is the party principally concerned) itself determine. It will fare as Truth would have it, and no otherwise. But it is more than the question of human chronology that is now in agitation. Behind that question as to the Antiquity of the Human Species lies the question as to the Origin of all Species, as to the place and connexions of Man in the entire scheme of Animated

Nature in our planet. Raised long ago in all varieties of ways by naturalists whose particular theories are exploded, this question has been raised again, and notably among ourselves, in forms that have brought our scientific chiefs into earnest debate, and gathered almost the whole population round them as spectators. The issue here too it is not for me to forecast. But observe how, if the views so recently announced should become general in any modification of them, Condillac's resolution of all human thought, feeling, belief, or faculty, into transformed sensation reappears in the world with its scope enlarged. Humanity itself then shades off by indefinite gradations into preceding forms of life. It is not at any particular point, however far back, assumed as the beginning of human history, that Empiricism need then abandon the battle, from the impossibility of accounting empirically for the then incipient organism, however poor and wretched it was. That organism itself, with all its stock of powers, was still, Empiricism might say, only transformed or concreted experience. Seas, ages, æons of experience had preceded it, whose essence was conserved and elaborated in its structure; and specimens of the intermediate organisms through which this one had been reached, and also the wrecks and shapes of myriads of others, lay strewn about, showing the measureless energy of

Nature, and the enormous struggle of sentient inventiveness which she had carried in her bosom, during periods anterior to the farthest ken of Man. And so, on and on, bursting the Vertebrate in the way, bursting type after type, Imagination, growing dizzier and dizzier in her ascent through an animated vagueness of she knows not what, pursues and still pursues that ideal of a by-past Eternity, at which Reason, following in her train, can take his stand and say, "Here we may stop; here experience begins; nothing here is *à priori.*" Utterly in vain! Whither goes the last phantasy of Science, still holding by the principle of continuity, transformation out of prior elements, the resolution of what is into what was? Whither but beyond conceivable sentiency itself on our Earth, nay beyond aught of a slush of vegetation conceivable as preceding sentiency, on through theories of a sheerly mineral geology, to alight at last on the steaming crust of a desolate planet of molten rotundity, itself the convolved shred of what was once a space-filling nebula? Here, from sheer fatigue, the imagination does rest for the present; here, if anywhere, it seems possible to whisper to oneself a faint persuasion as if one need not think of anything *à priori* to such a milk of thinness. Suppose the last word of Science then to be that all that exists is transformed nebula. With a thousand-fold more energy at such a last word in general knowledge than at Condillac's last word in psychological knowledge may Mr. Mill utter his protest. Is it such a mighty thing, such a stroke of universal explanation, simply to gather up the world and all its glories and to *call* them "transformed nebula?" No; but the particular question is as to the ultimate resting-place of that theory of Experience which Mr. Mill himself holds. If water is oxygen and hydrogen, why should we fear to say so? We want to trace Experience to its fountain-head.

It seems to me, I repeat, that by the recent crowding in of such new scientific conceptions there has been a disturbance of the relations of recent British Empiricism as represented hitherto in Mill and recent British Transcendentalism as thrown into form by Hamilton. Neither system seems to present its leading principle bent as one would like to see it into the curves and junctures of the most anxious thought of our time. Possibly Mr. Mill's system, from its comparative abstinence hitherto from the attempt to do so —from its being so much more the rich forthgoing of a philosophy the principles of which are avowed than a metaphysical wrestle for these principles—will have less difficulty in shaping itself to what it may recognize as the new requirements. It is by *metaphysical deficiency* that it falls short of such a system of more developed empiricism as one can conceive offering itself in the midst of these requirements. On the other hand, from the very elaborateness and exactness of the metaphysical part of Hamilton's Philosophy, from its consisting so peculiarly of a system of Metaphysics, it is possible that the complaint against it may be that of *positive incompatibility* at many points with present requirements. One can conceive a system of Transcendentalism that should be provided with answers to some questions, different from those which sufficed for Hamilton ere yet the questions had taken their present shape. Might not that Kantian scheme of the Mind of Man, for example, which represents it as a complex organism of so many *à priori* forms, neither more nor fewer, encounter now-a-days a kind of opposition that could not have been ready for it when it was first promulgated? Might not Science, in one of her new moods, object that it isolates Man as the last term of a series from all the preceding—nay, that it gives an account of Man fixed down, as it were, for inspection and analysis, at one moment (two or three thousand years long perhaps, but still a moment) of his own nominal existence? Is the organism itself stable? May not the very constituting *forms* of human thought have increased themselves, or changed perceptibly by a touch here and there, even within historic time, and may not the best present list that could be given of these forms be inapplicable to Man in the future? So I can conceive Science interrogating Transcendentalism, and perhaps explaining her meaning by means of a series of human crania chronologically arranged; and I do not think that such replies as Transcendentalism could give would suggest themselves easily out of Hamilton.

Always it is necessary, as I explained in the last chapter, to supplement any notion we may have formed of a system of Philosophy from a consideration of the Psychological Theory which it avows, by an independent look at the system in reference to its ruling Cosmological Conception. Not only have philosophers, as I there explained, been divided, psychologically, into the two great schools of EMPIRICISTS and TRANSCENDENTALISTS; they have been distributed, in farther recognition of the varying Cosmological Conceptions in which either Empiricism or Transcendentalism may be found housed (and not the less really housed because sometimes perhaps inconsistently), into such classes as *Nihilists*, *Materialists*, *Natural Realists*, *Constructive Idealists*, *Pure Idealists*, and believers in *Absolute Identity*. In the view of this classification, I said, Sir William Hamilton was to be ranked, by his own profession, in that class of Natural Realists whose representatives among philosophers have yet been few, while Mr. Mill, as I thought, might be ranked, with the great majority of philosophers hitherto, in the class of Constructive Idealists. Now, here also, I go on to say, it appears to me that the influx of recent scientific conceptions has disturbed the equilibrium between the systems of the two philosophers, or, if the fulcrum or middle point has remained the same, has occasioned a shedding off of much of British thought from that point in both directions towards the extremes.

Is it not precisely in the form of an alteration, or of alterations, of the cosmological conceptions that had served for us before, that the recent abundance of new scientific teachings and revelations has most visibly taken effect? What is that battle of Faith now going on among us, and painfully exercising so many minds, but a struggle between the expanded sort of cosmological conception which Science has seemed to be making imperative on the imaginations of us all and the little heap of propositions we have heretofore guarded so fondly at the centre as the true epitome to the reason of the whole physical vast of things? And what expanded sort of cosmological conception does Science seem to have been making imperative? We have just been speaking of it. In running back the difference of the two psychological theories to the extreme point to which Science seemed to be driving it up, we ended in a tumult of

Cosmology. Whither had we run ourselves back? Why—and this only because there seemed a defiance of any conceivable going farther—to a universal Nebula! Let rhythm re-suggest what prose is too shame-faced to repeat:—

> "*Our* hour is now: Erst, space was nebulous;
> It whirled, and in the whirl the luminous milk
> Broke out in rifts and curdled into orbs—
> Whirled and still curdled, till the azure rifts
> Severed and shored vast systems, all of orbs.
> Each orb has had its history. For ours,
> It blazed and steamed, cooled and contracted, till,
> Tired of mere vapouring within the grasp
> Of ruthless condensation, it assumed
> Its present form, proportions, magnitude—
> Our tidy ball, axled eight thousand miles."

And so, on and on, Geology taking up the wondrous tale, and navigating our ball and furbishing it, as she only knows how, through the boundless series of ages of her possession of it, till at length, not so very long ago, History meets her emerging into a glimmering light, and, the ball somehow having bred or been covered with populations of human beings, some of whom had made great advances, and formed civilizations, and taught themselves to read and write and think of high matters, we see at last a Greek Herodotus walking musingly round the margin of the Mediterranean, and collecting those legends of the past and those scraps of information respecting manners, customs, and monuments, for which we bless him and think of him with love! Thenceforward till now the voyage has been in a more familiar sea, and all has been simpler sailing.

Instead of trying, by farther description, and by involving each of the more important recent speculations of science in its proper place and measure, to body forth the cosmological Image which is becoming prevalent in educated minds, let me despatch the matter more swiftly by saying that any change or expansion of the cosmological Image that has recently taken place seems to be the result of a synthesis of three notions, each having its origin in scientific research:—

(1) There is the notion of *Evolution*, as a fact or law holding universally throughout existence. It is the notion that every existing state has grown entirely out of an immediately preceding state, has been evolved out of that state by using up all its elements or constituents. I need not stay to illustrate the notion. It is now tolerably familiar to most. A crude form of the notion existed long ago, and still figures, with a quantity of haze around it, in the word *Progress*. But, though *Progress* is a very good word, and may still most usefully be kept in service as express-

ing that advance from a worse state of things to a better which is the sort of evolution to be preferred and striven for, yet, for the general meaning now in view, *Progress*, both from its excess and its deficiency, is not nearly so good a word as its later substitute. *Evolution*, accordingly, has become the common word; it is more and more showing itself in our literature, and carrying the exact notion it expresses along with it. And the result of the diffusion of this notion, and of the exercise of it in the minds that have received it, has been that more men have been accustomed to *think back*, as it were, all the heterogeneous universe which we now behold, including our human society in the heart of it, through its preceding series of states making a complete rendition of all the contents of each state into the body of its predecessor, still in the direction of that simplest and homogeneous unity out of which all may be conceived as evolved. Observe, in this very statement of the notion of Evolution, the implied sub-notion that the course or method of Evolution is the gradual presentation of what was once simple and homogeneous in states more and more complex and heterogeneous. A name has been given to this sub-notion too. It has been called *Differentiation.*

(2) There is a notion which has not come into such distinct recognition as to have received a special name, but the existence and working of which in

many minds may certainly be detected, and which is hinted at in many current forms of speculation. I will call it the notion of *Interplanetary*, or even *Interstellar*, *Reciprocity*. Imperceptibly, by the action of many suggestions from different quarters, men have of late contracted or recovered a habit of interplanetary recollectiveness in their thoughts about things—a habit of consciously extending their regards to the other bodies of our solar system, and even to other sidereal systems, and feeling as if somehow *they* were not to go for nothing in the calculation of our Earth's interests and fortunes. Not of course the sort of interplanetary recollectiveness involved in the old dream of Astrology, during the prevalence of which dream men did, with an intensity which we seldom realize, though History would be a fool to forget it, bring down the high heavens into their being and carry the very stars as golden bees in their bonnets. It is not that we are becoming Guy Mannerings in ruined towers and again casting horoscopes. Nor is the habit of thought dependent on any continuance or revival of the old controversy as to the Plurality of Worlds. We are compelled to interplanetary recollectiveness in quite new ways. Seeing how we have conquered our little Earth physically, and brought it thoroughly into grasp with telegraphs and railroads, it has even been a whimsy of some minds that we might begin to foresee a time when terrestrial work alone would not suffice for the activity of the developed race of Earth's sons, and, in answer to their passionate longings, Nature might be bound to furnish them an outlet of enterprise in interplanetary connexions. But, such mere whimsies apart, very stringent teachings of real science are compelling to what may be called an interplanetary habit of consciousness. Those extraordinary recent revelations, by spectrum-analysis, as to the constitution of the Sun and of other celestial bodies, are they the curiosities merely of chemical speculation? No; the general thought of man drinks them in, and is different, with them, through a thousand correspondences, from what it would have been without them. Or, again, has no action of a vital kind been exerted upon general thought by those marvellous calculations, founded on the doctrine of the Correlation of Forces, as to probable endurance of that heat of the sun on which Science finds that all the movements, all the actions, all the life of our Earth and the rest of the solar system depend, and of which it views them as but conversions? I remember, indeed, that, when one of our most distinguished scientific men put forth a popular paper on the age of the Sun's Heat, stating the probability that in so many hundred millions of years the whole stock of heat would be exhausted, and we or our posterity should have to take the consequences, an English newspaper seriously objected to the publishing of such things, on the ground that, as the catastrophe was so far off, it could concern neither man nor beast to think about it. Here was an instance of a kind of pig-headedness, or indifference to ideas, which possess to a disastrous extent the current literature of Britain, and would move to indignation if it were not so comical. As if any man into whose mind this idea of the exhaustibility of the Sun's Heat, and consequently of the force energizing our system, had once entered, could ever think a thought about anything whatsoever that should not, in shape and colour, be influenced by that idea? In short, just as Science has made general, or is beginning to make general, by her teachings, the notion of the evolution of all the present cosmical variety and complexity of things from some vast indistinct beginning, so, by some of her late teachings, she has been persuading men to embrace in their regards all parts of the present complexity as still vibrating together, and to think of planets and stars and all starry systems, despite their enormous interspaces, as glittering dispersed in one entanglement.

(3) Distinct from either the notion of the past evolution of all things physical from some one homogeneous beginning, or from the notion of their present

inter-entanglement in all their places throughout the purlieus of Immensity, as still holding from that beginning by the threads of its mazy outrush—distinct from both these notions, but completing them and rounding them off towards the future, is the notion of the tendency of all things to *ultimate and universal collapse.* M. Comte, if I remember rightly, has an inkling of this speculation in one of its particular forms. Anticipating for the human race an almost indefinite career of farther development on this Earth, thinking humanity yet not near midway of the course of its mighty collective life, he nevertheless considers himself bound to announce it as an inevitable conclusion of strict science, that even this collective life of Humanity cannot go on forever—that there must come a period, however far distant, when all the elements of the collective organism of Humanity shall have been used up or brought into equilibrium, and when consequently the organism, like any other, must begin to decay. Some day, unless for a reserve of interferences of which we can foresee nothing, our Earth will be carrying not its present freight of nations, with their civilizations, governments, agricultures, literatures, and libraries, but only the unrecognisable wrecks of what had once been such, crawling over its surface, and degenerating, through stages of meaner and meaner vitality, back into shapelessness and extinction. But this prognostication of M. Comte's is as nothing compared with the prognostications to which Science has been led by the same principle. One might suppose, in considering M. Comte's anticipation, the coming-in, ere the period arrived for its fulfilment, of such a reserve of interferences, now unimaginable, as should hand on Man and his belongings, together with the tradition of our forsaken planet, into some wider mode of existence. But it is the collapse or winding-down of the whole solar system that recent Science, conjecturing onwards through time, has been prognosticating as inevitable in the distance. By a process which has been named the Equilibration of Forces, and which is slowly going on, it seems to be foreseen that a period will come when all the energy locked up in the solar system, and sustaining whatever of motion or life there is in it, will be exhausted, when the vivid play of its actions and interactions shall cease, and all its parts through all their present variousness will be stiffened or resolved, as regards each other, in a defunct and featureless community of rest and death. Nor is this all. Speculation dares to go with her mathematics beyond the bounds of the solar system itself, and, though professing to grope here in a region the possibilities of which transcend her accustomed grasp and make it falter and tremble, yet sees no other end but that all the immeasurable entanglement of all the starry systems shall also run itself together at last in an indistinguishable equilibrium of ruin, as beads or fleeces of oily substance hung in some gauze-work would trickle together in burning tears at the touch of fire, and be consumed in a steam. Thus, to something like that Universal Nebula out of which all things are fancied as evolved does Science, at her utmost daring, conceive of them as tending to be resolved again. Universal dissolution, universal rest, universal death, is her last dream of the drift of things in the infinite future. Or, if she will not let it be finally a dream of Universal Death, but will arouse herself even as she dreams, is it not by an act which she confesses to be incompetent to herself as yet—by a kind of convulsive shudder of her being at the touch of a ghostly hand, and an unconscious turning in her sleep? To this, however, there are some who think she ought to consent. Hence, with some, the notion of the tendency of all things back to a universal homogeneousness and collapse is relieved by the farther speculation that, when that state is reached, the process of evolution will somehow begin again. Again the Nebula will whirl; again there will be spun forth some wondrous entanglement of starry systems through a blue Immensity; again there will be dances of orbs round their central suns; again the orbs will have their strange particular histories; and again, when the maximum of diversity and speciality is reached, there will be a beginning of the revoke of all things into involution and integration again. Thus is introduced into the Cosmological Conception, as far as Science can carry it or consent that it can be carried, the ultimate notion or imagination of a vast *periodicity*. The Universe is a recurring beat or pulsation. It is a rhythm of alternate evolution and involution, expansion and contraction. It is the opening and shutting of a hand. It is a Nothing ever manifesting itself as a Something, and a Something ever returning into a Nothing.

By the action of these various scientific notions or speculations, there has been, I repeat, a disturbance of the prior distribution of British thought among the six traditional systems of which, so far as it discussed the cosmological problem at all, it seemed to have the option. Suppose these systems to be arranged in a line thus:—

1	2	3	4	5	6
Nihilism, or Non-Substantialism	Materialism	Natural Realism	Constructive Idealism	Pure Idealism	Absolute Identity

Then, I said, it was chiefly among the four middle systems, from *Materialism* to *Pure Idealism*, that recent British philosophical thought seemed to have distributed itself; and, if Sir William Hamilton and Mr. Mill were taken as the chief representatives of recent British philosophical thought, then, I added, the division seemed to be most marked at the very midmost point, between the two systems of *Natural Realism* and *Constructive Idealism.* Now, however, in consequence of the action of such recent scientific conceptions as I have been expounding, it seems to me that there have been drifts left and right, away from the middle point, towards the two extremes of the series. A large quantity of speculative thought has taken, I think, the Materialistic direction—a good deal remaining within the bounds of Materialism, but some passing on to a kind of Nihilism, which is David Hume's Nihilism over again, though reached by a different method. On the other hand, unless I am mistaken, there has been, or is now, a drift of a large quantity of speculative thought on through Pure Idealism, towards something like Schelling's and Hegel's doctrine of the Absolute Identity of subject and object. Lastly, though this is a more obscure matter, I am not sure but there might be recognised among us some yet inconsiderable quantity of thought which might be described as a blind struggling towards a logic that should profess to unite the two extremes, and intervolve the thought of Nothing inextricably, by a law of the intellect, with the thought of Absolute Being.

To this most excruciating pass, as it must appear to British souls, Science at the utmost seems to have conducted Metaphysics. How well the Laureate has expressed the real pain of the crisis! Always one of *his* peculiar merits is that he receives and ponders to the utmost the last scientific informations of the time, letting them sway his thoughts and occultly shape even the phrasing of his song; and no reader of the *In Memoriam* but must have noted this noble elegy, and its full philosophical significance :—

> 'So careful of the type?' But no.
>   From scarpèd cliff and quarried stone
>   She cries, 'A thousand types are gone:
> I care for nothing, all shall go.
>
> 'Thou makest thine appeal to me:
>   I bring to life, I bring to death:
>   The spirit does but mean the breath:
> I know no more.' And he, shall he,
>
> Man, her last work, who seemed so fair,
>   Such splendid purpose in his eyes,
>   Who rolled the psalm to wintry skies,
> Who built him fanes of fruitless prayer,
>
> Who trusted God was love indeed
>   And love Creation's final law—

Though Nature, red in tooth and claw
With ravine, shrieked against his creed—

Who lived, who suffered countless ills,
Who battled for the True, the Just,
Be blown about the desert dust,
Or sealed within the iron hills?

No more? A monster then, a dream,
A discord. Dragons in the prime,
That tare each other in their slime,
Were mellow music matched with him.

O life as futile, then, as frail!
O for thy voice to soothe and bless!
What hope of answer, or redress?
Behind the veil, behind the veil.

CHAPTER IV.

LATEST DRIFTS AND GROUPINGS.

In order to describe more exactly the present state of British Philosophy, I can take no better plan than that of attempting an enumeration of the chief currents and eddies of philosophical opinion that are now meeting and traversing each other at all angles within Great Britain.

I.

There may be grouped together a few eminent men speaking to the British public from the platforms of modes of thought announced as theirs long ago, and which they do not seek to adjust now, in any systematic manner, to the surrounding medium.

In this class may be again named Mr. Carlyle. We have seen how great, both extensively and intensively, has been *his* influence on the British mind of the last generation—how to omit the recognition of *him* from any history of recent British Philosophy would be to omit the part of Hamlet's father from the play of *Hamlet*. We all know, too, how his influence continues. No man is wider-awake than he to this day; no man catches more willingly and inquisitively, out of the roar of speculations and events around him, the tones that are significant. And, by his frequent voice in reply out of his characteristic solitude, or visibly in our presence, we know that he is listening, and not only listening, but always revolving the last news within his mind, and forming his judgments, and still caring for the state of Denmark. And, as for a generation past, whatever communication comes from that source flashes among us, in zig-zag, from coast to coast of our Denmark, and ends not even there. Nor, though the message may offend, and irritate, or even enrage, is it ever felt to be—what is the sole damnation of thought—irrelevant. But of the system or mode of mind out of which there still come these fresh communications, we have long had the theory before us as fully as it is ever likely to be. What a permanence of greatness in this personality! At whatever time of his life, and by whatever aid from without, Mr. Carlyle contrived to extricate himself so absolutely as it is clear he must have done from the coils of previous British systems, and to start with his own set of ideas and principles, certain it is that, since he began his career as a public teacher, we have seen him, more than most men, one and the same. Let him be supposed, then, remaining still gigantically apart on his particular well-known part of the stage, while we proceed with our general survey.

Occupying also their various particular positions, more or less known, from time past, and requiring here but to be mentioned, are such thinkers and writers as MR. ISAAC TAYLOR, DR. WHEWELL, DR. NEWMAN, MR. MAURICE, and MR. F. W. NEWMAN. There might be an interesting study of the mode of philosophical thought exhibited in the writings of each of these, and of its connexions with preceding powers and movements in British Philosophy. Partly because most of them are theologians, and have inwound their speculations with theological questions and controversies, I refrain from such a glance at each, as, even from our present point of view, each might merit. ——But I cannot but ask you to note how, in Dr. Newman's case, we have a splendid instance over again of the power of a purely metaphysical notion once formed and dwelt in, to dominate a man's whole life, and determine the nature of his practical activity. Dr. Newman had apparently at no time of his life concerned himself with philosophy, except in and through Theology; but he tells us, in his *Apologia* *pro Vitâ Suâ*, how he recollects that from his very boyhood he carried with him a certain constitutional frame or condition of mind, resembling, if I do not misinterpret his description of it, the Berkeleyan Idealism. All the external Universe seemed to him a deception, an angelic extravaganza, a spangled phantasmagory of zodiacal signs and hieroglyphics, a vivid environment of sacramental symbolisms and picture-writings, speaking to him of a great Being, besides whom and his own soul there was no other.* Dwelling long within the blazing cabalistic ether of this cosmological conception, till his soul had learnt its language and could think in no other, but tenacious of a principle which had also strongly possessed him from an early age, that of the necessity of dogma, Dr. Newman passed on, gradually but logically, into his peculiar ecclesiasticism, and became what he has become. It would be more difficult, in the case of Mr. Maurice, to refer the origin of a theological activity so different from Dr. Newman's to any recovering in its author's mind, by reading or native meditation, of any of the leading speculative systems in particular of which there is record in the history of philosophy. Mauricianism, as it is called, would require an explanation by itself, which could perhaps be given only by one imbued with it. It is to be ob-

* See *Apologia*, p. 56, p. 59, and pp. 88—91.

served, however, that Mr. Maurice, having written the history of Philosophy, must carry in his mind, even more than appears, a connected recollection of the alternations and vicissitudes of metaphysical systems that have characterized its course, and the means of thinking of his own Theology accurately in its historical as well as in its contemporary relations. That there is more than a relation of mere sequence between him and Coleridge (in whom again, as I have said, there was a resumption and re-issue of the elements of a rich and free native Anglicanism, the tradition of which had been long overborne or frittered away) seems to me a fair assertion, and, indeed, in Mr. Maurice's Theology, if nowhere else, I should find evidence that the influence of Coleridge's Philosophy, notwithstanding all that has intervened, is not exhausted in England.

In this place, as naturally as anywhere else, may be mentioned Mr. J. D. Morell. Of his various writings I do not know that any has contributed so much to the diffusion of philosophical notions, and of an interest in Philosophy, as his lucid and comprehensive "History of Speculative Philosophy in the Nineteenth Century," published nearly twenty years ago. It was a most welcome book at the time; and to it, along with Mr. Lewes's "Biographical History of Philosophy," our literary men, as well as readers at large, are indebted to this day for more of their best information on philosophical subjects than is always acknowledged.

II.

A very marked group of thinkers and writers among us may be distinguished, fairly enough, as the British Comtists.

Here let me take prejudice by the horns. No difference from Comte over the fundamental principle of his philosophy, no recoil or aversion of the spirit (let it be even as vehement as my own) from his final theory of things, ought to prevent or will prevent—save where fear of the Blatant Beast is allowed to measure men's words—a recognition of Comte's great services in the world of recent speculation. A figure full of interest to me—an interest compounded of admiration, mournfulness, and yet a sense of the comic—is that of the lonely Parisian, of little regard among the authorities of his country, and whom they had deprived almost of bread, persevering till his death in the work of building up, and finishing to its last detail and pinnacle, a system of thought in which, as he conceived, all Humanity, after its ages of weary wandering, might at last find rest. "Ho! all ye nations, and especially ye five, the *élite* of Humanity—Frenchmen, Britons, Germans, Italians, and Spaniards!

Ye have now nearly passed through the two stages, or modes of thought, through which, as I can prove to you, the mind of man must pass on all subjects whatsoever, before it teaches the third and last. It is time that this third stage should be prepared for you, and extended before your eyes in its reaches through a glorious future. This is *my* work; I am the herald, the apostle of Positivism. All the materials that have been accumulating for the new construction, all the hints for its design, have come together in me, and found the proper architect;—nay, not only have I been the architect, but I have been the builder from the foundation upwards, the carver, the gilder, the decorator. The vast construction is ready. Leaving all other systems, come, ye choicest spirits, my speculative kinsmen, from all ends of the earth; here we shall dwell together in unity, understanding and even reverencing the past, but regulating the present, and looking forward tranquilly to that future to which we shall have prescribed the true problem of Philosophy, Art, and Government, all in one—'the reorganization of human society, without God or King, through the systematic worship of Humanity.'" If there is something ludicrous to many in this over-estimate, in a man's own case, of what it can possibly be given to any one man to accomplish and leave permanent in the world, there is not the less something majestic in the intensity of conviction, the indomitable faith in ideas, which could lead to it. To our loss, we in Britain have too little of this spirit of self-assertion rather than too much. Given an intense idiosyncrasy, and a really powerful and inventive mind, and society around harms itself, rather than secures itself, by an intolerance of the speculative extravagances, the audacities of egotism, which might result, and by the habit of beating them back with coldness, witticisms, and derision. It is hard, indeed, for Teutonic flesh and blood to look on and see a Frenchman generalizing, to the utmost of his national manner when it breaks loose, without a longing to knock him down, and put him in a strait-waistcoat. There is such a confidence about him, such a systematizing rapidity, such an unhesitating sureness about things, where we Goths are clogged and restrained by traditional considerations and a sense of difficulty and complexity! But there is something superb, nevertheless, in the speculative movements of a first-rate French intellect. In the works of M. Comte, at all events, there is a well of thought and suggestion on all sorts of subjects, the value of which it does not need even an approach to acquiescence in his philosophical basis to appreciate. There are propositions and generalizations of his, more especially in the department of politics, the absorption of which into the general mind, or in the working-creeds of professional statesmen, would considerably transform and exalt what now passes for politics. Throughout Britain, indeed, this has been long perceived in many quarters; and, while Mr. Mill and others have expressed to the full their obligations to Comte, even when defining their increasing differences from him, others have been secretly helping themselves to Comte, and living on the results.

All in all, there is, I should say, a considerable tinge of Comtism through our present speculative literature. It is not, however, of those among us who have only in a general way received this tinge, as they would have received a tinge from any other powerful intellectual influence of their time, that I speak under the name of the British Comtists. Under this name I have in view a few writers and thinkers who in a more express manner adhere to Comte, or to an acknowledged adaptation of him. Even here, however, there are degrees. One may distinguish, even within Comte's own life-time, two Comtisms, of which those who were inclined to be Comtists had the option. There was the "Earlier Comtism," if I may so call it, represented in his completed *Cours de Philosophie Positive;* in which, though there was extravagance enough of opinion and expression to shock the British mind, there was still a reining-in of the intellect on this side of delirium. But this was ere long developed into the "Later Comtism;" in which, impelled by a sudden revelation that his system was deficient as yet on the sentimental side, the author suddenly broke down one of its gables, and did pass on, without his hat, into what irreverent lookers-on must really call delirium and moonlight. Out from that gable he built, as it were, a spacious verandah for a new Religion, attached to his Positive Philosophy under the name of the *Culte Systématique de l'Humanité.* Here there might be busts of three hundred and sixty-five selected eminent men of the past (a large proportion being, of course, Frenchmen), ranged in niches, as gods for ordinary daily worship throughout the year; besides more colossal busts of greater gods for the weeks and months, and a striking peculiarity of four black busts of History's most retrograde scoundrels, at quarterly intervals, to serve as devils, or desirable objects of execration; while within all, in a secret alcove, one might practise the sweetest and keenest of all forms of the worship of Humanity—the worship of Woman—by praying habitually to one's own mother, or wife!

Some form even of the later or sacerdotal Comtism, I believe, does exist among us in perfect earnest, and without seeking to conceal itself; but, as might be expected, it is chiefly the earlier or purely speculative Comtism, and that with modifications, that has any following in Britain. If I reckon Mr. Lewes and Miss Martineau among British Comtists in this sense, it must be only in as far as they themselves, in translating or expounding Comte, have signified their adhesion to his principles. Miss Martineau has had a career of thought and activity of her own too marked to make it conceivable that it can have merged absolutely in Comtism; and Mr. Lewes is too able and spirited a man, too cultured, of too frank and quick sympathies in all fine directions, that we should tie him down very stringently to his own enthusiastic expression, that "in the *Cours de Philosophie Positive* we have the grandest, because on the whole, the truest system which Philosophy has yet produced." * Still, there is a considerable amount of effective British Comtism among us—of that philosophy which abjures and protests against Metaphysics, or the thought of the supernatural in any form whatsoever, as by this time proved rubbish, and would direct the ploughshare of the human mind, in respect of the study of Man, exclusively to Physiology and Sociology.

Into this British Comtism have been absorbed, I think, all the relics, worth reckoning, of what was once native British Secularism. Absorption into Comtism has been an elevation for it.

* Lewes's *Biographical History of Philosophy*, Library Edition, p. 662.

To be named in close connexion with the British Comtists, though not decisively as one of them, is the late MR. BUCKLE. His great idea, that for which he lived and died, was the possibility of a Science of History. There was a paramount obligation of the human mind in the present age to the study of History in a scientific manner, with all possible aids from Physiology and the other sciences, in order to the discovery and establishment of a new body of truths bearing on the social well-being. In prosecuting this idea Mr. Buckle himself put forth a number of more or less suggestive conjectures and criticisms, and revealed also certain strong idiosyncrasies—in particular, his passion for liberty of thought, and his abomination of the theological spirit in all times and countries. There was a breaking away in him, too—as is often interestingly the case with enthusiastic Empiricists of his type—into a consolatory private transcendentalism of his own, accessible from his general system by a wicket to which he only had the key. But, on the whole, it must have been chiefly owing to the small amount of public familiarity there was in this country with exercises of speculation in the same general direction, and particularly with Comte's, that Mr. Buckle's doctrines ran about with such a clamour of rejection and acceptance. As far as I know, all that was essential in them might have been cut out of a corner of Comte, or out of that with a portion of Mill in addition—though I do not mean to say the author got at them by any such immediate method; and there was a crudity about his statements of them, an incoherence, and a sort of slap-dash contemptuousness towards whole centuries and civilizations of the past, on account of their using battle-axes, burning witches, wearing shoe-ties, or some trifle of that sort, from which the more comprehensive genius of Comte kept him free. It was Mr. Buckle's intellectual courage, his pugnacity for ideas that had roused and invigorated himself, that was his main merit. In our country it is a great merit, because still a rare one. Thinking, therefore, how largely he possessed it, and how prematurely and sadly *he* was cut off while others who have no such virtue are left, the words may occur to us:

> "How well could we have spared for thee, young swain,
> Enow of such as for their bellies' sake
> Creep, and intrude, and climb into the fold!"

III.

I will now name together two writers, not because they can be constituted into a class, but because each of them is so important individually that there is a propriety, on that account, in connecting them.

Associated with Mr. Mill by a mutual respect,

which has taken opportunities of expressing itself, and also by substantial adhesion in principle, is MR. ALEXANDER BAIN. His contribution to Philosophy is mainly his large system of Psychology in two volumes, entitled *The Senses and the Intellect* and *The Emotions and the Will.* It is perhaps the richest Natural History of the Human Mind in the language—the most fully mapped out, and the most abundant in happy detail and illustration. The author decidedly belongs to the school of Empiricism, and he roots his Psychology, more strenuously and extensively, I think, than any British psychologist since Hartley, in Physiology. But, from the fact that his Physiology is that of the present day, he does this with greater intelligibility and effect. He does not indeed reject from Psychology the method of the observation and registration of the phænomena of Mind, as flitting, however generated, in a supposed inner chamber of Consciousness; but he takes care to assert at the outset that this inner chamber is a mere phantasy or trick of the mind. Sweeping away even the imaginary sensorium, or central receptacle for impressions, of the older physiologists, he views Mind as presenting itself in *nerve-currents*, the *recoverability* of nerve-currents, and the *associability* of nerve-currents, on and on, in ever-increasing complexity and in ever-varying combinations. Beginning, therefore, with Brain and Nerve as the seats of the nerve-currents, and educing thence those simplest and most rudimentary states of mind which consist of instinctive muscular movements and sensations of the five senses, he proceeds to show how, out of these, by the processes of recoverability and association, all the facts of the mind, all the habits and faculties of men, all their cognitions and beliefs, all the varieties of aptitude, intelligence, character, and genius, may be conceivably built up. As he does this in a quiet, gradually synthetic way—leaving the sufficiency of his system to be judged of by his exhibition of its ability to work through, and account for, all the abundance of men's notions as to themselves and each other, rather than debating it formally—it is only incidentally, and here and there, that he touches on the great questions of Metaphysics. And yet his book, I should say, strews excellent new material over these questions, and, if attended to, will not leave their British forms precisely as they were. Thus, with respect to the battle of the two opposed psychological theories—that of Empiricism and that of Transcendentalism—Mr. Bain, I think, introduces a novelty in his Psychology. Rightly or wrongly, he places it to the credit of Empiricism; and, if rightly so placed, it would improve the position of Empiricists, including Mr. Mill, against their opponents. He finds, physiologically, that among the rudimentary facts of the human organism is that of a force of spontaneous movement, as well as an equipment for passive sensibility—a power of generating active nerve-currents from within outwards, as well as a liability to sensitive nerve-currents from without inwards; and through all the complications of his farther expositions he takes care to run this fund of automatic force, intermingled continually with mere sensation, as a something that may prove tantamount, when investigated, to a good deal of that *à priori* element, apart from sensation, for which Transcendentalists contend. Momentarily, as regards the individual human being, Mr. Bain, by this provision of a physiological substitute for at least somewhat of the *à priori* element of the Transcendentalists, does put a different complexion on the question between Empiricism and Transcendentalism, and alters the setting of it. As regards each individual, he provides, on physiological evidence, an ever-flowing fountain of necessary or innate impulse, independent of sensation from without, and intermingling with it. And, as thus, in the very beginning of his Psychology, he offers what may pass provisionally, in respect of the individual mind, as a physiological substitute, as far as it will go, for the important distinction of the Kantians between Form and Matter, so at the end of his work, where he comes round to his last word on the ultimate metaphysical question—the question of the trustworthiness of Consciousness in that conception of a double Universe, of Self and Not-Self, of Subject and Object, which seems to be compelled in every act of external perception—he makes the same notion reappear on an extended scale, so as to take effect upon the state of the controversy between the various systems of Realism on the one side and those of Idealism on the other. Movement and sensation, nerve-currents from within outwards and nerve-currents from without inwards, being rudimentarily and from the first moment the one radical contrast or antithesis in our feelings—this contrast, always accompanying us, and, though strengthened, enlarged, and educated by million-fold repetitions and associations, yet always remaining constant, swells out at last into that contrast between the extended visible immensity of an external world up to the stars, and a felt but invisible and unlike immensity of spirit within, which all men carry with them, and which has been the fascinating fact for Metaphysics. The notion of Self or Subject is a generalization of the feelings of Active Movement: the notion of Not-Self or Object is a generalization of the feelings of Passive Sensation. What, then, must be the answer of a philosopher to that question, as to the last certainty accruing from the total evidence of

Consciousness, to which philosophers may be expected to possess an answer, although common men, not for that matter philosophers themselves, except when they philosophize, need not entertain it? Where shall one rank oneself? Among Nihilists, among Materialists, among Natural Realists, among Constructive Idealists, among Pure Idealists, or among those who hold the doctrine of Absolute Identity? Curiously enough, Mr. Bain's premiss leads, on the one hand, out of any form of Idealism, towards a peculiar, and what may be called physiological, form of the doctrine of radical Identity. Though the two generalizations of Self and Not-Self, of the perceiving mind and of the world external to it, are carried apart practically by all men, and life consists in a perpetual hypothesis of their opposition, yet the psychologist, knowing that they have their roots inextricably united in the same organism, and knowing no more than this, is bound to proclaim, as the deepest fact of the phænomenal universe arrived at by his science, the identity, the inseparability, of Subject and Object. Of course, as it is within the bounds of his psychological theory of Empiricism that Mr. Bain takes up this position, his Identity-system is a very different thing, in its metaphysical bearings, from the Identity-system of some of the Transcendentalists. They, or any of their brother-Transcendentalists, would be entitled to run Mr. Bain back, with this physiological form of the Identity-system in his hands, along that eternal track which the controversy between Empiricism and Transcendentalism must pursue in the quest of the real beginning. Such farther interrogation, however, Mr. Bain implicitly declines. Except through Psychology, and consequently except through Physiology, he refuses Metaphysics. He does so, I believe, on definite principle. And, considering the great services he has done to Psychology by preserving adherence to his own method—the important novelties, I think I may say, which he has introduced into British Psychology in particular—we ought, most certainly, not to object to his system that it does not give us what it never undertook to give. Still, as Philosophy in its widest sense asks, and always has asked, for instruction as to the best mode of thought on those metaphysical questions, at their highest and most extreme range, which Mr. Bain declines to entertain, and as, at the present moment in particular, it is obvious to all that it is with these questions, as reset for it by an all-comprehensive and soul-exciting Cosmology, that British Philosophy is passionately grappling, Mr. Bain's treatise does not encircle all the requirements.

No such defeat can be charged against the other writer whom I am now to name—Mr. Herbert Spencer. Of all our thinkers he is the one who, as *it* appears to me, has formed to himself the largest new scheme of a systematic philosophy, and, in relation to some of the greatest questions of philosophy in their most recent forms, as set or reset by the last speculations and revelations of science, has already shot his thoughts the farthest. He both works out his Philosophy physiologically and psychologically from the centre, and—what seems to me an eminent merit in relation to the intellectual needs of the time—surveys it and contemplates it from the circumference cosmologically. Indeed, I should say that he is the British thinker who has most distinctly realized the absolute necessity that Philosophy lies under, of dealing with the total cosmological conception as well as with the mere psychical or physiological organism (and this from the demonstrable inter-relatedness of both), if it would grasp all the present throbbings of the speculative intellect. His writings take for granted this necessity, and make it plainer than it would otherwise be. Nowhere else are the various sciences so fished for generalizations that may come together as a whole to help in forming a Philosophy. Nowhere else, at all events, is there a more beautiful and fearless exposition of some of those recent scientific notions which I spoke of in the last chapter as affecting our views of metaphysical problems. There are parts of Mr. Spencer's writings, occupied with such expositions, which, from sheer scientific clearness, and adequacy of language to the matter, have all the effect of a poem. If even only for such renderings of high scientific conceptions, on the chance of their somehow taking possession of the popular soul, and uniting there to rectify previous forms of thought, he would deserve honourable recognition.

But Mr. Spencer does not stop short in the character of an interpreter between Science and Philosophy, handing on the conceptions of Science to that congress of all the Powers where they are to be adjusted and take effect. He assumes the work of the philosopher proper. He seeks to enmesh the physical round of things, as Science now orbs it to the instructed imagination, within a competent Metaphysic; he desires to fix in the centre a competent Psychology, consistent with this Metaphysic, and yet empirically and physiologically educed; and he would fill up the interior, or what of it the physical sciences leave void, with a competent Ethics, a competent Jurisprudence, a competent Æsthetics, a competent Science of Education, and a competent Science of Government and Politics.

In this great work he is still engaged; and it will not perhaps be till the whole is accomplished that there will be the means of determining either the sufficiency of Mr. Spencer's philosophy for the higher practical purposes of philosophy, or its exact intellectual relations to previous systems. Already, in consequence both of the decisiveness of his views and the variety of interesting subjects over which they extend, Mr. Spencer, more than any other systematic British thinker save Mill, has an avowed following both here and in America; and, if any individual influence is visibly encroaching on Mill's in this country, it is his. For my own part, believing that no type of man ought to be more precious to a nation than a resolute systematic thinker, and believing Mr. Spencer to be a very high specimen of this type, I anticipate nothing but good, nothing at least but a clearing away of the bad, from what he has already done or may yet do. And this I say, though differing as deeply and at as many points from Mr. Spencer as from any man whom I respect. His Metaphysic seems to me too merely negative; and this negativeness of character I trace through his views, so far as I know them, in Politics, in Æsthetics, and in all matters whatsoever. Also I think—or it may be the same thing in a particular form—he undervalues history, erudition, and the power of the historical element.

IV.

Although Hamilton is no more in the midst of us, Hamiltonianism is not defunct. But why should I say Hamiltonianism? All our British speculative thought, in every corner where intellect is still receptive and fresh, has been affected, at least posthumously, by the influence of that massive man, of the bold look and the clear hazel eyes, whose library lamp might have been seen nightly, a few years ago, by late stragglers in one of the streets of Edinburgh, burning far into the night when the rest of the city was asleep. Oh! our miserable judgments! Here was a man probably unique in Britain; but Britain was not running after him, nor thinking of him, but was occupied as she always is and always will be, with her temporary concerns and her riff-raff of temporary notabilities. And now one has to dig one's way to the best of him through the small-type columns of perhaps the most amorphous book ever issued from the British press. But some have done this, who had no inducement to do so except their love of Ideas, wherever they were to be found. Mill and Bain, who are fundamentally opposed to Hamilton's Transcendentalism, and Spencer, who is certainly not a Hamiltonian, all acknowledge their respect for Hamilton, and the obligations of British thought to his labour. And it was the gymnastic of Philosophy, its power to energize and elevate the mind in the pursuit of truth, more than agreement with any one supposed system of truth, whether his own or another, that he himself cared for. Hence, if I say that there are still

Hamiltonians among us, I do not mean that even those whom I call such adhere to Hamilton's doctrines, but only that to Hamilton they confess, more than others do, a sense of continued allegiance.

In England there is first to be mentioned Mr. Mansel, whose own works in Philosophy have earned him justly so high a reputation, and who has given a turn to one of Hamilton's doctrines, in connexion with a form of English Theology, for which, some think, the form of theology is more obliged to him than the Hamiltonian doctrine. Acknowledging specific obligations to Hamilton, but differing from him most of all precisely where Mr. Mansel's agreement is greatest, is Dr. McCosh of Belfast, in the last edition of whose *Intuitions of the Mind Inductively Investigated* will be found some express criticisms of the ontological applications of Hamilton's Philosophy by Mr. Mansel and Mr. Herbert Spencer. Along with Dr. McCosh, as also admiring Hamilton in the main, but dreading the consequences of his Relativity doctrine, may be named Mr. Lowndes, the author of a very shrewd and clear little volume recently published under the title of *An Introduction to the Philosophy of Primary Beliefs*; and there are still other writers that might be named in the same connexion.——Naturally, however, it is in Scotland, and among Hamilton's own pupils there, that Hamiltonianism lasts the strongest.

I can name one former student of Hamilton's now a minister in what would be accounted in England one of the straitest sects of Scottish Puritanism, and who has consecrated to the duties of that calling the powers of a mind among the noblest I have known, and the most learned in pure Philosophy. Any man who, on any subject of metaphysical speculation, should contend with Dr. Cairns, of Berwick-upon-Tweed, would have reason to know, ere he had done with him, what strength for offence or defence there may yet be in a Puritan minister's hand-grip. And, if I mention him so, it is to bring out a fact which we are too apt to forget in these days of increasing disrespect for the clergy—to wit, that it is impossible for any one to know, otherwise than by actual observation of society, and a habit of estimating men not merely by the apparent direction in which they are scudding, whether with the prevalent breeze or not (which the smallest ships may be doing), but by their weight and build all in all, what combinations of native power and of high speculative culture and insight may be found with what inherited positions and systems of belief, and honestly verifying them to their homeliest letter. Dr. Cairns is, in the main, though with considerable modifications, an adherent to Hamilton's speculative philosophy; and he has published interpretations and defences of portions of that philosophy as well as occasional expositions and criticisms of Kant and the later Germans. Freer and more at leisure by their positions to maintain Hamiltonianism, or to go on modifying it or leading it out of itself, are PROFESSOR FRASER, Hamilton's successor in the University of Edinburgh, PROFESSOR VEITCH of Glasgow, the joint-editor, with Mr. Mansel, of Hamilton's Lectures, and PROFESSOR T. SPENCER BAYNES, of St. Andrews—the last of whom, though a pupil of Hamilton and for some time his assistant, is of English birth. Thus, of the four Scottish Universities, three, so far as the express chairs of Speculative Philosophy are concerned, are in the possession of former pupils of Hamilton—the fourth, that of Aberdeen, having Mr. Bain for its philosophical chief. The influence of the three is exerting itself as yet chiefly, as Hamilton's own did so long, in the private conduct of their classes; nor is there sufficient public means of measuring and characterizing it. All three, however, have given proofs in occasional published writings of their ability and of their fitness to lead philosophic thought; and Mr. Fraser, in particular, besides teaching with admirable success, classes larger than Hamilton's ever were, has signalized his departure from some of Hamilton's views both in essays openly to that effect, and in some striking disquisitions, from a new point of view, on older philosophers, particularly Berkeley. On the whole, in his case, if not among the Scottish Hamiltonians generally, I think I see, along with a resolute adhesion to Transcendentalism in principle, a tendency to deviation from Hamilton's system of Natural Realism in the direction of Idealism. At all events, both Berkeley and Locke have received more extensive and profound attention from Mr. Fraser than has been common recently among thinkers of the Scottish school in Philosophy.*

V.

A frequent sign of a forward movement in Philosophy is an extravagant show of disrespect among those who represent it towards their immediate predecessors or their memory. The very sense of nearness causes antagonism. It is easier to do justice to philosophers between whose views and one's own the distance is great, than to those from whom one has just parted in order to shoot ahead.

Something of this kind, but rather implied than expressed, I find in that very remarkable book, *Institutes of Metaphysic: the Theory of Knowing and*

* See an article by Professor Fraser, entitled "The Real World of Berkeley," in *Macmillan's Magazine* for July, 1862, and another, understood to be by him, entitled "Berkeley's Theory of Vision," in the *North British Review* for August, 1864. A collected edition of Berkeley's works, of which Professor Fraser is to be the editor, has been announced as forthcoming from the Oxford University Press.

Being, by the late PROFESSOR FERRIER, of St. Andrews. It was published in 1854, while Sir William Hamilton was still alive. It is throughout a protest against Hamiltonianism, and an effort to lead on into a new system, having affinity with the post-Kantian metaphysics of Germany, and especially with Schelling and Hegel, but constructed by the author himself in a belief that, though there had been a struggle towards the true philosophy, and incessant and splendid glimpses of it in Plato, Spinoza, Leibnitz, and Berkeley, and then in Kant and his German followers, yet the all-important cardinal proposition had never been seized and once for all articulated. "It may be affirmed with certainty," he said, "that no man for at least two thousand years [since Plato, he meant] has seen the true flesh-and-blood countenance of a single philosophical problem." And what was the all-important cardinal proposition the missing of which had made the history of philosophy one such wide welter of occasionally illuminated confusion? It was this:—"Along with whatever any intelligence knows, it must, as the ground or condition of its knowledge, have some cognisance of *itself*." Starting from this proposition,—and proceeding through three sections of his treatise, entitled respectively "Epistemology, or the Theory of Knowing," "Agnoiology, or the Theory of Ignorance," and

"Ontology, or the Theory of Being"—Professor Ferrier deduced from it, or attached to it, a series of farther propositions, following each other numerically like the propositions in Euclid, and professing to be as strictly reasoned out, and offered in their totality as constituting an irrefragable system of Metaphysic or Necessary Truth. The last proposition in the "Ontology" may be here quoted, as exhibiting Mr. Ferrier's final landing-place in the question of the Absolute. "All absolute existences are contingent *except one;* in other words, there is One, but only one, Absolute Existence which is strictly *necessary;* and that existence is a supreme and infinite and ever-lasting Mind in synthesis with all things." Repulsive to the general taste as is a system of Metaphysics taking the form of a chain of such abstract propositions, like grinning death's heads, Mr. Ferrier's book is unusually rich in popular expositions of philosophical questions. The intervals between the propositions are filled with dissertations and elucidations of great literary power and picturesqueness, and containing passages eloquent with high feeling, and sparkling with wit. There are blasts, in particular, of measureless contempt against the Scottish psychologists as a body, and Dr. Reid as their type; there is a brave yearning of the spirit back into sympathy with the grander and more dynamic metaphysics of the past, unappreciated or misappreciated because of their higher nature—the metaphysics of Plato, Spinoza, and Berkeley; there is an inquisitive, and also sympathetic, looking across the seas towards the German Hegelianism, as if with the thought that noble elements might be brewing within that dark monstrosity to British eyes, if only it could be penetrated; and there are interesting historical sketches of the connexions of previous systems, and the mode of their gradual evolution. A fine speculative mind disappeared from Britain when Professsor Ferrier died.

What is of interest to us here is the attempt of British Transcendentalism, in Ferrier, to move out of the Hamiltonian system altogether, by leaving Natural Realism in disgust, and then not stopping even in any ordinary form of Idealism, but passing sheer on to the doctrine of Absolute Identity. The inseparability of subject and object, the identity of Knowing and Being—this was the doctrine to be hung up in the centre for ever as the all-irradiating, all-glorifying, all-cheering lamp of light. How it would strike to quick transparence all the gloom! How, seen at its highest, as the assertion of a one Absolute Mind in synthesis with all things, it need not fear, because it could overmatch and spiritualize, through and through, and round and round, any expansion of the cosmological conception that Science might empirically compel, if even into a vast periodicity from Nebula to Nebula again—clearing, as it would, the whole periodicity of its materialistic horror, or of its dread of being shored by a Nothingness; uniting Time past, present, and future in one Consciousness, making the stars, once more, but orbs or twinklings of Deity; and filling all within them, to the earth and the heart of man, with His presence and His love!—So, as I fancy, did the author represent to himself the consequences of his doctrine. Still, observe how closely the doctrine itself, in its simple verbal form, as respects the individual mind, corresponds, though belonging to a system of high *à priori* Metaphysic, with the doctrine of Mr. Bain, worked out physiologically, and stationed at the centre of his so different system. The systems are poles apart,—the one that of utmost Transcendentalism, the other that of the most exact Empiricism; but they revolve, as nearly as possible, on exchangeable pivots.

Since I began the preparation of these pages, there has come into my hands a book which enables me, I think, to point to a British representative of a metaphysical system beyond even Mr. Ferrier's, and a representative of which was wanting to fill the only place left vacant in our scheme.

Let me repeat our arrangement, for the eye, of the

six cosmological systems propounded and maintained by metaphysicians. It was as follows :—

1	2	3	4	5	6
Nihilism, or Non-Substantialism	Materialism	Natural Realism	Constructive Idealism	Pure Idealism	Absolute Identity

Assuming that the opposition of prevailing British philosophies, as recently represented in Hamilton and Mill, was most marked at about the mid-point of this series, or between Natural Realism and Constructive Idealism, there has been observable of late, I ventured to say, a drifting away of British thought from that middle point in both directions towards the extremes. There has been a drift leftwards, through Materialism or Materialistic Realism, towards Nihilism, or the conception of an ultimate nothingness, or, if the expression is preferred, the resolute non-conception of an ultimate anything. There has similarly been a drift rightwards, through more and more refined varieties of Idealism, towards the notion of Absolute Identity, or an eternal real Oneness of Subject and Object, of which all the vast cosmical periodicities from Nebula to Nebula, or whatever may be the terms, are to be conceived as living pulsations. Mr. Ferrier, as I have just said, seems, more distinctly than any other recent British metaphysician, to have carried Transcendentalism to this last point, and to have established, by so doing, a cousinship in this country with Schelling and Hegel. Well, was anything more to be done? It seems difficult to conceive that anything remained to be done. One might run backwards and forwards among the six schemes, returning from Nihilism or from Absolute Identity centrewards; but either to leap off Nihilism on the one hand, or to leap off Absolute Identity on the other, was a feat apparently beyond all rational gymnastic. Well, but what if the two extremes could be united? What if a logical bridge could be thrown at once from Nihilism to Absolute Identity, over-spanning all the intermediate systems? What if the mind could be hung as a pendulum, necessarily taking the exact arc from Nihilism to Absolute Being in its every swing, so that one swing of it, one single act of thought, should actually realize, apprehend, nay, repeat and represent, that vast cosmical beat of periodicity, from Nothing to completed Being, and from completed Being back to Nothing again?

At such a suggestion we Britons naturally feel uneasy. We would rather not have our mind swung so! "For any sake, don't," we cry; "we haven't been accustomed to it. Absolute Oneness, if you please, or Nihilism, if you please; we should not so much mind which; but who can live on a shuttle between them?" And yet this is precisely what he whom his admirers regard as the last of the world's great metaphysicians tells us we must do, and indeed are doing every moment, whether we know it or not. And who is he? Hegel, the terrible Hegel, the brain-benumbing Hegel—on scraps of whose doctrines modern Germany is said to have been living for forty years, but whose entire system no German soul even is believed to have yet fathomed or got round; who himself said, after his system had been before the world for a sufficient time, and hundreds had been doing their best with it, "There is only one man living that understands me, and *he* doesn't." What Hegel gave to the world, as principally wanted and as the foundation for all else, was a new *Logic*, or science of the necessary laws of Thought; and in this *Logic* the foundation-principle was the identity, the inseparability in thought, of the idea of Being and the idea of Nothing. The most abstract thought of man, that in which he ends by the most intense effort of reason, is the idea of pure Being; and absolutely and in every way, this idea is the same as the idea of pure Nothing; and each merges into the other necessarily; and both are forms of one combining idea, the idea of Becoming. And this alternation between the idea of Nothing and the idea of Being, through the idea of Becoming, is the law of every thought that man thinks or can think. Every thought is a poise, a beat, a pulsation between the two contradictories, comprising them both in one organic act, as inseparable, though distinguishable. And this law of Thought is also the law of Being; and Logic, which is the science of Thought, is also the science of Being. Logic and Metaphysic are identical. What takes place in every thought also takes place in every fact. "Nowhere in heaven or in earth is there anything, that contains not both these—Being and Nothing." And, on the largest scale, with respect even to the vast cosmical periodicity itself, the entire rounded object of the cosmological conception, the same, according to Hegel, if I understand him, is the desired explanation. The Universe is a thought, a beat, a pulse, of the Absolute Mind. The apprehension of the logical law of this thought constitutes our Metaphysic; and again this Metaphysic reappears as the Logic of our own minds, and of each of their minutest acts. In the minutest act of our minds is the same secret—logical, physical, metaphysical—as in the entire Universe!

Of course, we by no means see the complete Hegel in this speculation, even if it has been rightly stated. It is only the most abstract form of that one special principle the leaven of which threw German Philosophy, as received by Hegel from Kant, through Fichte and Schelling, into a new universal ferment. Hegel had his Philosophy of Nature, his Philosophy of History, his Philosophy of Art, his Politics, &c., in addition to his Logic, but declared to be in consistency with it. He had also his Theology, which he discriminated from the Pantheism of the mere Identity-system as it had remained in Schelling's hands. By the new Hegelian law of the pendulum-movement of the mind between Nothing and Being, it was not Pantheism, but a theology much more at one with the common theology, that was necessitated. And, in point of fact, most of the recent religious developments of Germany, orthodox and heterodox, Catholic and Protestant, Straussian and anti-Straussian, refer themselves to Hegelianism. A tincture of Hegel has also appeared, with various effects, in the most recent speculative literature of France. It is, I think, a later influence in the French mind than that of Cousin or that of Comte. I trace it in the writings of Proudhon, if not in those of Renan.

This influence, for better or worse, has broken in among ourselves. MR. JAMES HUTCHISON STIRLING—of whom I know nothing more than I am now stating, but who is certainly no common person—has just published, in two handsome volumes, an exposition of Hegel, entitled, *The Secret of Hegel: being the Hegelian System in Origin, Principle, Form and Matter.* It consists partly of translations from Hegel's Logic, partly of introductions, comments, &c., by Mr.

Stirling himself, relating to Hegel, and to all things in heaven or earth, from a Hegelian point of view. A passage from the book, which I quoted in my first chapter, will have given an idea of the author's views and style. He thinks that there have been three, and only three, all-comprehensive philosophical minds in recent Europe—Hume, Kant, and Hegel—and that any search for the real stuff of philosophy out of these three, except in the way of historical and biographical episode and filling-up, is labour lost. But, as Kant ate up all Hume, and redigested him, and Hegel ate up all Kant and redigested *him*, Hegel is the appointed food for these generations. Knowing Hume from long ago, it has been the labour of Mr. Stirling's own life to master Kant and Hegel. He was almost beaten by Hegel; it has taken him years to work himself into a knowledge of Hegel's system; it was like going round and round a monstrous block of flint, but he thinks he has succeeded. He has prepared an exposition of Kant and an exposition of Hegel for the British public; but, for various reasons, he has published his exposition of Hegel first. What the British public will say to the gift I can anticipate. They will say nothing at all; or they will say that, if this is Hegel in English, he might as well have remained in German. Mr. Stirling's translation of Hegel, and even some parts of his exposition of Hegel in his own words, are more Hegelian than Hegel himself. Yet the book deserves a cordial welcome, not only as introducing Hegel among us more authentically and laboriously than hitherto, but also as introducing, in Mr. Stirling himself, a new British philosophical writer of great, if somewhat uncouth, strength. There is every probability, I should say, that he will be yet better known; and, indeed, in addition to the exposition of Kant which he has ready for publication as a companion to the present work, he has announced, since the present work was published, a farther contribution to Philosophy in the shape of a special criticism of Sir William Hamilton's Logical opinions. This is one out of many signs that our British literature of Speculation is most healthily on the increase at present. In Mr. Stirling's present volume he speaks of Sir William Hamilton throughout with what I cannot but consider unpardonable disrespect and irreverence; but, as it is from the conceived vantage-ground of a knowledge of Kant and Hegel possessed by no one else in Britain that Mr. Stirling thus steps forth as an iconoclast, and as he is impartially iconoclastic all round among our recent British philosophical writers from this same conceived vantage-ground (Mr. Buckle, for example, is termed "a conceited schoolboy," and Coleridge and Mr. Mill are mentioned only sneeringly), one feels at least a roused anxiety about the message which Mr. Stirling himself may be bringing, and a roused interest in the way he may be able to comport himself in bringing it. We have only as yet his first publication to judge from. My impression of *it* is that it is certainly an uncouth and turbid book, but yet with more in it both of *heat* and of *light* of certain kinds than I have met with for a long time. As presented by this book, Hegel's Philosophy, I should say, will appear among us with such welcome as might be given to an elephant, if, from the peculiar shape of the animal, one were uncertain which end of him was his head.

VI.

If only on the principle that bulk entitles to recognition, it would be wrong to omit, in an enumeration of the elements composing the present state of British philosophical opinion, a distinct reference to British Swedenborgianism and the widely-diffused forms of analogous belief represented in the so-called literature of Spiritualism or Spirit-manifestations. Without entering on a criticism of these peculiar creeds, or trying to distinguish their forms and degrees—from the mere Animal-Magnetism of Baron Reichenbach and others, which professed to be nothing more than an enlargement of the science of nerve in certain curious directions, up to the wildest recent imaginations of an interfusion of the ghostly with the normally-physical—it will be enough to note what seems to be the one common mode of thought which these creeds in all their forms seek to contribute to Philosophy, and the fact that they do contribute which, in spite of whatever exaggeration and whatever admixture of delusion and folly, is perhaps a sufficient reason why they should exist. The chief influence, then, of all these forms of speculative research or bewilderment, worth noting here, seems to be one of a cosmological kind. What they all inculcate, from the most moderate Animal Magnetism up to the most involved dreams of the Swedenborgians and Spirit-rappers, is simply the idea that our familiar phænomenal world, or cosmos, may not be the total sphere of the phænomenal, or even of the phænomenal as it may possibly be brought within our apprehension by appropriate experimentation and artifice. The idea is old enough. Shakespeare has furnished us with an expression of it which we are never tired of quoting, and which has been a godsend to the Spiritualists in particular. It is where Horatio and Hamlet compare their impressions after the disappearance of the Ghost:—

Hor. O day and night, but this is wondrous strange!
Ham. And therefore as a stranger give it welcome.
There are more things in heaven and earth, Horatio,
Than are dreamt of in *your* philosophy.

With or without a ghost at hand to enforce the lesson, all philosophers of mark have taken care to provide a similar protest against that "Horatio" spirit (if it be not maligning Hamlet's friend to call it such) which would identify the sphere of the hitherto known with the sphere of all phænomenal existence, or even of the knowable. It is an obvious corollary of the doctrine of the Relativity of Knowledge; and we have seen how both Mr. Mill and Sir William Hamilton recognize it as such. "The existing order of the Universe, or rather of *the part of it known to us*," is a phrase of Mr. Mill's, which we have already quoted; and Mr. Mill is most careful always to speak in this manner, so as to foster, rather than discourage, in his readers, the habit of conceiving that our cosmos may be but that snatch of a measurelessly greater and more complex phænomenal totality which is possible to the present conditions (these perhaps not fixed, nor the same at all) of our sentiency. So also Sir William Hamilton. We have quoted his striking illustration of his doctrine of Relativity by the supposition of the total universe of the phænomenal as "a polygon of a thousand, or a hundred thousand, sides or facets," to only three or four of which we may be organically related by our senses or faculties. But, indeed, he went farther. He contended for "the recognition of occult causes" as a duty of Philosophy—

that is, for the admission that there are credible and attested phænomena in our present experience which we are unable as yet "to refer to any known cause or class." He specially cited the "phænomena of Animal Magnetism" as an instance, expressing his surprise at the "difficult credence" accorded to these phænomena in Britain (he was writing in 1852) in contrast with the "facile credence" accorded to what he considered the baseless pretensions of Craniology.*

Now, so far as Swedenborgianism and its cognate "Spiritualism" have had any appreciable influence on recent British Speculative Philosophy, that influence has consisted, I believe, in their having diffused through the philosophical mind (whether from any background of real facts or no is a different question) a stronger disposition than existed a little while ago to acknowledge the existence of occult causes—a stronger form of the always philosophical notion that the phænomenal cosmos of our sentiency is not necessarily the phænomenal cosmos of all contemporary sentiency. I am confirmed in this by observing that this is the sort of representation of the alleged phænomena of spirit-rapping, clairvoyance, apparitions, &c., given by that British believer in these phænomena who has the greatest independent philosophical reputation, and whose name is always cited by

* Appendix to *Discussions*, pp. 611, 612.

the spiritualists as that of their weightiest supporter. "When it comes to what is the cause of these phænomena," says this writer, in a remarkable preface to a recent book on spirit-manifestations, "I find I cannot adopt any explanation which has yet been suggested. If I were bound to choose among things which I can conceive, I should say that there is some sort of action of some combination of will, intellect, and physical power, which is not that of any of the human beings present. But, thinking it very likely that the universe may contain a few agencies—say half a million—about which no man knows anything, I cannot but suspect that a small proportion of these agencies—say five thousand—may be severally competent to the production of all the phænomena, or may be quite up to the task among them." * This is precisely Hamlet's rebuke to Horatio over again, though in different language. It suggests simply that we may be under a mistake in our habit of conceiving of the cosmos orbed forth to us by our present science and experience as if it were the total cosmos of actual existence.

* "From Matter to Spirit: the Result of Ten Years' Experience in Spirit-manifestation by C. D.; with a Preface by A. B. 1863." The extract is from the Preface, the writer of which, though signing himself only "A. B.," was announced so generally at the time of the publication of the book to be Professor De Morgan that it would be an affectation of etiquette not to name him here. For ingenuity and sceptical suggestiveness, as well as wit, I know nothing in the "Literature of Spiritualism" comparable to this brief Essay.

It grounds this suggestion, however, on certain alleged facts, believed in by the author, which seem to him to prove that, even within the orb of our present cosmos, and intermingling with its affairs, there are hosts of occult agencies, of which, by momentary accidents, or by known artificial arrangements, we may be so far made cognisant as to hear, as it were, the rustle, and feel the touch, of their passing wings. Now observe that, in all this, there is no implication respecting the alleged phænomena, that, were they true even to the utmost extent of the most open-mouth credulity, they would bring us a single inch nearer an Ontology, or knowledge of the central Absolute. This is, indeed, what the mob of ladies and gentlemen who amuse, excite, and stupefy themselves with "mediums" and "séances" do always assume; but the drift of the present critic's remarks is very different. The result at the very utmost, according to him, would only be an enlargement of our notions of the phænomenal, and by no means an acquaintance with noumena—a perception that there were more things in *our* "heaven and earth" than had usually been dreamt of in our philosophy; but by no means a vision of any Empyrean or Heaven of Heavens beyond the heaven and earth of the phænomenal. Our present conception of the Cosmos might be burst and honeycombed—which might be attended with useful soul-shaking and an overpowering flood of mystery; but, after all, it would be only a new Cosmology that we should have, and not in the least an Ontology. In short, if we inweave the whole substance of the speculation with that preceding philosophical doctrine of Relativity into which it seeks to fit itself, the matter shapes itself as follows: —It has been the general admission of Philosophy that knowledge is in proportion to the grasp, or mode, or faculty, of the particular sentiency knowing. Now, there are, within our view, countless gradations of sentiency, all busily existing—from those infinitesimally minute creatures which the microscope reveals to us swarming in and in among the mere interstices of things till invisibility is reached, up to ourselves, the chief possessors of the Earth, and the last and highest of the visible scale. Make out a chain of these sentiencies, and of each it must be supposed that it has its cosmos, its proportionate apprehension or cognisance of the phænomenal. The minutest microscopic animalcule has *its* little nip of a cosmos, *its* little pin-point apprehension of existence, be it even existence in a water-drop, or in the fibre of another animal's muscle. As we rise higher in the scale, the same thing is borne in upon us by more distinct evidence. Imagine a mole disturbed in a field during its brief ramble above-ground for food on a summer night. Has not the sleek, black, and almost eyeless little sentiency its momentary notion of a cosmos, though that notion may go but a very little way, may be compounded chiefly of petty subterranean experiences, and may include nothing of that wonder of the shimmering lawns around, and none of those glimpses of the moon, which make the walk poetic to the man whose approach has disturbed it? And so through the nobler animals—the watch-dog in his lair, the lion roaming the forest—till "the paragon" is reached. Must our supposition of a series of phænomenal worlds, each the construction of its particular native sentiency, and outsphering and transcending each other according as the sentiency increases in grasp—must this supposition be closed abruptly when we come to Man? One reason may be alleged why it should. Man, as the last term of the series, is able to look inward on the whole range of the preceding terms till the microscope fails him. Well, does he not everywhere mark this peculiarity—that each sentiency is aware of at least some of the sentiencies higher than itself, and includes these sentiencies in its cosmos? Animalcules are alert to escape the bigger neighbours that would make them their prey; the mole, little fellow, has experimental evidence of the existence of owls as sharp and indubitable as if he could take their portraits; the dog sees and knows of men, and will fly at them, or look them in the face and understand what they say. But in the cosmos of man what sentiencies or intelligences are there of which man is sensibly aware as preterhuman? According to orthodox modern science, none. He is himself the extreme of known sentiency; and, when he looks out from himself, so far as physical experience can teach him, it is into a void. He may, if he chooses, exercise his imagination so as to fill that void with ideal forms of sentiency and intelligence transcending his own, and for such an exercise of imagination he may be made more apt by constitutional peculiarities or by the form of his religious belief. Science, though disinclined on its own account to such idealizing or personification of the metaphysical, need not prohibit it, if certain conditions are observed. One may even figure to oneself that the entire human cosmos is to the totality of phænomenal existence but as one of those glass globes in which, in a lighted drawing-room, in these days of aquaria, some of the guests may be seen studying the little forms of filmy and filamentous life attached to stones or weeds, or the movements of the small fishes as they go round and round, speculating confusedly with their eyes what is all that glamour beyond the globe and away in the distances of the room. Science will not prohibit even this image to any who may find it satisfactory—only taking care to point out that it fails in exactness. Some of the creatures in the glass globe do testify that their sentiency extends beyond the glass. Though it may not take in much of the spectacle of the room, or be aware of the flirtation going on in one corner of it, or the discussion on the politics of Brazil going on in another, yet it distinctly recognises the finger touching the outside of the glass, and shuns or follows the tracing. In that cosmos of man which the image compares to the glass globe, what is there analogous to this? Here it is that the heterodox science of the Swedenborgians and the spirit-manifestationists steps in to differ from orthodox science. It is maintained by them that the tradition of the vulgar in all times as to the occasional apprehension by man's sentiency of the real activity of other sentiencies that are distinctly preterhuman has had a foundation in fact. It is maintained that the percentage of such sentient contact among men with this preterhuman world may have exhibited historical increases and diminutions in the past, and that it may depend on such conditions as either suddenly to expand itself without solicitation from man, or to be capable of artificial solicitation and extension. And so—on the faith of masses of alleged experience and experimentation, in which not even the respect that ought to be felt for men of great intellectual power entertaining the faith, nor yet the most studious disposition of Philosophy to act on Hamlet's rule of "giving welcome to the stranger," ought to restrain one from declaring that there has been more of the silly, the disgusting, and the hideous in every way, than in almost any other social extravagance of our time—out of these alleged experimentations what are the items of belief which the out-and-out manifestationists would seek to add to our philosophy? Religion, independently of Science, had already offered two beliefs that might fill for the imagination of the pious the realms beyond Appearance—the belief in the indestructibility, and perpetual discriminated duration somewhere and somehow, of all human sentiencies of the human degree that had ever once existed; and the belief in Angels, or superior Spirits, good and bad, also leading lives of inscrutable and preterhuman modes. To these beliefs the manifestationists, or the extreme of them, have sought to add a doctrine which, if developed, would assert nothing less than the phænomenal recoverability within the Cosmos of all sentiency that had ever belonged to it, and the phænomenal presentability within it, on occasion or summons, of other and non-native sentiencies, angelic or demonic. But, go as far as they may, it is still only a cosmos that they figure, still only a world of the phænomenal.

In this little exposition, it will be perceived, there has been a bearing on the question between Realism and Idealism as alternative systems of cosmological conception. In that supposition of a chain of sentiencies up to man, each grasping or construing its particular cosmos according to its amount of relatedness to a potential sum-total conceived as existing, it is the realistic hypothesis that seems most natural. It seems most natural to assume an external totality remaining the same in its own nature, whether there were any sentiency to grasp it or no, and apprehensible in different degrees of extent and intricacy by different sentiencies, though by none wholly. In confirmation of this the fact may be dealt on that, where the means of comparison among animals exist, notions of the phænomenal world possessed by one do not seem to contradict those possessed by another. The dog's world seems to corroborate man's, and man's world the dog's, and on this feeling generalized not only our sport but all our action proceeds. Is not this as if there were a basis of independent reality to which every sentiency helped itself according to its appetite, but in such a manner that all can co-operate? Not even so, however, need the Idealist be nonplussed. Viewing the cosmos of each sentiency as a pure construction of that sentiency out of its subjective affections, he may find the reason of the manifest co-operation of the sentiencies in a law of relation among themselves, producing a unanimity of illusion.

VII.

MR. MILL ON SIR W. HAMILTON.

Let us return to surer ground. As, in the beginning of our review of recent British Philosophy, Mr. John Stuart Mill was the thinker of whom it seemed necessary to make mention almost first of all, and as there is no thinker whom it has been necessary to mention more frequently in the course of the review, so it chances that here, at the end of the review, Mr. Mill is the last in the field. Since the greater portion of the preceding pages was written, two publications of Mr. Mill's have been given to the world, expounding his philosophy in that shape in which its chances of remaining the dominant British philosophy of this generation may be best discussed. To one of these publications—the *Westminster Review* article on the Philosophy of Auguste Comte—we have been able already to make such reference as seemed requisite. The other, and by far the more important, has been reserved till now. It is Mr. Mill's *Examination of Sir William Hamilton's Philosophy, and of the Principal Philosophical Questions discussed in his Writings.*

Certainly, if the British public, or that portion of it which is interested in philosophy, had been allowed to hint to Mr. Mill the sort of volume that would be most acceptable from him after so much else that they would not willingly let die, this is the volume for which they would have petitioned. With the right instinct of high combat Mr. Mill has singled out that recent British thinker who is universally regarded as the most formidable representative of the antagonistic philosophy, and has undertaken the battle with that philosophy over again in the form of a duel with *him*. That it is, in seeming, a duel of the living with the dead, none regrets more than Mr. Mill. "In thus attempting," he says, "to anticipate, as far as is yet possible, the judgment of posterity on Sir William Hamilton's labours, I sincerely lament that, on the many points on which I am at issue with him, I have the unfair advantage possessed by one whose opponent is no longer in a condition to reply. Personally, I might have had small cause to congratulate myself on the reply which I might have received, for, though a strictly honourable, he was a most unsparing controversialist, and whoever assailed even the most unimportant of his opinions might look for hard blows in return. But it would have been worth far more, even to myself, than any polemical success, to have known with certainty in what manner he would have met the objections raised in this volume. I feel keenly, with Plato, how much more is to be learnt by discussing with a man who can question and answer, than with a book, which cannot."* Thus it is, in the warfare of thought, no less than in cruder and older warfare, that a true knight speaks and thinks of his dead opponent.

> "The Percy leanèd on his hand,
> And saw the Douglas dee;
> He took the dead man by the hand,
> And said, 'Wo is me for thee!'"

But, though there is this chivalry of feeling towards the memory of his antagonist throughout Mr. Mill's volume, and there is not a word in it that does not show the most anxious desire to do that antagonist justice, I must confess that, on the whole, Mr. Mill's estimate of Sir William Hamilton's intellect, and of the worth of his services to British thought, seems to me lower than was to be expected from so fit a judge. The praises that a man bestows must be valued according to his habit in the matter of praising; and adjectives which from one man would mean much will disappoint from another. Again and again Mr. Mill uses expressions about Sir William Hamilton which, if they stood alone, would seem sufficiently

* Page 3.

high-pitched. He frequently praises Sir William Hamilton's ability, his candour, his industry, and especially his great erudition. Yet, when all these expressions of admiration, taken together, are viewed in the light of the summary appreciation of Sir William Hamilton with which the volume is wound up, and when the total estimate thus resulting is compared with the corresponding estimates which Mr. Mill has given of other philosophers, not to speak of his more casual eulogies of various writers miscellaneously on account of this or that pleasing to him in their stray performances, the impression, I repeat, falls short of the just expectation. It is not only because, contemporaneously with Mr. Mill's judgment of Hamilton, there has appeared his so much more enthusiastic appreciation of M. Comte—though this does make the contrast more striking. M. Comte was a great European thinker; and they are but few that would compare Hamilton's intellectual efficiency, or probable influence, all in all, with M. Comte's. But, when I find Mr. Mill saying, for example, of such a distinctly inferior British thinker as Archbishop Whately, that he "has done far greater service to the world, in the origination and diffusion of important thought, than Sir W. Hamilton, with all his learning," * my sense of proportion is jarred. Such

* Page 553.

an opinion comes upon me as a phenomenon requiring to be accounted for.

Partly it may be because Mr. Mill's acquaintance with Sir William Hamilton's writings is not of old date. One's recollections of early friends are more affectionate than of later. Or, again, the cause may be looked for in a certain high form of party-spirit, which is no more unnatural in a philosopher than in a politician. It is not unbecoming that one should have a superior affection for those of whose opinions one approves, and who are one's colleagues and auxiliaries in urging things in the direction in which it is one's deepest conviction that they should go. Philosophy, as well as politics, will be in a strange pass when there is no discount against a man for being on the opposite benches. Mr. Mill's language seems to imply that, on the whole, he thinks Sir William Hamilton the greatest representative of the Transcendental Philosophy of late times in Britain; but then, as he thinks this philosophy a wrong philosophy, it may be his private opinion that no mind holding by it can be first-rate. Yet, a generous controversialist may, after all, have a greater respect for the powers and character of some antagonist than for those of any of his own colleagues, and may even recognize that antagonist's state of mind as less removed from his own—removed, say, only by a single oscillation of the pendulum, whereas the interval in the case of the best of his colleagues may be measured by two, or four, or ten oscillations. Now, as Mr. Mill has given proof, in other instances, of more than usual capacity of this kind of feeling, it is to be inferred that there is something in the total style or form of Sir William Hamilton's intellect that has prevented *him* from becoming the object of the feeling.

If I am not mistaken, something of this result is to be attributed to a habit of preference, on Mr. Mill's part, for a quality of intellect which he seems frequently to have in view under the names *fertile* and *fertility*. "A fertile thinker" is one of his most characteristic phrases of praise; and what he seems to mean by such a thinker is one who yields his readers a large number of socially available propositions. I was going to say "marketable propositions;" and, if the expression were understood as implying nothing derogatory, but simply as describing truths or ideas adapted to the state of the intellectual demand, fitting felt needs, and useful at once for helping things on, it might not be amiss. One descries, at least, a certain ruling of Mr. Mill's critical judgments by his own principle of Utilitarianism—a high and widely sympathetic principle, certainly, in his interpretation and exemplification of it; but still such as must exclude from his liking modes and displays of intellect that are greatly impressive to others, who admire on no such definite principle, but, as it were, instinctively and at large. Barbaric pearls and gold, we should say, would have small chance with Mr. Mill. Hence, doubtless, in part, his great admiration of M. Comte. *He* was pre-eminently a fertile thinker; his writings are fields of valuable generalizations; whoever visits them, if he should read but a few pages, may carry away in his pocket one or two propositions that will serve for the purposes of a leading-article, a speech in Parliament or even (though then the authority need not be quoted) a discourse from the pulpit. With Sir William Hamilton it is, at first sight, very different. One may say of him, indeed, that his greatest and most characteristic merit among his contemporaries consisted in his having been, while he lived, the most ardent and impassioned devotee to the useless within Great Britain.

> "Plague on't!" quoth Time to Thomas Hearne,
> "Whatever *I* forget *you* learn."

What all the world besides had forgotten and given up, Sir William Hamilton, for that very reason, would overhaul and bring back into notice. Hence the unparalleled extent and range of his erudition. Hence also the profound bent of his own speculative endeavours. Problems which immediately preceding British speculation had ruled to be obsolete, in its own mere hurry to get on, were *his* daily and nightly meditation. He even avowed (and this is one of the points on which Mr. Mill professes inability to agree with him) his preference for philosophy considered as a gymnastic for the soul over philosophy considered as a purveyor of available truths. The toil, the labour, the pain of philosophizing seemed to him valuable to the individual spirit, apart from any teachable results. Of course, just as Mr. Mill would justify the toil and the pain of philosophizing by bringing them within the scope of his principle of utility, or of the utmost of pleasure for all sentient existence, so Sir William Hamilton, in passionately consenting to such toil and pain for himself, both confessed his own overpaying delight therein, and foresaw, in a cloud, plenty of future utilities. But try him by any standard. What a writer he was! What strength and nerve in his style, what felicity in new philosophical expressions! Throw that aside, and try him even in respect of the importance of his effects on the national thought. Whether from his learning, or by reason of his independent thinkings, was it not he that hurled into the midst of us the very questions of metaphysics, and the very forms of those questions, that have become the academic theses everywhere in this British age for real metaphysical discussion? Throw this aside too, and let it be said of Sir William Hamilton that, simply and by whatever means, he did more than any other man to reinstate the worship of Difficulty in the higher mind of Great Britain. On this ground alone I should have expected, still on the principle of utility, a considerably higher recognition of his services from Mr. Mill than he has been able to accord. Mr. Herbert Spencer, it seems to me, speaks of Sir William Hamilton with a juster sense of proportion. He even goes so far as to confess, for himself, a greater indebtedness, for special doctrines and suggestions, to Hamilton than to Comte.

One tribute Mr. Mill has certainly paid to Sir William Hamilton, which amply compensates all omissions. He has written, in reply to Hamilton, a book which will probably take rank as the ablest and profoundest of even Mr. Mill's works. Were I to say that, in the process of studying and answering Hamilton, Mr. Mill has become twice the metaphysician he was, the expression might be over the mark; but that Mr. Mill has been moved by this antagonism to bring out twice the amount of his metaphysics ever brought out before, will, I think, be questioned by no competent critic. It is, indeed, a splendid treatise. Almost at the outset of this volume we quoted from an early essay of Mr. Mill's a passage of lamentation over the low state into which Speculative Philosophy had fallen in Britain at the time when it was written. What does Mr. Mill say in the present work? "The justification of the work," he says, "lies in the importance of the questions to the discussion of which it is a contribution. England is often reproached by Continental thinkers with indifference to the higher philosophy. But England did not always deserve this reproach, and is already showing, by no doubtful symptoms, that she will not deserve it much longer. Her thinkers are again beginning to see, what they had only temporarily forgotten, that a true Psychology is the indispensable scientific basis of Morals, of Politics, of the Science and Art of Education; that the difficulties of Metaphysics lie at the root of all science; that these difficulties can only be quieted by being resolved, and that until they are resolved, positively if possible, but at any rate negatively, we are never assured that any human knowledge, even physical, stands on solid foundations." * Now, if Mr. Mill was one of those who began that revival of Philosophy in Britain of which he here speaks, and if for thirty years he has been one of the chief powers in the revival, he appears before us in this very volume as likely to expedite, in a manner more vigorous than ever, that

* Page 2.

farther desirable stage of the revival which shall lead us out of our insular discredit, and enable us to hold up our heads with the best that is going in Europe. Tons of popular literature might be spared for a volume such as this! It will make men think. It is Britain that will proximately be benefited, but the volume will probably have a wider influence.

Considering how invigorating to the mind of the nation at the present moment would be such a battle of purely philosophical opinion as might be raised over Mr. Mill's volume, one must hope that the volume will rouse opposition. It is certain to do so. Replies may be expected, first of all, from the Hamiltonians—whether those who adhere in the main to Hamilton's system, or those who do so only partially. Mr. Mansel will, no doubt, come forward, if only in defence of his own peculiar theological application of one of Hamilton's doctrines. Something may surely be looked for from Professor Veitch and Professor Spencer Baynes; and these are points on which Professor Fraser, notwithstanding those deviations from some of Hamilton's most important views of which his writings have given evidence, will probably think that Mr. Mill has missed his way, or failed in his attack on Hamilton. If Dr. Cairns of Berwick-upon-Tweed could be induced to lay aside other work till he should have written a defence or re-explication of the Hamiltonian Philosophy in reply to Mr. Mill, I should expect that Mr. Mill's regrets at not being able to look for such an answer as the gladiator himself would have given, and to receive *his* "hard blows in return," would be in some degree assuaged. But, indeed, it is not only the Hamiltonian philosophy that is assailed in Mr. Mill's volume, nor is it the adherents of any one school of speculative thought that it may be expected to rouse. At one point or another every form of philosophy, not reducible to Mr. Mill's own ultimate interpretation of Locke's Empiricism, is thrust at in the volume through the ribs of Hamilton; and our pre-Hamiltonian British Transcendentalists, as well as our Ferrierists, our Kantians, and our Hegelians (so far as there are such among us), may all feel themselves challenged. There are several points on which Mr. Herbert Spencer, in consequence of his modified agreement with notions of Hamilton, is involved by name in Mr. Mill's criticisms.

My own impression is that Mr. Mill has made good at least one general criticism respecting the character of Hamilton's Philosophy as it is presented to us in his remaining writings collectively—to wit, that it is a philosophy of imperfect junctions. There are blocks and obstacles, as if of unremoved embankments, between its several parts. One doctrine, pursued at one time, does not always meet or lead into another, pursued at another time, or seem as if it could meet or lead into it; much less is there any spacious central terminus whither the various doctrines are seen to converge, and from which access to any of them might be direct and easy. Mr. Mill, applying a simile suggested by Sir William Hamilton himself, has expressed this very happily. "I formerly quoted from him," he says, "a felicitous illustration drawn from the mechanical operation of tunnelling; that process affords another, justly applicable to himself. The reader must have heard of that gigantic enterprise of the Italian Government, the tunnel through Mount Cenis. This great work is carried on simultaneously from both ends, in well-grounded confidence (such is now the minute accuracy of engineering operations) that the two parties of workmen will correctly meet in the middle. Were they to disappoint this expectation, and work past one another in the dark, they would afford a likeness of Sir W. Hamilton's mode of tunnelling the human mind." * Every reader of Sir William Hamilton that has tried to rethink his main doctrines so as to connect them must have experienced something of this feeling; but Mr. Mill's specific enumeration of the imperfect junctions, or actual inconsistencies and incompatibilities,

* Page 551.

between the several parts of Hamilton's philosophy, will greatly increase the feeling. Mr. Mill suggests that one cause of this incompleteness or imperfect centralization of Hamilton's speculative labours may have been "the enormous amount of time and mental vigour which he expended in mere philosophical erudition, leaving, it may be said, only the remains of his mind for the real business of thinking." So far as this suggestion is true, however, does it not furnish an excuse admitting also of admiration? Was it not the character of Hamilton's erudition that it recovered not mere irrelevant facts and dry bones of defunct ingenuities, but thoughts and forms of thought on all philosophical questions which leaped again into vitality and the full interest of relevancy the moment they were re-stated by his powerful pen, and some of which modern philosophy had voted to be impedimenta only in its too great hurry to get on? Was it not a service to Philosophy to compel it to re-assume these so-called impedimenta, if they were not such, but data and difficulties necessary to all philosophizing that would find itself solid and efficient in the long run? At all events, was not Hamilton's own conception of a complete fabric of Philosophy rendered hereby so much more laborious that to have failed to finish the fabric, or even to leave an adequate conjecture how it might be consistently finished, was hardly a discredit to one man's life?

Of those of Mr. Mill's criticisms of Sir William Hamilton which fall within our scope in these pages, the greater portion resolve themselves into a criticism, repeated from all points of view, of Hamilton's doctrine of the Relativity of Knowledge in connexion with his system of Natural Realism. Accepting the doctrine of the Relativity of Knowledge, and thinking it a most important doctrine, and indeed the foundation-doctrine of all sound philosophy, Mr. Mill argues again and again through the earlier chapters of his volume, that there is a radical incompatibility between this doctrine, in any sense in which it would be worth keeping, and that Natural Realism with which in Hamilton's Philosophy it stands incorporated. "If what we perceive in the thing," says Mr. Mill, "is something of which we are only aware as existing, and as causing impressions on us, our knowledge of the thing is only relative. But, if what we perceive and cognise is not merely a cause of our subjective impressions, but a thing possessing, in its own nature and essence, a long list of properties, Extension, Impenetrability, Number, Magnitude, Figure, Mobility, Position, all perceived as 'essential attributes' of the thing as 'objectively existing'—all as 'Modes of a Not-Self,' and by no means as an occult cause or causes of any modes of Self—(and that such is the case Sir W. Hamilton asserts in every form of language, leaving no stone unturned to make us apprehend the breadth of the distinction) then I am willing to believe that, in affirming this knowledge to be entirely relative to Self, such a thinker as Sir W. Hamilton had a meaning, but I have no small difficulty in discovering what it is." * Again, after farther discussion, Mr. Mill thus sums up:—"It has been shown, by accumulated proof, that Sir W. Hamilton did not hold any opinion in virtue of which it could rationally be asserted that all human knowledge is relative, but did hold, as one of the main elements of his philosophical creed, the opposite doctrine of the cognoscibility of external things in certain of their aspects, as they are in themselves." † Now, with all deference to Mr. Mill, we cannot see that he has here fairly apprehended Sir William Hamilton. Whether Sir William's doctrine of Natural Realism is true or false is one question; and it is a question on which Mr. Mill, in other parts of his volume, where he defends the Idealistic theory of external perception, and developes it with reference to the so-called "primary qualities" of matter, has pressed Sir William very hard. He has also, I think, convicted Sir William of a somewhat fast-and-loose

* Page 21. † Page 31.

habit in his use of the word Relativity, and of a want of sufficient care to distinguish that sense in which he alleged that we possess an intuitive, or face-to-face knowledge of certain properties of matter "as it is in itself," and that sense in which he denied the possibility of any knowledge of "things in themselves." But, as we have already tried to show, while anticipating this very objection (see *antè*, pp. 119—122), there seems no necessary incompatibility between Sir William Hamilton's Natural Realism, or doctrine of the cognoscibility of certain attributes as belonging to matter itself, independently of the mind knowing, and a very distinct and substantial sense of the doctrine of Relativity. Referring to our previous observations on this subject, we need only repeat that the difference between Sir William Hamilton and Mr. Mill seems to be wholly *cosmological*, and not at all *ontological*. They both agree that only the phænomenal can be known, but they differ as to what is to be taken as the sum or composition of the phænomenal. Sir William Hamilton, as a natural Realist, holds that in the phænomenal cosmos there are two directly known constituents—a phænomenal world of Matter, that has to be thought of as persisting the same in itself apart from any percipiency that may be brought to bear upon it; and a phænomenal agency of mind, so related to this world of matter as to apprehend some of its real or independent qualities. There is a cognising phænomenon, and a phænomenon cognised in certain items of its own independent phænomenal nature. This doctrine may be wrong; and, as we have already said, it gives a kind of wrench to the cultivated or etymological notion of the meaning of the word "phænomenal," to be called upon to imagine a phænomenon, or world of phænomena, subsisting with no percipiency to which it could be phænomenal. But, instead of the word "phænomenon" use the word "nature" or "creation," and it is difficult to see why Sir William Hamilton could not have held his particular cosmological system of Natural Realism, its tenability once allowed, in perfect consistency with a very sturdy doctrine of the incognoscibility of the Absolute. The two creations, Mind and Matter, might roll on together in a joint cosmos, so related that the one might have a conviction that it toothed at some points into the independent constitution of the other; and yet both creations might be thought of as equally melting away, in the last study of them, into an Absolute unknown. Mr. Mill's error seems to be in supposing that, when Sir William Hamilton spoke of our direct cognisance of certain qualities of matter as it is in itself, this was equivalent to saying that we know something of Matter as a Noumenon, of Matter in the absolute. He never meant this, and he guarded himself in several incidental sentences against such a construction of his meaning. But, as we hinted, it might have been better if he had done so at greater length, and with a stronger partition between his cosmological and his ontological statements.

Leaving Mr. Mill's criticisms of Sir William Hamilton after this mere reference to one of the chief of them, let us note such re-explications of Mr. Mill's own philosophical opinions, intermingled with the criticisms or arising out of them, as may bring our views of the principal articles of his metaphysical system down to the latest date.

The most likely charge against Mr. Mill's previous writings, we said, might have been that they left a sense of metaphysical deficiency. While the charge against Sir William Hamilton is that of imperfect junctions of the constituent portions of his system at the critical points, the charge against Mr. Mill, with reference to his previous writings, I can conceive to have been that of a limpid evasion of the chief metaphysical difficulties as felt by others. As an instance take the fact that in his beautiful essay on Utilitarianism he devoted but a few sentences to what seemed to be the very knot of the whole question—the psychological genesis of the idea of *right;* the conversion of the *Prodest* into the *Oportet;* the evolution of the participle in *dus* out of never so much of the past participle passive; the demonstration how or why, if it were granted that moral actions are those done with a view to the greatest possible diminution of pain and promotion of pleasure throughout the sentient universe, there should have arisen in connexion with this class of actions the notion of moral obligation to do them, unless on the principle of some *à priori* or connate notion of rightness that fitted itself on to that class of actions. The apparent deficiency in Mr. Mill's writings of which this has been felt to be an instance, may be attributed in part to the ease with which Mr. Mill had grasped for himself the connexions of his system, and could evolve everything in it, to his own satisfaction, inductively out of experience. In part, however, it may have been owing to the peculiarity of Mr. Mill's literary style and method. Sir William Hamilton's style and method are such as to force his ideas upon his readers in their individual distinctness. He heaps them up, as it were, in mounds, each crowned by a signal-flag, so that there can be no mistake about it. His plan is generally something like this: "On this subject there are three opinions. *Primo*, there is such and such an opinion; and that is the opinion of such and such philosophers (naming them). *Secundo*, there is such another opinion; and this is what is held by so-and-so and so-and-so (naming them). *Tertio*, there is this third opinion (describing it), and this is the opinion that I hold." Hence it results that there is hardly ever any difficulty in pinning Sir William Hamilton to his opinions, and, if they are inconsistent with each other, the inconsistencies almost solicit observation. Mr. Mill, on the other hand, though admirably exact in his criticisms of the opinions of others, generally presented his own views on philosophical subjects in what may be called clear liquid lapses of exposition, over which one floated with an agreeable sense of facility, feeling all the while a fine and full element of meaning underneath one—which meaning, however, it was more difficult, afterwards, than in Sir William Hamilton's case, to concentrate into definite propositions for the purposes of recollection and controversy. Sometimes, even, there was a feeling as if there must have been points of rocks concealed under the clear flow of the stream.

Whatever truth there may be in these remarks as applied to Mr. Mill's previous writings, all critics will admit that, to a great degree, they cease to be applicable to the present volume. I am not sure but there are traces in it of effects of Sir William Hamilton's bold and strenuous rhetoric on the manner and language of his opponent. At all events, in studying Sir William Hamilton and replying to him, Mr. Mill has felt the necessity of taking a harder grasp of some of his chief philosophical opinions than before, and re-issuing them in a more distinct manifesto.

I.

There is a most interesting restatement in this volume of Mr. Mill's peculiar cosmological Idealism. The chapters containing this restatement (Chapters XI., XII., XIII.) are, I should say, in some respects, the best in the whole volume. They form, I believe, a valuable contribution of new reasonings and happy forms of phraseology to one branch of metaphysics. Let me give as much of their substance as seems necessary by way of extension of our previous account of Mr. Mill's Idealistic doctrine.

Sunt cogitationes, There are Thoughts or Feelings—such is still, Mr. Mill seems to hold, the one radical fact, or phænomenon of the Universe, from which all Philosophy must be developed. Beyond this fact, that there are thoughts, feelings, sensations, cogitations, we cannot, by any analysis, go. Perhaps *cogitations*, though not the word used by Mr. Mill, is the word that would best convey his conception of those ultimate phænomena out of which all else must start. For what he insists on, in the same breath in which he fastens attention on these ultimate phænomena, is the fact of what may be called a curdling tendency among them—a tendency among them to form associations with each other, according to relations of coexistence, succession, and likeness. Given sensations or feelings and their physical sociability (I say *physical*, for as yet no notion of Mind as a distinct entity, nor indeed of Matter either, must enter into the conception, though I think Mr. Mill inadvertently permits it to enter in some parts of his language even thus early in his account of things)—given these, and all the rest is an evolution thencefrom. The most notable agency in the evolution is that of the repetition of certain associations between sensations or the phænomena of feeling till they seem indissoluble or inseparable. It is this Inseparability of Association (why Mr. Mill should say "Inseparability" I do not see: he seems entitled only to "Unseparatedness") that has been the agency in generating what are now our most constant cognitions and beliefs. It is through the action of the principle of association among the ultimate phænomena called feelings that we see taking place, first of all, that enormous self-separation of the phænomena into two orders or aggregates—that now called Mind or Self, and that now called Matter or Not-Self. The correct theory "maintains," says Mr. Mill, "that there are associations, naturally and even necessarily generated by the order of our sensations and of our reminiscences of sensation, which, supposing no intuition of an external world to have existed in consciousness, would inevitably have generated the belief, and would cause it to be regarded as an intuition." * And the notion of Mind or Self admits, he contends, of "a similar analysis." † In other words, that duality of Self and Not-Self which is now the paramount fact or rule of all consciousness known to us has been generated out of the curdling or inter-association, according to laws of co-existence, succession, and likeness, of phænomena in which, in their prime or crude state, no such notion can have subsisted. But, now that the notion does subsist, now that the entire Cosmos seems to revolve on the poles of this antithesis, what is Philosophy to make of it? Is Philosophy—cognisant as it now is of the fact that all has been the product of a process of cogitation, or association on and on, among feelings in ever-growing complexity—to uncoil the complexity to the uttermost, and, reaching a succession of associable feelings or sensations, describable as phænomena, but undistinguished as either of Matter or Mind, to proclaim *that* as the basis or ultimatum of the Cosmos? This would be nearly the conception of the *Non-Substantialists* or *Nihilists*, as represented by Hume. But Mr. Mill, as before, shows no anxiety for going so far

* Page 192. † Page 204.

back, unless where he thinks there may be benefit in a bath of such final scepticism as may wash away from the mind all notion of knowledge where we do not absolutely know but only assume that we know. Nor is he content with such a rise out of Non-Substantialism as, economizing assumption the most possible, and assuming only one kind of substance, or cause of phænomena, behind the phænomena themselves, should offer *Materialism* or *Pure Idealism* as the alternative. Whatever may be his reserve of scientific opinion as to the probable origin of sentiency, the cosmological conception which he states and defends as the best working conception for Philosophy, is, as before, that of *Constructive Idealism.* But here is perhaps the chief novelty of his volume. It is a new and refined form of Constructive Idealism that he now propounds—a form so expressed that, while it will serve, he thinks, as a working conception fitted for all the essential purposes of philosophy or science, philosophy and science may sink back through its meshes at will into all desirable vagueness and quest of the homogeneous.

"As Body is the mysterious something which excites the mind to feel, so Mind is the mysterious something which feels and thinks"—thus, after all sorts of caveats and explanations, we found Mr. Mill willing formerly to sum up his doctrine of Constructive Idealism. He does not now reject this mode of speech, but he substitutes another which is much more abstract. If we examine our assertion that we are cognisant of a world external to ourselves, and of ourselves as having a being distinct from that world, what is it, he asks, that we really imply? Nothing more or less than this—that there seem to be two durations, distinct from each other, though in contact from moment to moment, in each of which we are aware, in every momentary contact, of a great deal more than is ever then momentarily present. Take first our notion of an external world. "What is it we mean when we say that the object we perceive is external to us, and not a part of our own thoughts? We mean that there is in our perceptions something which exists when we are not thinking of it; which existed before we had ever thought about it, and would exist if we were annihilated; and, further, that there exist things which we never saw, touched, or otherwise perceived, and things which never have been perceived by man. This idea of something which is distinguished from our fleeting impressions by what, in Kantian language, is called perdurability—something which is fixed and the same while our impressions vary—constitutes altogether our idea of external substance. Whoever can assign an origin to this complex conception has accounted for what we mean by the belief in matter." * Developing this idea farther—calling attention to the fact that each petty patch or flash of present sensation that we experience seems to us to certify a vast background of permanent possibilities of sensation out of which it is but the momentary emergence, and which we know to be common to other sentient beings besides ourselves, while the present emerging patch or flash is ours in particular—Mr. Mill finds in the phrase "permanent or guaranteed possibilities of sensation" all that he thinks included, or requiring to be included, in the notion of an external world. "Matter, then," he says, "may be defined a Permanent Possibility of Sensation. If I am asked whether I believe in matter, I ask whether the questioner accepts this definition of it. If he does, I believe in matter; and so do all Berkeleians. In any other sense than this I do not." † Similarly, in the same notion of a present shifting experience reposing on and certifying an infinitely wider non-present of possibilities, Mr. Mill finds all that seems necessary for a definition of Mind or Self. "Our notion of Mind, as well as of Matter, is the notion of a permanent something, contrasted with the perpetual flux of the sensations, and other feelings or mental states which we refer to it—a something which we figure as remaining the same

* Page 192. † Page 198.

while the particular feelings through which it reveals its existence change. This attribute of permanence, supposing that there were nothing else to be considered, would admit of the same explanation when predicated of Mind as of Matter. The belief I entertain that my mind exists when it is not feeling, nor thinking, nor conscious of its own existence, resolves itself into the belief of a Permanent Possibility of those States." * Mr. Mill goes on to point out that this "permanent possibility of feeling," constituting our notion of Self, is distinguished by certain important differences from the "permanent possibilities of sensation" constituting our notion of an external world. Still Mind, as well as Matter, resolves itself, Mr. Mill concludes, into a patch of present upon the ground of an unlimited non-present—into a series of feelings varying and fugitive from moment to moment, in a sea of possibilities of feeling. "Thus far," he says, "there seems no hindrance to our regarding Mind as nothing but the series of our sensations (to which must now be added our internal feelings), as they actually occur, with the addition of infinite possibilities of feeling, requiring for their actual realization conditions which may or may not take place, but which, as possibilities, are always in existence, and many of them present." † And again, more briefly,

* Page 205. † Page 206.

"My Mind is but a series of feelings, or, as it has been called, a thread of consciousness, however supplemented by believed possibilities of consciousness, which are not, though they might be, realized." *

Such is Mr. Mill's new version of his system of Constructive Idealism. It is likely, I think, to be a good deal canvassed in future metaphysical discussions. The objections that most naturally arise to it are the following:—

It does not, as it stands, seem to answer the actual and total conception which we all have of even the *present* constitution of the cosmos. It seems to break down at least on the side of Mind or Self. It does not seem, on that side, to answer the felt requisites so well as either the old Constructive Idealism of Berkeley and others, which supposed a permanent substance or entity of Mind, determined by some external cause or causes to imagine a world of material objects, or the system of Pure Idealism, which supposes a substance or entity of mind self-determined to the same exercise. A patch of present on an unlimited ground of a non-present, a series of feelings varying and fugitive from moment to moment in a sea of possibilities of feeling—this does not seem to be all that our notion of Mind or Self includes. It includes an organic

* Page 208.

union somehow of the present with the non-present, the identity somehow, in one conscious organism, of the *was*, the *is*, and the *is to be*. In a passage of singular candour, Mr. Mill has himself anticipated and stated this objection to his theory of Mind. After disposing of certain "extrinsic" objections to the theory he announces an "intrinsic" difficulty which it seems to him "beyond the power of metaphysical analysis to remove." This difficulty presents itself in the mental phænomena of memory and expectation. "Besides present feelings and possibilities of present feeling," he says, "there is another class of phænomena to be included in an enumeration of the elements making up our conception of Mind. The thread of consciousness which composes the mind's phænomenal life consists not only of present sensations, but likewise, in part, of memories and expectations. Now what are these? In themselves, they are present feelings, states of present consciousness, and in that respect are not distinguished from sensations. They all, moreover, resemble some given sensations or feelings of which we have previously had experience.—But they are attended with the peculiarity that each of them involves a belief in more than its own present existence. A sensation involves only this: but a remembrance of a sensation, even if not referred to any particular date, involves the suggestion and belief that a sensation of which it is a copy or representation actually existed in the past; and an expectation involves the belief, more or less positive, that a sensation or other feeling to which it directly refers will exist in the future. Nor can the phænomena involved in these two states of consciousness be adequately expressed without saying that the belief they include is that I myself formerly had, or that I myself, and no other, shall hereafter have, the sensations remembered or expected. The fact believed is, that the sensations did actually form, or will hereafter form, part of the self-same series of states, or thread of consciousness, of which the remembrance or expectation of those sensations is the part now present. If, therefore, we speak of the Mind as a series of feelings, we are obliged to complete the statement by calling it a series of feelings which is aware of itself as past and future; and we are reduced to the alternative of believing that the mind, or Ego, is something different from any series of feelings or possibilities of them, or of accepting the paradox that something which, *ex hypothesi*, is but a series of feelings can be aware of itself as a series."* Nothing could be fairer or braver than this statement by Mr. Mill of the intrinsic objection to his proposed theory of Mind; for he goes on to confess his conviction of its insuperability. "The

* Pp. 212, 213.

truth is," he continues, "that we are here face-to-face with that final inexplicability at which, as Sir William Hamilton observes, we inevitably arrive when we reach ultimate facts; and, in general, one mode of stating it only appears more incomprehensible than another, because the whole of human language is accommodated to the one, and is so incongruous with the other that it cannot be expressed in any terms which do not deny its truth. The real stumbling-block is perhaps not in any theory of the fact, but in the fact itself. The true incomprehensibility perhaps is, that something which has ceased, or is not yet in existence, can still be, in a manner, present—that a series of feelings the infinitely greater part of which is past or future, can be gathered up, as it were, into a single present conception, accompanied by a belief of reality. I think by far the wisest thing we can do is to accept the inexplicable fact, without any theory of how it takes place, and, when we are obliged to speak of it in terms which assume a theory, to use them with a reservation as to their meaning." * This, I venture to say, is the most memorable passage, in its philosophical consequence, in the whole of Mr. Mill's volume. Were I to say that it reveals a trap-door opened by Mr. Mill himself in the floor of his own philosophy, I should say what others will feel as well

* Page 213.

as myself. What concerns us here is that Mr. Mill avows that the difficulty he has stated leaves his definition of Mind insufficient unless with the accompaniment of a paradox. What is the advantage, then, of propounding such a definition? Why not adhere to the notion of Mind in the older Constructive Idealism, which regarded it as the unknown substance, or entity, or organism, which feels and thinks? Whatever objections there may be to the words "substance" and "entity," let them die a natural death. If the notion of Mind as "a series of feelings with a background of possibilities of feeling" is not complete without the rider that "the series of feelings can be aware of itself as a series," or that "something which has ceased, or is not yet in existence, can still, in a manner, be present," then the word "substance," with all its faults, seems a very exact etymological equivalent for both notion and rider.

A second objection to Mr. Mill's new version of Constructive Idealism, in competition with other cosmological systems, is that it is confessedly only a useful working conception of the present constitution of the Cosmos, which we may rest in by voluntarily stopping short of an ulterior scientific conception. When Natural Realism speaks of a substance Mind, and an independent substance Matter directly known to some extent by Mind, and calls these the two constituents or factors of the phænomenal cosmos, it professes to give the results of its utmost analysis of the cosmos. When Materialism resolves present Mind into *quondam* Matter, it also professes to go the whole length of the analysis to which it is competent. When Pure Idealism asserts the contrary, and maintains that so-called Matter is but a figment of Mind, this also is its final account of the sum-total of the phænomenal. Nay, when the older Constructive Idealism set up a substance or principle called Mind, and supposed it actuated by some force out of itself in its ideas of external objects, not the less was this proffered as an analysis to the utmost of the total world of phænomena. But Mr. Mill's new Constructive Idealism does no such thing. When it speaks of the Cosmos as consisting of a series of feelings carrying in itself a sense of permanent internal possibilities of feeling, and aware of itself as in the midst of permanent external possibilities of sensation, it professes nothing more than an analysis arrested at a convenient point for practical purposes. Scientifically, it avows its own ability to carry the analysis farther. These present notions or facts of Mind and Matter, it avows, are ultimately to be conceived as generated out of a prime original of phænomena, definable in their original state neither as mind nor matter, but only as feelings or sensations and their associabilities. *Sunt cogitationes; fuerunt cogitationes*—this is the ultimate statement to which we are led back. A curdling together of phænomena, such as we now call feelings or sensations—this is the fact of the Cosmos at its uttermost. It is but a secondary or subsequent fact, that out of this curdling there has resulted that vast self-differentiation of the curdled material whereby it has happened that now, in every act of thought or perception, there is, as by a necessary law of our being, a discrimination bursting asunder, or mutual release and disengagement, of two notions—the notion of an external world of permanent possibilities of sensation, whirled away from us in extension up to the clouds and the stars; and the notion of a distinct internal persistency of feeling, living on amid this extension, and uniting in its consciousness the past, the present, and the future. Now, is not Mr. Mill's Constructive Idealism only an account of the secondary fact—an account of our notions of Ego and Non-Ego as they have been generated for us out of a prior and simpler consistency referred to by himself, and describable neither as Ego nor Non-Ego, but only as cogitations or associable phænomena of feeling? If Mr. Mill is forced back to the very end of the avenue which his own system opens to the view, does he not cease to be, cosmologically, a Constructive Idealist, in any preservable sense of the term, and lapse into something else? It is difficult to see what name already in use would then describe his cosmological conception in its ultimate form. Owing to his describing the ultimate cosmical phænomena as "feelings," and thus inducing us to think of them, however vaguely, as phænomena of what we now call the mental or ideal order, there would still be a character of general Idealism in his system. His ultimate resolution of things would involve a preference for the language of the idealistic over that of the materialistic hypothesis. What he would invite us to think of as the prime "matter" of the Universe would be describable, at all events, as "matter of feeling." Yet it would by no means be Idealism, as hitherto understood, to which we should thus be brought; for, in Idealism, as hitherto understood, the prime or genetic phænomena have always been feelings imagined as functions of some personality or personalities, whereas in Mr. Mill's system personality is itself a mere notion evolved out of the phænomena, and therefore not to be imported (though I think he does himself inadvertently import it) into the primary contemplation of them. In some respects it is the Nihilism or Non-Substantialism of Hume to which Mr. Mill would seem to be brought back, for in that system there is no denial of anything of phænomenal fact that Mr. Mill seems to think it necessary to keep. But, as Mr.

Mill does perhaps make more of the natural associabilities of the prime phænomena than Hume, a more positive name than Nihilism or Non-Substantialism is desirable for his system. On the whole, if I were allowed to invent a term, I should say that Mr. Mill, cosmologically, is now a *Cogitationist.* The ultimate fact of the phænomenal world, as recognized by him, is neither Matter nor Mind in any present sense of these terms, but a cogitation or coagulation of phænomena which may be called feelings; out of which cogitation or coagulation it has happened, in virtue of the laws regulating it, that there is now that stupendous fact of all present, or at least of all human, sentiency—the instinctive furling off, in every conscious or perceptive act, of a conceived external world of possibilities from a conscious and persisting personality. If we stop at this fact—which we may do for most practical purposes—our cosmological system may be that of the new Constructive Idealism; but, if we persevere in the analysis, we end in *Cogitationism.*

But can we end even here? Is even this Cogitationism, as it is propounded, ultimate? For, as we have said, it is still a kind of Idealism. Those prime phænomena, out of the coagulation of which, according to their laws of associability, he represents our cosmos of Matter and Mind to have been wholly evolved, are, he is always studious to remind us, phænomena definable as feelings. What we have to start with, in his scheme, as the prime cosmical matter, is still a matter of feeling—the facts or phænomena of a crude original sort of sentiency, which has not yet worked out the distinction of Ego and Non-Ego, but is only engaged in working it out. He will not even part with the word "consciousness;" but, holding by the expressions "thread of consciousness," and "series of states of consciousness," as, in his opinion, equivalent to Mind, he follows up the "thread" or "series," in the case of each individual being, still calling it consciousness, back into that infant confusion of first sensations with first muscular movements wherein the notions of Self and Not-Self are to be conceived as lying yet unseparated and indistinct. Beyond this he does not go. But will the theory serve us to the last extreme? Mr. Mill has spoken of the difficulty of conceiving how that which, *ex hypothesi* in his theory of Personality or Mind, is but a series of feelings, can be aware of itself as a series, or can grasp the non-present in the present. He has represented this as the one stumbling-block in the way of his total theory of Mind and Matter—the final mystery or inexplicability which he can only accept, without attempting a solution. But are there not mysteries on the back of this one?

How, for example, about our belief in the existence of other sentiencies, or "threads of consciousness, "or successions of feelings," contemporaneous with our own—whether our human fellow-creatures, or the inferior sentiencies of all grades, from the largest quadrupeds down to microscopic animalcules? Mr. Mill sees no difficulty here. He thinks his theory may be easily relieved from that "extrinsic" objection which Reid threw in the way of Idealism, when he maintained that it would leave us without evidence of the existence of our fellow-creatures. Reid, Mr. Mill argues, was here under a complete mistake. What is there, he asks, in the admission that Self or Personality is nothing but a "succession of feelings" or "thread of consciousness," that should prevent our believing that there are other selves besides our own —human, or inferior to human, or even hyperphysical and divine—provided only these selves are regarded also but as "successions of feelings" or "threads of consciousness?" Among my permanent possibilities of sensation there are recurring appearances—say of bodies like my own, shaped and moving and behaving like my own, and yet felt not to be my own—whence I infer that there are around me other human minds or possibilities of feeling besides myself; and from similar marks or signs I conclude, with equal certainty, that there are hosts of sentiencies not human.

Now, it is not the mere dizzying intricacy of the conception that would so arise that should prevent us from allowing that Mr. Mill may be in the right here against Reid. But the intricacy is worth noting. According to Idealism, when I meet a man walking in the street, he, as part of my Non-Ego, or possibilities of sensation, is really a production of my Self or series of feelings, and yet I may know that the compliment is returned, and that I, as part of *his* Non-Ego, am a production of *his* series of feelings. Again, what is the butterfly I see fluttering in the garden but a little object accounted for by the self-evolution of my consciousness or series of feelings, respecting which object nevertheless I am bound to conclude that it also is a little series of feelings, working out its life as self and not-self within the sphere of my Not-Self? Or, again, do not the French Emperor and the whole of the French nation exist for me but as a portion of the aggregate possibilities of sensation that have been generated out of the experience of that series of feelings which constitutes Me, and yet, on the other hand, as neither the French Emperor nor the French nation ever heard of my existence, must I not think of my series of feelings as a something lodging not yet realized amid the possibilities of sensation appertaining to those transmarine threads of consciousness? In short, what, according to the Idealistic theory, are the millions of human beings of whose existence on the earth contemporaneously with myself I am so well aware, and the countless hosts of inferior contemporary sentiencies with which Zoology amazes me, but multitudinous "threads of consciousness" whirring and spinning their lives within the bounds of that which is but a poem of my consciousness, and making *their* poems there, all of which are different from mine, and some of which outsphere mine? Illustrations of this kind might be multiplied, not in the least for the purpose of ridiculing Idealism, but only for the purpose of exhibiting the involutions of idealism within idealism to which the thinking out of the theory leads. Of the Idealists metaphysically, as of the Ptolemaists physically, it may be said that there is an interest in knowing

> "how they will wield
> The mighty frame; how build, unbuild, contrive
> To save appearances; how gird the sphere
> With centric and eccentric scribbled o'er,
> Cycle and epicycle, orb in orb."

Whether Mr. Mill has adequately met the alleged difficulty of reconciling such an idealistic theory as his with the belief in the independent existence of contemporary sentiencies I cannot undertake to say, not having been able to think his explanation out to my own satisfaction. It seems to me, however, that the explanation is too summary, as it stands. It is not in the least doubted that Idealism may work out the notion of the existence of other beings besides self. It seems only to be questioned whether, on the idealistic hypothesis, this notion must not be regarded as an illusion. For what is the idealistic hypothesis, as entertained by Mr. Mill? Is it not that the sum-total of existence for each sentiency is its own series of feelings worked out? What I am aware of as really existing in *my* thread of consciousness, *my* series of feelings. If, in the course of my series of feelings, there occurs to me the notion of another series of feelings out of me, I may certainly call that an existence, inasmuch as it belongs to my series of feelings. But do I not leap beyond the fact when I set up this second or notionary series of feelings in independent existence, as emancipated from me, nay, as approaching me for the first time out of circumjacent vacancy where I had nothing to do with it, and even as capable of making *my* series of feelings, of which it is the creature, *its* creature in return? Yet is it not in this sense that we believe in the existence of our fellow-mortals? How can one thread of consciousness be aware of another conceived thread of consciousness as anything more than its own conception? Will it be replied by Mr. Mill that this kind or amount of existence is the same that the first thread of consciousness claims for itself? It does not seem to be so. The Ego and Non-Ego of any thread of consciousness *are*, according to Mr. Mill, conceptions of that thread of consciousness experimentally arrived at; but he has never said that the thread of consciousness itself is only a conception of the thread of consciousness. The thread of consciousness constituting each man is followed up at last to a specific original of feelings and their associabilities which formed that man's peculiar infant existence, and was as yet the neutrum of his Ego and Non-Ego. The existence which each man predicates of himself is, according to Mr. Mill, derivability from that neutrum; but is the existence which each man predicates of his fellow-creatures also derivability from that neutrum? If, then, I admit the *notion* of the existence of my fellow-creatures to be a product of the experience of my thread of consciousness, must I not admit also that this notion corresponds to a *fact* of which my experience can give no account? But is this Empirical Idealism? Is it Empirical Idealism first to resolve the whole of my Non-Ego into my acquired notion of permanent possibilities of sensation, and then to have to admit, respecting those moving bits of my Non-Ego in which I recognise alien threads of consciousness or possibilities of feeling, that their existence is not rooted within my being?

Let me not be misunderstood. An Idealism or Cogitationism that should start with the assumption that there is in the universe a plurality of minds, sentiencies, threads of consciousness, already discriminated from each other in the nature of things, might very well explain the supposed existence of Matter on the idealistic principle, and might adopt Mr. Mill's definition of Matter as the happiest and most exact that has yet been given. Each of these minds, sentiencies, or threads of consciousness comes to be aware of "permanent possibilities of sensation," which it figures, according to its ability, as a substantial world of matter, external to itself, but the cause of which may be in others minds or sentiencies. The cause of all those sensations which each of us feels, and which we body forth in so mighty a framework of imagery, may be not, as the Natural Realists hold, the actual existence out of us of any material objects at all such as we suppose, but only the perpetual uniform determinations of our minds so to think in consequence of influences or suggestions from other minds—say hyperphysical intelligences or one Supreme Mind. By this kind of Idealism, which was very much Berkeley's, the Universe might be simplified into Thought or Notion. But it postulates plurality of minds or threads of consciousness in the present universe; and here it is that Mr. Mill's Cogitationism seems to differ from it. For, in Mr. Mill's system, not only is Matter resolved into a conception of each particular thread of consciousness, worked out by the laws of association from its experienced feelings, but the existence of other sentiencies or threads of consciousness is resolved into a conception of each particular thread of consciousness, arrived at in the same way. Now, if it is a conception merely, how can I predicate the existence of other minds in the same sense in which I predicate my own? In the case of my own, I have the guarantee of the fact of the thread of consciousness which has come at the conception; and, if I run back that fact to the utmost, I come still, Mr. Mill admits, to the indestructible fact of a specific initial cogitation of phænomena called feelings, a specific neutrum of Ego and Non-Ego, emerging out of a previous complexity of things, or let it be out of nothingness. But, in the other case, I have no such guarantee; and, unless I can assume the contemporaneity of other minds as vouched somehow in the initial neutrum of my own consciousness, or can break through that neutrum, so as to see it but as one in a crowd of other neutra, prior or contemporaneous (both of which suppositions Mr. Mill's Empiricism would disallow), then I can predicate the existence of other threads of consciousness only in the sense that they are notions of my thread of consciousness. When I say that *I* exist, I do not mean, nor does Mr. Mill's Cogitationism oblige me to mean, that my thread of consciousness is a notion of my thread of consciousness; but, when I say that my fellow-creatures exist, in what other sense Mr. Mill's Cogitationism allows me to say it than that these fellow-creatures are notions of my thread of consciousness, I confess I cannot see.

But farther. Let all difficulty be supposed overcome about the reconciliation of Mr. Mill's theory with the belief in the existence of a countless plurality of minds and sentiencies contemporaneous with our own. Let it be supposed also that the theory is perfectly reconcileable with our belief in those ages of mind and sentiency, anterior to the present, and sustaining or constituting the history of things down to the present, of which we have assurance in record and in science. Has not recent science been making another conception incumbent upon us—the conception of a point in backward time at which not only human sentiency, but all sentiency whatever, disappears from the scene, and yet the Cosmos is not annihilated, but there remains a more or less substantial priority of non-sentiency, which had a history of its own? Is it not worth while to look at Mr. Mill's Cogitationism, or at Idealism generally, in connexion with this conception? A while ago the necessity of such a test of cosmological Idealism was not likely to be thought of. The emergence of the completed Cosmos from an Absolute Unknown was imagined as instant or sudden, and all known sentiency, including that of Man, was imagined as introduced into the Cosmos within, at latest, the first week of it. Idealism, whose principle it is that *esse* is synonymous with *percipi*, had only, as it were, to find the means of supporting metaphysically a shell of *esse*, consisting of the heavens and earth with all their material garnishment, for a brief day or two; after which the arrival within this shell of a competent native provision of sentiency, or plurality of perceiving powers and forms, relieved the chief amount of the strain. But it is different now that the advent of sentiency into the universe is conceived as gradual. There are long tracts of an *esse* which could not be a *percipi* at all to any native sentiencies, save of kinds decreasingly inferior to man; and again, beyond these, there are farther æons of an *esse*, claiming to be thought of as by no means nothing, but a real and true ongoing of phænomena, though bereft of all native percipiency whatever. How does cosmological Idealism, or Mr. Mill's Cogitationism, reconcile itself with this scientific conception?

There is one plan, which I suppose was the plan of the old Idealists in regard to that brief interval over which *they* had to tide of a material *esse* in the Cosmos before the advent of a native percipiency. It is the plan of deputation to prior mind or percipiency. For the interval which the older Idealists had to tide over, they could suppose the shell of the material universe sustained or suspended, as it were, as an idea or conception in the thoughts of non-native or hyperphysical intelligences, or in the creative mood of Deity himself—this conception waiting for the native sentiencies that were to leap on to it, or arise within it, and were to inherit it as a prompting-ground for their continued constitutional thinkings. By a little adaptation the same plan of deputation might be available for present Idealism. A world of some kind might be sustained in existence backward, far beyond the era of man, by fancying it as the conjoint function of such inferior native sentiencies or percipiencies as were anterior to man. Or, if such a world seemed too mean, resort might be had immediately to that transcendent "metaphysical aid" which would have finally to be resorted to, in any case, when all native percipiency had been exhausted to the dregs, and there still remained a vast priority of *esse* refusing to be abolished. Hyperphysical intelligences, to whom our human measure of time is naught, might be reading the marvellous poem of creation and celebrating its completion in chorus ere yet there was appearance of any native sentiency in that creation to take up the song. Or He to whom a thousand years are as one day, and one day as a thousand years, and of whom we are told that, surveying the emanation of His mind, He pronounced it good—might not *He* have continued the necessary contemplation? Of this mode of thought Idealism may avail itself, as I believe all religious human feeling must avail itself of some analogous mode of thought in the long run, whether it calls itself Idealism or not. But it is to be observed that it imports a transcendent reality into Idealism. It does not require the particular reality characteristic of Natural Realism—*i. e.* a real block and history of a material world, distinct from all the minds or sentiencies appertaining to it, and to which they help themselves according to their capacities; but it requires, as a substitute, a reality of previous idea or thought, transmitted as a housing and pasturage for the sentiencies, minds, or threads of consciousness arriving within it, and furnishing them with the suggestions that determine *their* perceptions and thinkings.

What is the relation of Mr. Mill's Cogitationism to Absolute Idealism we shall presently see. Meanwhile, it does not appear that it is of any such plan of deputation as that just described that he would avail himself in respect of the problem in question. He holds, apparently, that his phrase "permanent possibilities of sensation," taken as expressing that Non-Ego or material world which each individual mind works out for itself, is amply sufficient to cover, for that mind, all requisites of conceivability back to the Nebula. He does not depute the burden of sustaining the conception of a world not yet tenanted by man, or by any sentient forms, upon supposed non native or hyperphysical intelligences; but, leaving the question of the existence of such intelligences open, he thinks that each human intelligence is capable of sustaining the burden for itself without going beyond the process of its own thoughts.

Now we cannot see how Mr. Mill makes this out. There is not the least objection to his phrase "permanent possibilities of sensation" as an equivalent for the material world. It is a phrase admirably chosen in many respects, and one which Natural Realists, as well as Constructive Idealists, might accept as expressing what they agree in before they begin to differ. All schools, indeed, agree that there are "permanent possibilities of sensation;" and the sole question among them is as to the nature of the cause of these permanent possibilities. Natural Realists find the cause in an actual external material world with which the mind is so constituted as to hold intuitive commerce; Constructive Idealists find it in some agency, physical or hyperphysical, determining the mind to uniform sensations or images, but not necessarily in the least like them in its own nature; Absolute Idealists find it immediately in the thoughts of the Divine mind. In each case there is a *substratum* for the possibilities—a something out of which they are imagined as springing, and which is independent of the mind of the individual percipient. But in Mr. Mill's Cogitationism there is no such substratum allowed or taken for granted. Each mind, or thread of consciousness, is supposed to work out its notion of an external world by a process confined to itself; and it is the notion of "permanent possibilities of sensation" so worked out by each mind for itself that Mr. Mill must hold to be a sufficient notion of a material world wherewith to cover all that that mind may be called upon, by history or science, to believe in as existing or having happened before its own birth, or before the era of humanity on the earth, or before the era of any forms of sentiency on the earth, or back, if need be, to the imagined convolutions of a universal Nebula. But *is* any such notion of "permanent possibilities" as may be worked out by the process of the individual consciousness sufficient for this immense burden? As far as I can see, it is not. For either the "permanent possibilities" are only a notion of the individual mind, evolved in the course of that mind's development out of its original condition as a mere neutrum of Ego and Non-Ego, a mere bundle of feelings; or they are more than a notion, and answer to a fact in the nature of things beyond the individual mind taken in its whole evolution from the first moment. If they are a mere notion, what happens? One mind may then fill antecedent time with any cloud of possibilities it chooses, and it may elect to fill it with those precise possibilities which history and science represent as real occurrences. But in all this it is only filling antecedent time with a notion; and a notion won't do. For it is out of antecedent time, and in consequence of the conditions of antecedent time, whatever they were, that the mind must think of itself as having come to exist; and, if the sole contents of antecedent time are a notion of the present mind, then the mind that has formed the notion must think of itself as springing out of the notion which itself has formed. Physics and metaphysics are then at war. The world of antecedent existence is, metaphysically, the child of the conceiving mind, and this child is, physically, the ancestor of its own mother. Mr. Mill then cannot mean that the "permanent possibilities of sensation," which he offers as equivalent to all we know of an external world, are a mere notion of the individual mind conceiving them, and nothing more. Well, then, let us take the other alternative—that these "permanent possibilities" are indeed a notion of the individual mind, but a notion which it knows or believes to answer to a fact in the independent nature of things. Here we should be all right; only this is precisely the position with respect to our belief in an external world from which Mr. Mill's Empirical Cogitationism seems to seek to drive us. That the mind, without going beyond its own experience, may form a notion of "permanent possibilities of sensation"—let it be granted that his theory is competent so far; but, if what is wanted is that the mind may form such a notion, and also know or believe that the notion corresponds to a fact in the nature of things, then how his theory will suffice, unless by knocking a hole in itself, it is difficult to conceive. For to form such a notion, and to know or believe that the notion does not end in itself, but shakes hands with a fact in nature—what is this but to have an intuition, to acknowledge a structural compulsion to an act of faith, to refer out of the mind to a basis or security for its conceptions in things beyond?

In order to account, therefore, for our belief in an antecedent history of things, whether back to the Nebula, or to any other point that may be taken as the proper cosmical beginning, must not Mr. Mill considerably enlarge that ultimate inexplicability to which (at the peril, as it seemed, of the principle of his own philosophy) we found him willing to confess? If the mind is to be spoken of as a "series of feelings" (which is the definition of Mind he contends for), then, he admitted, an inexplicable mystery must be acknowledged in the mind's constitution. It must be thought of as "a series of feelings which is aware of itself as past and future." The alternative was that either the definition of mind as "a series of feelings" must be abandoned, and the mind must be thought of as "something different from any series of feelings or possibilities of them," or the paradox must be maintained that "that which, *ex hypothesi*, is but a series of feelings can be aware of itself as a series." Keeping his definition, Mr. Mill must be supposed to have accepted the accompanying paradox. "The true incomprehensibility," he said, "perhaps is, that something which has ceased or is not yet in existence can still be in a manner present—that a series of feelings the infinitely greater part of which is past or future can be gathered up into a single *present conception accompanied by a belief of reality.*" Observe the last phrase. It exactly expresses what we have arrived at in examining the reconcileability of Mr. Mill's Cogitationism with the mind's knowledge of a world pre-existing itself. Only "as a present conception accompanied by a belief in reality" will Mr. Mill's Non-Ego or "permanent possibilities of sensation" cover our knowledge of an antecedent history of things. It is not the "present conception," but the accompanying "belief in reality" that is the required factotum. But it is a "belief in reality" of a wider range than Mr. Mill then particularly bargained for, though he must surely have been aware of its elasticity even to the present requirement. For then he was thinking only of the life of an individual mind, and only of as much of that life as consisted in the mind's self-consciousness. Even so, in order to account for the indubitable experience of every mind within its own life, it was necessary to suppose an organic union of the successive moments of that life in a sense of identity or personality. It was necessary to suppose that a series of feelings could be aware of itself as a series—that perhaps something which had ceased, or was not yet in existence, could still be, in a manner, present. But for the requisites of our present problem must not this mystery be enlarged? In order to account for a certainty in a world preceding ourselves, must not each series of feelings, constituting a self, be aware of itself not only as a series, but as a series that is not foreclosed at its own nominal beginning, but depends on a vaster series? In the *total* self, as well as in each moment of that self, must there not be a sense of a something past which is still in a manner present—*i. e.* of a bequest into self of a something that was not self? No mere gathering up of the past or future moments of the single thread of consciousness into a single conception will suffice. There must be a conception of the thread of consciousness transcending the whole thread of consciousness—which conception would be worthless unless accompanied by a belief in a reality corresponding. What the reality is may be phrased in various ways, by Materialists, Natural Realists, Constructive Idealists, and Absolute Idealists. The belief in some reality or other, supporting or yielding "the permanent possibilities of sensation" of which one figures the past as composed, is what all systems alike require; and, if a single series of feelings, evolving itself from an initial neutrum, could generate the conception of the "permanent possibilities," how else could it add the required belief in a corresponding reality than through some necessity so to believe, inwrought in the very nature of the neutrum?

Whatever farther objections may arise to Mr. Mill's new cosmological doctrine will mostly resolve themselves, I fancy, into the question, on which we have just been trenching, of the reconcileability of the doctrine with his principle of Empiricism. We proceed, therefore, to a remark or two on Mr. Mill's volume in as far as it illustrates his present state of feeling with respect to the fundamental principle of all his philosophy hitherto. Had we adhered to our former order of topics, we should have taken this point first. But there have been reasons for the slight difference of arrangement.

II.

Mr. Mill's volume, we now therefore say in the second place, is wholly, and from first to last, a reassertion of his psychological theory of Empiricism against the opposite theory of Transcendentalism. As it is the latest, so it is the most uncompromising and most thoroughgoing, British manifesto in favour of Empiricism. Its very purpose is to reassert Locke's principle in a form adapted to the latest developments of opinion, and to exhibit afresh its unversal competency. Not only is this the implied drift of every chapter and page, but there are portions of the volume specially devoted to a re-explication of the principle of Experience and a demonstration of its sufficiency for every possible requirement of philosophy. More particularly, there is brought forward, under the name of "the law of inseparable association," a reserve of strength in the experimental principle, which Mr. Mill believes that the Transcendentalists, and especially Hamilton and Mansel, have uniformly ignored.

Now, with all our admiration of Mr. Mill's arguments, and with every willingness to admit that, in consequence of some of them, Transcendentalism may have to change some of its dispositions and re-intrench itself (which is always the effect of a good attack, as Empiricism has itself confessed again and again by its own behaviour in like circumstances), we must avow our general conviction that Mr. Mill has left the battle perfectly renewable on the side of Transcendentalism. We see not the least reason why, notwithstanding the immediate hurrahing that there will be on the other side, and among mere bystanders, over so vigorous and well-conducted an onslaught, Transcendentalism may not be as lively among us as ever, and quite confident of its power, if equally well led, to inflict as valiant a retaliation. Indeed we must say that there is hardly any one of the old stock arguments of the Transcendentalists against Locke's principle that Mr. Mill's volume seems to have robbed of its real force. Leibnitz's "*intellectus ipse*," the well-known illustration of the impossibility of conceiving that two straight lines should enclose a space, and many more of the like, seem to me to survive all Mr. Mill's reasonings in the present volume, and to start up again as popularly available as ever. There is no use, however, in going back on these old forms of objection to the theory of Empiricism. Let us look at the theory in respect of its compatibility with that cosmological system of Constructive Idealism, or, as we have called it ultimately, Cogitationism, which Mr. Mill has advanced in its interest. For it *is* expressly in the interest of the principle of Empiricism that Mr. Mill has advanced his new cosmological conception. Of all our natural, or, as the Transcendentalists say, intuitive beliefs, there is none surely more natural, more intuitive, than our belief in the distinction or independent reality of these two things—an external world or Non-Ego, and an internal personality or Ego. If, then, the origin of this belief can be empirically accounted for, Empiricism may be said to have been crucially tested. Now Mr. Mill's new cosmological Idealism is propounded expressly to show that Empiricism can stand even this test. It is offered as a proof that the most immense and consequential of all our so-called natural beliefs can be accounted for on the principle of Experience without any *à priori* supposition. Let us view it afresh in this particular light.

First, as to the possibility of accounting empirically for our belief in an external world. "I proceed," says Mr. Mill, breaking ground first on this part of his subject, "to state the case of those who hold that belief in an external world is not intuitive, but an acquired product." And how does he proceed? "This theory," he proceeds, "postulates the following psychological truths, all of which are proved by experience. . . . It postulates, first, that the human mind is capable of expectation—in other words, that, after having had actual sensations, we are capable of forming the conception of possible sensations. . . . It postulates, secondly, the laws of the Association of Ideas. So far as we are here concerned, these laws are the following: 1st. Similar phænomena tend to be thought of together. 2nd. Phænomena which have either been experienced or conceived in close contiguity to one another tend to be thought of together. The contiguity is of two kinds—simultaneity and immediate succession. . . . 3rd. Associations produced by contiguity become more certain and rapid by repetition. Where two phænomena have been very often experienced in conjunction, and have not in a single instance occurred separately, either in experience or in thought, there has been produced between them what has been called Inseparable, or, less correctly, Indissoluble Association; by which is not meant that the association must inevitably last to the end of life, that no subsequent experience or process of thought can possibly avail to dissolve it, but only that, as long as no such experience or process of thought has taken place, the association is inevitable. . . . 4th. When an association has acquired this character of inseparability—when the bond between the two ideas has been thus firmly riveted—not only does the idea called up by association become, in our consciousness, inseparable from the idea which suggested it, but the facts or phænomena answering to these ideas come at last to seem inseparable in existence."* If these postulates are granted, there is no difficulty whatever, Mr. Mill holds, in showing how a notion of an external world or Non-Ego, including all that either people in general or the majority of philosophers require to be bound up in that notion, may have grown up factitiously, as a mere product of experience. For out of these conditions there would inevitably be formed a habit, or call it instinct, of the mature mind, in every act of sensation or conception, to regard what occurred in that act as only the immediately present flash out of an infinitely wider area of permanent external possibilities of sensation, more or less accessible. And what more than this need any theory of the external world include? Why assume the notion of a Non-Ego as an original or intuitive datum of consciousness, when we can see so clear a way in which, though it was not in consciousness from the beginning, it not only might, but must have grown up there, so as now to be perpetually and irresistibly present?

* Pp. 190, 191.

Of course, even were this analysis of our notion of the Non-Ego to be accepted with acclamation as absolutely and in every particular satisfactory, Mr. Mill cannot mean that it would establish the principle of Empiricism. It would only establish the Berkeleian Idealism. It would show that one most important notion or belief—that of the existence of an external world—need not be held primitive, but may be resolved into *prior* notions or beliefs; but, so far from shutting us up therefore to the theory of a factitious origin for our notions and beliefs in general, it would seem even to work the other way. By retiring the *à priori* element from one wing, in which its presence seemed unnecessary, it would only mass that element in closer strength on the other wing. For what does the speculation amount to? To what else than this—that, given a mind, or thinking principle, endowed with a capability of expectation, and with *à priori* notions of likeness, coexistence, and succession (and in this capability and these notions there seem to be included the notions, or mental forms, of Time and Number, or Plurality, if not also some others), then the notion of an external world might well be a mere result or factitious product of the experience of such a mind? But surely, in what is here begged or postulated, in the shape of structural pre-equipment for the mind ere the notion of an external world could be generated out of its experience, the Transcendentalist has a pretty large allowance of the sort of thing he wants. Not at this stage, therefore, can Mr. Mill think for a moment that the argument is closed.

But what if he can account empirically for the notion of Mind too? Then the whole field will be swept, and not a wrack of the mirage of Transcendentalism need disturb the universal clearness of the view. To this feat, accordingly, Mr. Mill next addresses himself. Having demonstrated, in one chapter, that, according to the correct psychological theory, the belief in matter "is but the form impressed by the known laws of association upon the conception or notion, obtained by experience of contingent (*i. e.* non-present, but possible) sensations," he proceeds, in another chapter, "to carry the inquiry a step farther, and to examine whether the Ego, as a deliverance of consciousness, stands on any firmer ground than the Non-Ego—whether, at the first moment of our experience, we already have in our consciousness the conception of Self as a permanent existence, or whether it is formed subsequently, and admits of a similar analysis to that which we have found that the notion of Not-Self is susceptible of." What the issue of the inquiry is we have already seen. It is that the sole effective notion we all have, or can want, of Mind, is that of a series of feelings reposing on, or, as we may say, navigating, infinite permanent possibilities of feeling. It *is a flashing-on of consciousness* from moment to moment, each flash giving a horizon of a limited present, but conveying also the irresistible conviction of endless other horizons of a non-present or possible. Now the question is not about the acceptability of this definition of Mind—a definition which I can conceive heated, and coloured, and glorified, till it should have charms for the poet no less than for the metaphysician. The question is as to the possibility of an empirical origin for the notion of Mind or Personality, taken as so defined. When Mr. Mill says that such a conception of Mind or Self admits of a "similar analysis" back into experience to that of which the notion of Not-Self has been shown by him to be susceptible, what does he mean? Does he require for the evolution of the notion of the Ego the same postulates as in the case of the Non-Ego? Hardly the same, surely, though he says nothing on the subject. For what were these postulates? "That the human mind is capable of expectation—that, after having had actual sensations, we are capable of forming conceptions of possible sensations:" also the four laws of the Association of Ideas—to wit, (1) that "similar phænomena tend to be thought of together;" (2) that phænomena experienced or conceived as either simultaneous or immediately sequent, "tend to be thought of together;" (3) that associations of this second class "become more certain and rapid by repetition," till, by very frequent and uninterrupted coincidence, they may acquire a character of inseparability; (4) that, when an association of ideas has acquired this character of inseparability, the notion of inseparability is transferred from the ideas to the phænomena thought of. Mr. Mill cannot surely want this cumbrous allowance of postulation for the evolution of our conception of an Ego out of conditions in which it was not originally present; or, if he does want it, we may be a little astonished. For what would be virtually his offer in such a case? What but that, if there were given him a mind endowed with the capability of expectation, and structurally equipped with the notions of likeness, coexistence, and succession (involving Time and Plurality), then he would undertake to show that out of such a mind's experience of phænomena there might be generated the notion of "present feelings with a background of permanent possibilities of feeling." Would not this be very much as if out of a four-horse stage-coach one were to offer empirically to produce a tandem or gig? Empirically!—yes, save for the slight *à priori* concession of the four-horse coach! Of course, I repeat, Mr. Mill cannot possibly have meant any such absurdity. But he does not sufficiently guard against the chance that it might be attributed to him. The very title of his chapter, "The Psychological Theory of Matter, how far applicable to Mind," suggests that the process of the evolution of belief explained in the preceding chapter as accounting for the origin of the notion of Matter, is to be carried on into this chapter as accounting also for the origin of the notion of Mind; and I am much mistaken if the unwary reader of the second chapter does not fancy that he has the full benefit still of the postulates of the first. There is no formal abrogation in the second chapter of these postulates, nor any re-expression of them to suit a new problem, to which, as they stand, their very phraseology is repugnant; nor is there any sufficient suggestion of a new process whereby that which was spoken of in the foregoing chapter (provisionally, it must be supposed) under such terms as "the human mind," "we," "our," &c., and figured as a structure of very definite forms and capabilities holding converse with phænomena, might be now seen to melt itself into the required "series of feelings with permanent possibilities of feeling." In other words, Mr. Mill, in order to account empirically for the notion of the Non-Ego, postulates in one chapter an Ego which is wonderfully like the ordinary Ego of the Transcendentalists; this Ego he resolves in the next chapter into a form so different from the Ego postulated that it would be interesting to know how, if he were compelled to go back and work with *it* as a substitute for the postulated Ego, he would be able to repeat his preliminary exposition of the derivativeness of the notion of Matter: but as to how this second notion of the Ego is arrived at, there is, within the limits of the chapter, no detailed explanation.

We are not left in the dark, however. We can fall back on the theory of Cogitationism as, from various hints here and elsewhere, we can see that Mr. Mill would work it in that earlier stage of the process when as yet neither the Ego nor the Non-Ego has been developed in the crude consciousness, but there is only the initial neutrum of both. Here, of course, we cannot speak of a mind observing phænomena, and forming conceptions and expectations according to the laws of the association of ideas by likeness, coexistence, and succession. That is a form of language not applicable till the mind is supposed sufficiently extricated from the phænomena of sensation and movement to be able consciously to watch them as something distinct from itself. We have not yet got at Mind in this sense. What we are at work with is the material out of which the notions both of mind and matter are evolved. What is that? Feelings and their associabilities; a certain curdling or cogitation of phænomena definable simply as feelings;

that first kind of consciousness in which the Ego and the Non-Ego lie confused or intertwined. It is out of this state of things that Mr. Mill maintains that our notions of Matter, as "a permanent possibility of sensation," and Mind, as "a permanent possibility of feeling," might be generated empirically and without any *à priori* assumption.

It seems to me that a very large amount of *à priori* assumption is implied in the very terms of the statement. It is assumed, in the first place, that there are certain predetermined associabilities among the phænomena of feeling from the first—that they tend to come together, or to grow together, according to certain laws or rules of associability pre-imparted to them. It is assumed, in the second place, that the phænomena themselves are, atomically, if I may so express it, or in their own individual nature, apart from their associabilities, of a certain kind, and no other, by *à priori* derivation:—(1.) *The Associabilities.* These must be represented now not as associabilities by conscious likeness, coexistence, or succession (for these, with the involved notions of Time and Plurality, are surely mental notions, the origin of which requires to be accounted for as much as the origin of the notions of Matter and Mind, and can hardly have been earlier), but rather as physical or physiological associabilities, which we can characterize in the retrospect, as likenesses, coexistences, or successions, but which, as acting among the phænomena themselves, may have involved much not so describable. If we take Mr. Bain's phrase "nervous currents" as furnishing the physical equivalent to the phænomena of feeling, then we may say that coexistent or immediately consequent nervous currents tend by repetition to form permanent associations, and also perhaps (though this is farther-fetched) that *like* nervous currents tend to occur together; or there may be other definitions of the associabilities of nerve-currents that Physiology has yet to find out. Mr. Mill abstains from the phrase "nerve-currents—preferring to talk consistently with his metaphysical Idealism, according to which, if the nerve-currents are the causes of the feelings, yet as these nerve-currents, like all other things and existences, are only conceptions or notions of their own effects, the effects must have the precedence in metaphysical discourse. This is very characteristic. That there are feelings is certain; that there are nerves or human bodies at all is but an item in that conception of a material world which the Idealist maintains to be merely a conception; and, though it may be an irresistible part of the conception that the nerves originate or occasion the feelings, it would be doing wrong to Idealism, in metaphysical argument, to start with the nerves. But among these "phænomena of feeling" which Mr. Mill, as an Idealist, consistently does start with, he recognises associabilities not the less describable in the retrospect as associabilities by likeness, coexistence, and succession. Without these precise associabilities among the crude phænomena of feeling there would not be the result he seeks—*i. e.* the generation of those notions of Mind and Matter, of an Ego and a Non-Ego, which each mature mind has. But, as these associabilities are laws pre-imparted to the phænomena, and regulating most stringently the process of their cogitation, how can the process be said to be empirical? Precisely what Transcendentalism asserts in opposition to Empiricism is that in every process there must be conceived a derived or *à priori* element on which the result depends. It matters not how far the inquiry is moved back. If the mature human mind is taken, then Transcendentalism asserts that there is an *à priori* element in *it*—forms or necessities of its structure, according to which it must and does think. If a certain coagulation of phænomena, called feelings, is taken as that out of which the human mind was convolved into completed being, equally there Transcendentalism undertakes to place its finger on something and say, "That is *à priori*." The associabilities of the feelings are *à priori;* their reason and origin transcend the process itself. (2). *The Feelings them-*

selves. There is an *à priori* element here too. What the result shall be depends on the *à priori* kind or nature of the atoms, as well as on the pre-imparted associabilities by which they are drawn into combinations. Else why should there be differences of sentiency? "Feelings" or "phænomena of feeling" is an indiscriminate Atlantic of a phrase. In fact, there must be millions of *kinds* of "feelings" or "phænommena of feeling," all in busy, already discriminated existence, out of *à priori* depths of the Unfathomable; so that, even if the same associabilities prevailed among them in common, the results could never approximate. There are feelings and feelings. Why, in one case, should the result of the cogitation of feeling be a dog, or an earwig, rather than a man? Why but because there was an inherent *dogginess* or *earwigginess* in the given kind of associable feelings, which, whatever the associations formed among the feelings, would not let the result be anything else than a dog or an earwig? Is there nothing *à priori* in this?

Deliberately I have brought the question between Empiricism and Transcendentalism to this pass, knowing what will be said. "What is the mighty difference," it will be said, "between Empiricism and Transcendentalism, if *this* is Transcendentalism? Would Empiricism deny aught of what you have here called it Transcendentalism to maintain? If it is the sole difference between Transcendentalism and Empiricism that the one maintains that in every thing, or process, there is an *à priori* or inherited element, necessarily assisting to determine what shall be the history of the thing or the result of the process, while the other maintains that this also, on our mounting higher in the evolution, may be resolved into experience—if this is all, is it not only the old story of looking at the gold-and-silver shield from opposite sides, and pronouncing it golden or silver according to the side looked at?" Not so; I cannot think that it is so. Send Transcendentalism and Empiricism back, tugging with each other on the very terms described, through all stages of the evolution from the present moment, and at every stage Transcendentalism is the mode of thought that keeps the field, while Empiricism must still be the fugitive. That is something. And at the utmost, when the Nebula, or whatever else may be deemed primordial and homogeneous in the phænomenal evolution, is reached and rushed through by the two combatants, the pursued and the pursuing, is there not a mighty consequence in the ultimate victory? If Empiricism, fugitive till then, can then turn at bay and conquer, it can only be because its back is against Zero, against Nihilism, against a wall of absolute blackness. If

Transcendentalism is still courageous and sure of the victory, it can only be because it sees in the middle of the wall of blackness a blazing gate, and knows it to be the gate whence the chariots issued and issue of an external *à priori*. And here perspective is as nothing. Wherever we stand, it is either the wall of absolute blackness that terminates our view, or the blazing gate shoots its radiance to where we are and move.

III.

Mr. Mill having, throughout his volume, re-asserted the principle of Experimentalism or Empiricism against that of Transcendentalism in philosophy, and having, in one portion of his volume, put forth, as the proper consequence of this principle when applied to our notions of Matter and Mind, that developed system of cosmological Idealism which I have ventured to call Cogitationism, it becomes interesting to inquire, finally, in what attitude, on the platform of such a total metaphysical system of Empirical Idealism, he leaves his readers standing in view of the permanent ontological questions, or questions of the Supernatural.

Partly, we have already had hints and informations on this subject. Accepting the doctrine of the Relativity of all knowledge, but declaring the doctrine to be incompatible, in any sense in which it would be worth keeping, with that cosmological system of Natural Realism with which Sir William Hamilton tried to associate it—nay, ultimately identifying the doctrine with the principle of Experimentalism itself, and denying by implication its compatibility with Transcendentalism—Mr. Mill, as we have seen, agrees with Sir William Hamilton, or even outgoes him, in his formal repudiation of Ontology. All our knowledge, he declares, can only be of the relative or phænomenal; of Noumena, Absolute Causes, or Things in themselves, we know, and can know, nothing. Again and again this declaration is made. It pervades the entire volume. We have now to note, however, two respects in which, notwithstanding this formal agreement with Sir William Hamilton in the repudiation of all Ontology, Mr. Mill is by no means at one with Sir William on that last frontier of speculative philosophy where the shore of the ontological is supposed to be reached.

(1.) Under the name of Faith, Sir William Hamilton affirmed, as Mr. Mill has himself explained, much which he declared to be utterly unpredicable in the name of Reason. There is, he thought, a structural necessity of the human mind whereby it is compelled to believe much that it cannot know—to accept inexplicabilities, nay, inconceivabilities, as nevertheless facts. It was on this principle (avowed, but not sufficiently explained) that Sir William Hamilton, notwithstanding his speculative doctrine of ultimate Nescience, or the incognisability of the Absolute, assumed, with a fervour equal to that of any Ontologist, the veritable Absolute of the Theists. Now, although Mr. Mill has had at one point to resort practically for himself to an ultimate salvo which looks very like Faith—although to stop a hole in his theory of Mind, he has had to assume an inexplicability, an inconceivability, a paradox, as nevertheless a fact—yet in his general philosophy, he provides no room or function whatever for Belief as distinct from Knowledge. If we assert a Deity, it must be as a legitimate inference from the phænomena of our experience; if we predicate certain attributes or actions of this Deity, there also must be rational inferences from the facts that come within our observation, investigated according to the ordinary principles of reasoning. In other words, if Theism and Theology are to sustain themselves at all, it can only be by the *à posteriori* argument, and not by any form or forms of the *à priori* one. This is certainly an interesting intimation of Mr. Mill's opinion to professional theologians. That Bridgewater Argument from Design which has been so much derided of late is, after all, he asserts, the only argument on which Theism can make any stand;

and the much-abused method of Paley, both in Natural Theology and in the matter of the Christian Evidences, was, after all, the only right method. If Paley fails, or rather if Paley's style of argument fails, all is over. Herein, I say, there is certainly a difference between Mr. Mill and Sir William Hamilton—a difference which will be construed by many as giving the advantage to the Hamiltonian system in connexion with Theism and Theology. For, without foregoing whatever may be of worth in the *à posteriori* argument, Sir William would reach Theism and Theology also, or primarily, through faith, or an *à priori* necessity of our mental constitution; and, since our surfeit of Paley and the Bridgewater Treatises some time ago, this is the kind of warrant for Religion that has seemed deepest and strongest to most Theists.

(2.) *Per contra*, however, Mr. Mill makes some corrections of Sir William Hamilton's doctrine of Relativity, or our nescience of the Absolute, which may be taken as relieving that doctrine itself from certain supposed impediments to rational religious belief. For example, Sir William Hamilton's assertion was that in our notion of the Absolute there is nothing positive whatever—that our sole conception of the Absolute is that of "a negation of conceivability." And Mr. Mansel, expanding the statement, declares the Absolute and the Infinite to be but "names indicating, not an object of thought or consciousness at all, but the mere absence of the conditions under which consciousness is possible." Many critics of Hamilton, while agreeing with his doctrine of the Relativity of Knowledge, or the Unknowableness of the Absolute, have dissented from this extreme form of it, which would allow in our notion of the Absolute nothing else than a negation or paralysis of all conception. Mr. Herbert Spencer, for one, has argued at some length against this as "a grave error," even while expounding approvingly Sir William's main doctrine of Relativity.* He contends for the necessarily *positive* character, however vague, of our consciousness of the Unconditioned. In our notion of the Unlimited, he argues, our consciousness of *limits* is abolished but not the consciousness of *some kind of being* stretching out and away into an illimitable. Here—and with considerable similarity in the mode of argument—Mr. Mill follows and corroborates Mr. Spencer in his criticism of Sir William Hamilton's Philosophy of the Conditioned. (Chapter VI.) So long as we use the abstractions, "the Absolute," "the Infinite," he says, it may be possible to assert that our corresponding conceptions are utterly void of any positive element—are in fact simple failures to conceive any meaning at all. But couple the predicate

* Mr. Spencer's *First Principles*, pp. 87—97.

"Absolute" or "Infinite" with a subject—say "Infinite Space," or "Absolute Goodness"—and then the mind is conscious of a tolerably positive element in the compound effort of thought. When we think of space as infinite, we think away the limits, but we do not cease to think of it as continuing to be space; when we try to imagine absolute Goodness, we fail in realizing the predicate "absolute," but the Goodness remains in our thoughts substantive enough. Or, if what we mean by the abstractions "the Absolute," "the Infinite," be (as Mr. Spencer understands, and as Sir William Hamilton himself doubtless understood, when he used these phrases independently), "Absolute Existence" or "Infinite Being," then still, Mr. Mill would say (as Mr. Spencer has said), there is a positive element, however vague and general, present in our conception—inasmuch as we still think of Existence or Being as that something whose absoluteness or infinitude is inconceivable. Nor is all this without consequence. Not unimportant as regards Sir William Hamilton's own philosophy, the error (as Mr. Mill and Spencer agree in considering it) in his statement of the doctrine of Relativity, as bearing on the question of rational Theism, swells into immense proportions in Mr. Mansel's express application of the Hamiltonian doctrine to Christian Theology. Accordingly, Mr. Mansel's whole elaboration of Hamilton's Philosophy of the Conditioned in its bearings on Religion is assailed by Mr. Mill in a separate onslaught (Chapter VII.). "He maintains," says Mr. Mill, speaking of Mr. Mansel, "the necessary relativity of all our knowledge. He holds that the Absolute and the Infinite, or, to use a more significant expression, an Absolute or an Infinite being, are inconceivable by us, and that, when we strive to conceive what is thus inaccessible to our faculties, we fall into self-contradiction. That we are nevertheless warranted in believing, and bound to believe, the real existence of an absolute and infinite being, and that this being is God. God, therefore, is inconceivable and unknowable by us, and cannot even be thought of without self-contradiction; that is (for Mr. Mansel is careful thus to qualify the assertion), thought of *as* Absolute, and *as* Infinite. Through this inherent impossibility of our conceiving or knowing God's essential attributes, we are disqualified from judging what is or is not consistent with them. If, then, a religion is presented to us, containing any particular doctrine respecting the Deity, our belief or rejection of the doctrine ought to depend exclusively upon the evidences which can be produced for the divine origin of the religion; and no argument grounded on the incredibility of the doctrine, as involving an intellectual absurdity, or on its moral badness as unworthy of a good or wise being, ought to have any weight, since of these things we are incompetent to judge." * Mr. Mill's opinion of this doctrine being that it is "simply the most morally pernicious doctrine now current," he spares no pains in denouncing and exposing it. There is probably no portion of his volume which will be read with keener popular relish, or more frequently quoted from, than precisely that which contains his attack on Mr. Mansel.

It is an attack, as we have hinted, which the prevailing theology will pretty unanimously adopt, with thanks to Mr. Mill. For, however common it has been with theologians to avail themselves of a mild form of Mr. Mansel's doctrine, and by the single averment that God's ways are not as our ways, to bar or silence rational objections to particular dogmas of Theology, yet Mr. Mansel's doctrine in full, as he propounds it, is one from which all theologians, save a few, would undoubtedly shrink. Whatever mysteries, or inexplicabilities, or inconceivabilities there may be in Religion, few theologians would contend for that kind of mystery which should maintain that, precisely *because* our sole notion of the Absolute or Deity is that of a Being respecting whom we can make no predicate whatever, or respecting whom we can only say that he unites all possible predicates, including

* Pp. 88, 89.

even those that are contradictory of each other, while at the same time none of these predicates have the same meaning that they would have if applied to a human being, *therefore* no objection is to be made to a Religion, miraculously attested, on account of the intrinsic nature of any of its teachings. What is called Rational Theology, at all events, has never committed itself to this. Now here Mr. Mill comes to the help of Rational Theology. He does not enter on the question of the possibility that any evidence whatever could attest to us that a Revelation had come from Deity, if we had no preliminary notion of Deity whereby to be sure that the Revelation had come from Him—no other notion of the source of the revelation than that it was the inconceivable home of no attribute, or of no attribute in a human sense, or of all opposite attributes simultaneously, and all in non-human senses. He confines himself to an indignant protest, in the name of reason, against the notion that such a Deity could be, on any terms, the object of the religious sentiment. Only in so far as Deity can be conceived as a Being endowed with those attributes (goodness, wisdom, justice, power, &c.) which we love and reverence in men, and with those attributes in the very sense in which they are predicated of men, albeit in Deity they are regarded as raised to the degree of infinity and in that respect *are* rolled beyond all grasp of our comprehension—only in as far as Religion can offer such a Deity, ought reason, or morality, or common sense, or the heart of man, Mr. Mill argues, to have satisfaction in Religion or to tolerate it in the world. But he sees nothing in the doctrine of the Relativity of Knowledge, or Incognisability of the Absolute, rightly interpreted, to deprive men of such a conception of Deity, if it can be otherwise fairly arrived at by induction from the phænomena of experience. Speaking in behalf of those "Rationalists," or believers in a "Rational Theology," against whom Mr. Mansel's arguments are principally directed, he says that they may "hold with Mr. Mansel himself, the doctrine of the relativity of human knowledge," and yet not be "touched by his reasoning." For they may reply to Mr. Mansel thus: "We cannot know God as he is in himself; granted: and what then? Can we know man as he is in himself, or matter as it is in itself? We do not claim any other knowledge of God than such as we have of man or of matter. Because I do not know my fellow-men, nor any of the powers of nature, as they are in themselves, am I therefore not at liberty to disbelieve anything I hear respecting them as being inconsistent with their character? I know something of Man and Nature, not as they are in themselves, but as they are relatively to us; and it is as relative to us, and not as he is in himself, that I suppose myself to know anything of God. The attributes which I ascribe to him, as goodness, knowledge, power, are all relative. They are attributes (says the rationalist) which my experience enables me to conceive, and which I consider as proved, not absolutely, by an intuition of God, but phænomenally, by his action on the creation, as known through my senses and my rational faculty. These relative attributes, each of them in an infinite degree, are all I pretend to predicate of God. When I reject a doctrine as inconsistent with God's nature, it is not as being inconsistent with what God is in himself, but with what he is as manifested to us. If my knowledge of him is only phænomenal, the assertions which I reject are phænomenal too." * In short, whatever theology is content to offer itself not as an ontology or science of the Absolute itself, but simply on the same terms as any other science, or as a generalization of certain phænomena in the supposition that they are the phænomena or effects of a Divine personality antecedent to all nature, is safe, Mr. Mill holds, from all injury from the doctrine of the Relativity of Knowledge, as understood by true philosophy, and can only be assailed, as any other theory might be, on ordinary logical grounds. Such a the-

* Pp. 98, 99.

ology has only to prove itself to be the only adequate theory or generalization of the phænomena, or of certain phænomena of nature, to make itself good; and it is only a theology that should profess itself to be more than this, to be a revelation of the absolute or noumenal Existence underlying all phænomenal nature, that true Philosophy must condemn beforehand.

In all this, however, Mr. Mill has spoken only vicariously, or by way of showing the compatibility of certain views with certain defined conditions, provided they have fulfilled certain other defined conditions. What one wants to know is the final attitude in which, according to Mr. Mill's own judgment of his system of Empirical Cogitationism all in all, it ought to leave men in respect of the great religious questions.

Here the last word of Mr. Mill's volume seems to be simply what is implied in the very quotations in which he has spoken vicariously. It is a reiteration of what we have seen him assert in his article on Comte's Philosophy—to wit, that, so far as is yet visible, true philosophy (*i. e.* Empirical Idealism or Empirical Cogitationism) may fairly leave these questions *open*. The most explicit statement to this effect in his own name, occurs, I think, in the chapter in which, after expounding his idealistic or cogitational theory of matter, he considers how far the same theory is applicable to mind. It had been objected by Reid to the idealistic theory that it left no evidence of the existence of our fellow-creatures, and no evidence of the existence of God. We have seen how Mr. Mill disposes of the first part of the objection—to wit, that the theory would leave us without evidence of the existence of other created minds or sentiencies besides our own. This part of the objection disposed of, Mr. Mill proceeds to answer the second part. "As the theory," he says, "leaves the evidence of the existence of my fellow-creatures exactly as it was before, so does it also with that of the existence of God. Supposing me to believe that the Divine Mind is simply the series of the Divine thoughts and feelings prolonged through eternity, that would be, at any rate, believing God's existence to be as real as my own. And, as for evidence, the argument of Paley's Natural Theology, or, for that matter, of his Evidences of Christianity, would stand exactly where it does. The Design argument is drawn from the analogy of human experience. From the relation which human works bear to human thoughts and feelings, it infers a corresponding relation between works more or less similar, but superhuman, and supernatural thoughts and feelings. If it proves these, nobody but a metaphysician needs care whether or not there is a mysterious substratum for them. Again, the arguments for Revelation undertake to prove by testimony that, within the sphere of human experience, works were done requiring a greater than human power, and words said requiring a greater than human wisdom. These positions, and the evidences of them, neither lose nor gain anything by our supposing that the wisdom means only wise thoughts and volitions, and that the power means thoughts and volitions followed by imposing phænomena."* The result of all which is that, if Theism will consent that the Divine Mind, for whose existence it contends, is knowable only as our own minds are knowable—to wit, as a series of thoughts and feelings, but these thoughts and feelings transcendently hyperphysical or Divine, or, again, as a thread of consciousness, but that consciousness transcendently hyperphysical or Divine—then Theism may remain an open question And so, on the same terms of consistency with the mode of thought of Empirical Cogitationism, other questions of the supernatural, of similar moment, may also remain open questions.

Now, without returning on objections previously urged against the reconcileability of Mr. Mill's idealistic theory with any knowledge of the existence of other created sentiencies or threads of consciousness tantamount to that which we have of our own exist-

* Pp. 210, 211.

ence (which objections, however, if valid in that connexion, would be as valid now against the reconcileability of the theory with the required knowledge of the existence of a Divine Mind—*i. e.* the knowledge of such a mind as more than a mere notion or conception of our own), let me simply say that I can see no interpretation of Mr. Mill's fundamental principle of Empiricism according to which those questions of a Supernatural which he would keep open ought not to be, at once and for ever, *closed* questions. Empiricism, so far as I can see any meaning in it, leads inevitably at last to Zero, Absolute Nihilism, or the resolute non-conception of an ultimate anything. It must either stop there, or transmute itself at that point, for the nonce, into an enormous all-including Transcendentalism. Unless as the name for the determining eternal *à priori* whence all else has proceeded, and has inherited law, structure, form, necessity, through every stage of the evolution, I can see no meaning whatever for the word Deity. If Mr. Mill vindicates the belief in such a Deity as compatible with true philosophy, well and good. Only how he can then assert that the true philosophy is that which supposes that every notion, belief, faculty, or power of the human mind is entirely generated out of experience, without the coefficiency of any innate or structural tendency, form, capability, necessity, or determination, passes my comprehension. I cannot conceive anything as resulting from the experience of a zero; and, unless I start with a human mind definable as zero, I must allow a very definite amount of *à priori* bequest in that human mind wherewith to grasp and mould experience. Or, if Empiricism pushes the dispute farther back, and, allowing that bequest, undertakes to resolve *it* into prior experience, still, at every stage, the assertion recurs, "We are not yet at zero; something is *à priori*, something structural and predetermined, even here." Or, if at last, somewhere behind the Nebula, we do reach Zero, or Nothingness, what becomes of Deity? Is Deity at the back of the original zero or nothingness out of which all else has been evolved or convolved empirically? Then either Zero would have remained such, and, as *ex nihilo nil fit*, there would have been no evolution whatever, or else the true origin of the whole evolution is not zero but Deity. But, on this last supposition, what meaning, such as that claimed for it, remains in the principle of Empiricism?

Waiving this objection, however, and allowing Mr. Mill's reservation of the question of Deity and other cognate questions as open questions in philosophy to be perfectly consistent with *his* interpretation of the principle of Empiricism (for which it may very well happen that *mine* is but a blundering substitute), let me look farther at that notion of Deity for which Mr. Mill insists that a space is open in his philosophy. Let us look at it in its connexion with his cosmological theory of Idealism or Cogitationism. Here, I think, there are curious results. For what is the Deity or Divine Mind whose existence then remains an open question. A Divine, or transcendent, superhuman, thread of consciousness, or series of thoughts and feelings. *Ex hypothesi*, no other Deity is allowed than a Deity conceivable according to the sublimed analogy of our experience of our own minds. Now, what I say is, not that such a Deity of Idealism may not be a sufficient Deity for all the needs of religion or the human mind, but only that there seems to be an interesting consequence of such a notion of Deity, which Mr. Mill's Cogitationism implies, but which he has left undeveloped. Was it not involved in Mr. Mill's theory of the human mind as a thread of consciousness or series of feelings, that there must have been a crude period in the history of that consciousness or series of feelings, when as yet it had not worked out the notions of the Ego and the Non-Ego, but existed only as a confused neutrum of both? Is this analogy to be transferred to the Divine Mind? If so, what do we end in? In what but the Absolute Idealism, or Absolute Identity-system, of Schelling and Hegel, which supposes an aboriginal Absolute Neutrum, of which the universe as a whole is to be conceived as the external forthrushing or Non-Ego, and Deity personally as the self-consciousness, or Ego, accompanying the forthrushing?

Yes, that final alternative to which we seem to be led up by all other modes of purely speculative thought seems to be also the alternative to which Mr. Mill's Cogitationism leads us up. It is the alternative of *Nihilism* or *Summation in an Absolute.* The choice between these alternatives seems to be the question that is left open. But to say that it is left open at all is, I apprehend, the same as saying that one has to choose, now as heretofore, between Empiricism and Transcendentalism in philosophy. This, it seems, though with the scope and meaning of the two terms marvellously enlarged by science, is still the essential distinction. Logically, Empiricism seems to have its only termination in Nihilism, while Absolute Identity seems to be but the modern principle of Transcendentalism reasoned back universally to its uttermost. Are we here in that predicament where it is only an act of faith, an impassioned throe of the soul obeying its own structural necessity, that can effect the solution? Are we in presence of the last and most gigantic possible form of that difficulty which is said to lie at the root of all our thinkings about anything whatsoever, and to be the very law of our thinkings—the perpetual balance of two propositions, mutually contradictory, and both inconceivable, yet one of which must necessarily be true? Or where is the logic, Hegelian or any other, that shall really dare the stricter solution of uniting the two extremes, by showing how in one organic beat or swing of thought there may be comprised the whole arc between Nothingness and Absolute Being? On these questions, as well as on all the crowd of homelier questions which concern the practical filling-up of any metaphysical system to fit it for the needs and uses of the human soul, much remains to be said, and much presses on me that might be said. But it will be more consistent with the nature of this work—which professes to be only a historical review of recent British Philosophy, with interspersed criticisms—if I stop, for the present, exactly at this point.

THE END.

www.ingramcontent.com/pod-product-compliance
Lightning Source LLC
LaVergne TN
LVHW020216110826
845151LV00003B/731
9781425533526